THE CHRISTIAN CATACOMBS OF ROME

History, Decoration, Inscriptions

THE CHRISTIAN CATACOMBS OF ROME

History, Decoration, Inscriptions

Vincenzo Fiocchi Nicolai
Fabrizio Bisconti
Danilo Mazzoleni

SCHNELL & STEINER

Die Deutsche Bibliothek - Cataloguing in Publication Data:

The **christian catacombs of Rome** : history, decoration, inscriptions /
Vincenzo Fiocchi Nicolai ; Fabrizio Bisconti ; Danilo Mazzoleni.
[Engl. transl. by Cristina Carlo Stella and Lori-Ann Touchette]. -
2. ed. - Regensburg : Schnell und Steiner 2002
  Dt. Ausg. u.d.T.: Roms christliche Katakomben. - Franz. Ausg. u.d.T.:
  Les catacombes chrétiennes de Rome. - Ital. Ausg. u.d.T.: Le
  catacombe cristiane di Roma. - Span. Ausg. u.d.T: Las catacumbas
  christianas de Roma
  ISBN 3-7954-1194-7

English translation by Cristina Carlo Stella and Lori-Ann Touchette, Rome

2nd edition 2002
© by Verlag Schnell & Steiner GmbH,
Leibnizstrasse 13, D-93055 Regensburg

Typography, plates: Visuelle Medientechnik GmbH, Regensburg
Printed by Erhardi Druck GmbH, Regensburg
ISBN 3-7954-1194-7

INTRODUCTION

Many initiatives have been sponsored by the Pontificia Commissione di Archeologia Sacra for the upcoming Great Jubilee Year of 2000. This volume deals with the Christian catacombs of Rome and presents the current state of research and knowledge concerning these extraordinary monuments, that provide the most tangible and eloquent testimony of Early Christianity.

As President of the Pontificia Commissione di Archeologia Sacra and the Commissione Artistico-Culturale del Grande Giubileo dell'Anno 2000, I gladly welcomed the invitation of Dr. Albrecht Weiland, Director of Schnell & Steiner Press, to prepare this work on the Christian catacombs of Rome. Three specialists in this field were entrusted with the task of presenting the salient aspects of these significant monuments.

Professors Vincenzo Fiocchi Nicolai, Fabrizio Bisconti and Danilo Mazzoleni are well known for their studies of the topography, decoration and epigraphy of catacombs. As members of the Pontificia Commissione di Archeologia Sacra and lecturers at the Pontificio Istituto di Archeologia Cristiana, they have a profound knowledge of all aspects relating to the Christian catacombs in Rome, not only scientific and monumental issues, but also the delicate issue of protection and conservation.

In this period, many publications will appear on Christian Rome that also deal with its ancient period and the catacombs. This volume is intended to represent the official publication on the Christian catacombs of Rome, prepared directly by members of the Pontificia Commissione di Archeologia Sacra. This institution, founded in 1852 by papal mandate, is concerned with the task of studying, protecting and conserving these stimulating testimonials of Christian antiquity. Through association with this commission, it has been possible to publish the most recent and up-to-date graphic and photographic documentation of the excavations and restorations carried out in the last few years in preparation for the Jubilee.

Therefore this publication fits perfectly within the series of initiatives planned by the Pontificia Commissione di Archeologia Sacra as we approach the Jubilee Year. It should be a useful and valuable didactic tool for visiting the catacombs of Rome, that, as the Holy Father has noted on numerous occasions, represent mandatory destinations for all the pilgrims who will come to Rome in the year 2000 from all over the world.

Mons. Francesco Marchisano
Titular Archbishop of Populonia
President of the Pontificia Commissione di Archeologia Sacra

CONTENTS

HISTORY, DECORATION, INSCRIPTIONS

Introduction
by Mons. Francesco Marchisano

I. Vincenzo Fiocchi Nicolai
   THE ORIGIN AND DEVELOPMENT OF ROMAN CATACOMBS

II. Fabrizio Bisconti
    THE DECORATION OF ROMAN CATACOMBS

III. Danilo Mazzoleni
     INSCRIPTIONS IN ROMAN CATACOMBS

I. THE ORIGIN AND DEVELOPMENT OF ROMAN CATACOMBS

Vincenzo Fiocchi Nicolai

1. THE TERM "CATACOMB"

According to archaeological terminology, the word "catacomb" means an underground Christian cemetery of large dimensions, characterised by an elaborate network of galleries and *cubicula* (square or rectangular chambers) used intensively for burial. The use of this term to refer to these ancient monuments is first attested at the end of the 10th century, in connection with a local hypogean (underground) cemetery at Subiaco (Latium)[1]. However, the word was already used in a derivative sense in Naples during the 9th century to indicate the burial-place to which the body of one of the earlier bishops of the city was transferred[2].

The term derives from the Roman toponym *catacumbas*, that during the fourth century indicated a location at the 3rd milestone of Via Appia, characterised by the presence of hollows and wide sandstone cavities (*catacumbas* from the Greek κατὰ κύμβας or "near the hollows")[3]. From the third century onwards, one of the most important and extensive underground cemeteries of the city was laid out in this area: the cemetery of S. Sebastiano, that the ancient sources call the *cymiterium catacumbas*[4]. This funerary area was famous in the early Medieval period, and remained one of the few burial sites still accessible and regularly visited after the abandonment of the catacombs in almost precisely this period. Its significance in this period explains the extension of the name of this Appian complex (at least by the early Medieval period) to other sites with the same characteristics.

The ancient name of Early Christian underground cemeteries in Rome, however, was different. Visitors to ancient catacombs, such as S. Jerome or the Spanish poet Prudentius, attest that between the mid-fourth and the beginning of the fifth centuries they were designed simply as *cryptae* (Jer., *In Ezech.*, XII.40 = PL, 25, col. 375; Prudent, *Perist.*, XI. l.154 = CSEL, 61, p. 417). The term also occurs in several inscriptions found in underground cemeteries, where it is used to indicate galleries and hypogea for funerary use[5].

2. THE HISTORY OF SCHOLARSHIP

As mentioned earlier, during the Medieval period, almost all of the catacombs in Rome were abandoned. The transferral of the bodies of martyrs buried there to churches within the city also signified that frequent visits to the catacombs ceased almost entirely[6]. Only four or five of the more than sixty catacombs that have emerged from archaeological excavation[7] were still accessible during this period. These catacombs were in areas connected with suburban basilicas (S. Sebastiano, S. Lorenzo, S. Pancrazio, S. Agnese, S. Valentino) from which the bodies of the titular saints had never been removed and transferred to the city[8]. Nevertheless, only a very limited area of these catacombs remained accessible. Sections of other underground cemeteries must occasionally have been reachable as a result

Pl. I
Catacomb of Commodilla: Cubiculum Leonis

1 Copy of the plan of the Catacomb of S. Sebastiano, drawn by Philippe De Winghe at the end of the 16th century

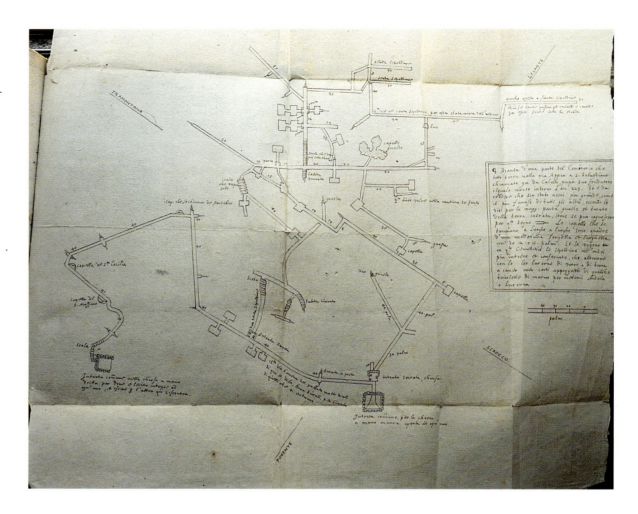

of landslides, earthquakes, or through shafts that opened accidentally in suburban vineyards. The first Renaissance visitors penetrated into the "labyrinth" of the catacombs through these chance openings. Their presence in these underground passages from the first half of the fifteenth century onwards, is proven by signatures traced in charcoal, red lead, or graphite in various areas[9].

In the second half of the fifteenth century, members of the famous *Accademia Romana degli Antiquari* of Pomponius Laetus, who were quite influential in the cultural milieu of Rome in this period, were assiduous visitors to several Roman catacombs. This group, it seems, was driven by simple curiosity and love of antiquity to frequent the catacombs[10].

The first person to approach underground cemeteries in a scholarly manner was the Augustinian Onofrio Panvinio in the middle of the sixteenth century. Based on a pioneering investigation of ancient historical and topographical sources, he was able, within the context of a study dedicated to Early Christian funerary rites, to reconstruct the names and locations of 43 urban cemeteries[11].

Onofrio Panvinio was the leader of a group of scholars who in the second half of the sixteenth century focused new scientific interest on the catacombs. The times, however, were ripe for a valorisation of these ancient monuments. The Counter-Reformation movement was interested in the material evidence of Early Christianity since, through a

10

"targeted" interpretation, it was capable of confirming the dogmas of the Roman Catholic Church[12]. The Roman Oratory of S. Philip Neri promoted the study and frequentation of catacombs, both to draw on them as a source of spiritual renewal as well as to recover useful sources for a more accurate reconstruction of the history of the Early Church[13]. In such a religious and cultural climate, the chance discovery of a completely intact new catacomb contributed decisively to the arrival of ancient underground Christian cemeteries at the forefront of the scholarly world[14]. Found on May 31, 1578 on Via Salaria, the catacomb, now known as the "Catacomba Anonima" of Via Anapo, was the first to come to light since antiquity. This find catalysed the attention of not only the Ecclesiastical hierarchy of the time, interested in the new monument primarily for apologetic reasons, but also that of the first scholars of Christian antiquity active in Rome in this time. The Spanish Dominican Alfonso Ciacconio and the Flemish scholars Philippe De Winghe and Jean L'Heureux explored the new site and described its paintings, sculptures and inscriptions with the "secular" intention of illustrating and commenting on them[15]. In particular, Ciacconio and De Winghe were driven to explore other underground cemeteries (fig. 1). In this same period, the Roman Pompeo Ugonio, within a study dedicated to stational churches, also took pains to describe several catacombs then open to the public, citing the literary sources that illustrated their history[16]. At the end of the sixteenth century, the Maltese Antonio Bosio (1575–1629), who laid the foundations of Christian archaeology, joined this group of experts (fig. 2). Bosio was the first to conceive the idea of a complete illustration of underground Christian Rome. His scholarly methodology was based on the systematic collection of historical and topographical sources. His work differed from the early attempts of Panvinio since it was carried out in greater depth and included a careful analysis of the individual monuments (in exceptional cases he even resorted to archaeological excavation). Based on this documentary evidence, this "Christopher Columbus" of Roman catacombs (as G.B. de Rossi called him), was able to recover and document about thirty new underground cemeteries in his forty years of research activity[17]. His "comparative" method, based on both architectural and topographical sources, was a great novelty destined to prepare the way for the methodology of future scientific studies.

Nevertheless, Bosio's innovative approach was not followed by those who occupied themselves with Roman catacombs immediately after him. From the middle of the seventeenth century, for two centuries, the underground cemeteries of Rome were studied out of mere antiquarian interest for their iconographic material and the grave goods that they preserved (as in the studies of Bar-

2 Portrait of Antonio Bosio (PalazzoMagistrale del Sovrano Militare Ordine di Malta, Rome)

3 Charcoal graffito that mentions the "quarry of saintly bodies" in a cubiculum of the Catacomb of Marco, Marcelliano e Damaso

only partial information concerning such investigations[21].

In the mid-nineteenth century, catacomb archaeology finally emerged from the darkness that enveloped it after the death of Bosio. The Jesuit Father Giuseppe Marchi approached the study of underground cemeteries with renewed attention to the analysis of the monuments and historical contextualisation[22]. In 1851, Pope Pius IX established the Pontificia Commissione di Archeologia Sacra, entrusted with the protection and scientific exploration of the catacombs[23]. Giovanni Battista de Rossi (1822–1894), the founder of the modern science of Christian archaeology, resumed research following the methodological lead of Bosio in these years. He based his studies on the careful analysis of the monuments correlated with examination of the primary sources, now studied in greater detail with a new critical approach. The systematic adoption of archaeological excavation as a means of investigation allowed de Rossi to discover numerous and important new sections of the catacombs. The discovery of a considerable number of tombs of Roman martyrs and bishops made it possible for him to identify many underground necropoli based on the sources that recorded the presence of these particular tombs. Thus, he was able to shed light on the intricate historical topography of suburban Rome. De Rossi's extensive knowledge of historical, literary, hagiographic, epigraphic, and art-historical issues allowed the Roman scholar to produce a much more complete and exhaustive picture of the monuments analysed. The critical rigour and novelty of his method of investigation and the tone and historical tension that sustained it represent even today a fundamental heritage for all those who approach the study of catacombs[24].

The extraordinary discoveries of de Rossi aroused a considerable flurry of interest. Between the end of the nineteenth century and the first decades of this century, his three students, Mariano Armellini, Orazio Marucchi and Enrico Stevenson, were particularly active in the Roman catacombs. They

toli, Bottari, Marini, Serout D'Agincourt). Alternatively, they were of interest for the contribution that they seemed to provide, in the very lively debate between Catholics and Protestants, in support of the religious convictions of the former, and thus, with forced exegetical interpretations[18]. Moreover, during these centuries, the underground cemeteries were the object of systematic plundering by a group of specialised workers (the so-called *corpisantari*), who, often on official commissions from the highest Ecclesiastical hierarchy, dedicated themselves to the extraction of the presumed bodies of martyrs from these catacombs (fig. 3)[19]. The dispersal of valuable data provoked by these destructive excavations, that were regulated (but in fact institutionalised) by a Pontifical Decree in 1668, was extremely serious[20]. The work of Fabretti, Boldetti, Marangoni, and other "Custodians of the Sacred Relics and Cemeteries", set in this cultural and chronological context, allow us to recover produced many important studies including the first comprehensive syntheses of underground cemeteries[25]. In his research dedicated primarily to the study of the art-historical production in the catacombs, the German Joseph Wilpert successfully integrated the scientific activity of this group of archaeologists[26]. In the 1920s and 30s, the incipient building expansion of Rome in the area of the ancient suburbs provoked numerous new discoveries. These were scientifically analysed by Enrico Josi, the author of many important contributions on underground Rome[27]. During this same period, the Swiss Paul Styger produced a general critical revision of the origins and topographical development of Roman catacombs, based on a more accurate interpretation of the architectural evidence[28]. In the post-war years and in these last decades, the underground cemeteries of Rome have been the subject of studies that are always more attentive to the material evidence and conducted following modern criteria of investigation. The studies of Antonio Ferrua, Umberto Maria Fasola, Louis Reekmans, Francesco Tolotti, Pasquale Testini, Hugo Brandenburg, Aldo Nestori and the last generation of scholars have greatly increased our knowledge of this subject.

3. THE ORIGIN OF THE CATACOMBS

In the period of the first modern discoveries of the sixteenth and seventeenth centuries, a curious belief began to spread that the catacombs served as places of habitation or refuge for the Early Christians during the persecutions. This legend was fed, among other things, by the incorrect interpretation of several ancient sources. For example, the passages of the Roman *Liber Pontificalis* allude to the residence of some Popes "in the cemeteries" (meant evidently in the broader sense of the term, including existing buildings situated above ground) (LPI, pp. 161, 207, 227, 305–306). Similarly, the murder of Pope Sixtus II along with his deacons is set "*in cimiterio*", in the area of the Catacomb of S. Callisto, on 6 August, 258, during the persecution of Valerian (Cypr., *Ep.*, 80 = CSEL, 3/2, p. 840)[29]. In reality, as is well known, the catacombs were exclusively funerary areas used for the burial and funeral rites of members of the Early Christian communities.

Their existence, like that of the Christian cemeteries above ground, cannot be dated earlier than the end of the second century. In fact, the literary sources and monumental evidence agree in placing the first appearance of collective and exclusive funerary areas for Christian communities in this period.

In Africa, Tertullian (*Scap.*, 3.1 = CSEL, 76, p. 11) records the presence of "*areae sepulturarum nostrarum*" at Carthage around 203. Its ownership by the Christian community was strongly opposed by the pagan plebeian population. The protest of the people, "*areae non sint, areae eorum non fuerunt*", suggests that the institution of these communal cemeteries cannot have dated to a much earlier period[30]. Again, Tertullian, in his *Apologeticus*, written around 197, refers to the existence of a "communal fund" created by the community, with spontaneous monthly contributions by the members, to guarantee proper burial for even the poorest of them (Tert., *Apol.*, 39.5–6 = CSEL, 69, p. 92).

In Alexandria, the existence of collective cemeteries is attested in the first decades of the third century, in a passage by Origen (*Hom. in Jer.*, IV.3.16 = SC, 232, p. 264–265).

Also at Rome, in more or less the same years, the first mention of a communal area is found: the cemetery of S. Callisto, whose operation was assigned by Pope Zephyrinus (198–217) to the well-known deacon and future Pope Callistus (Hippol., *Philosoph.*, IX.12.14 = GCS, 26, p. 248). The Greek term τὸ κοιμητήριον, used to indicate the communal funerary area of the Christians, is attested for the first time at Rome in this document. The literal significance of the word, "dormitory", expresses well the concept that the Christians had of death, that is, of a temporary break while awaiting the res-

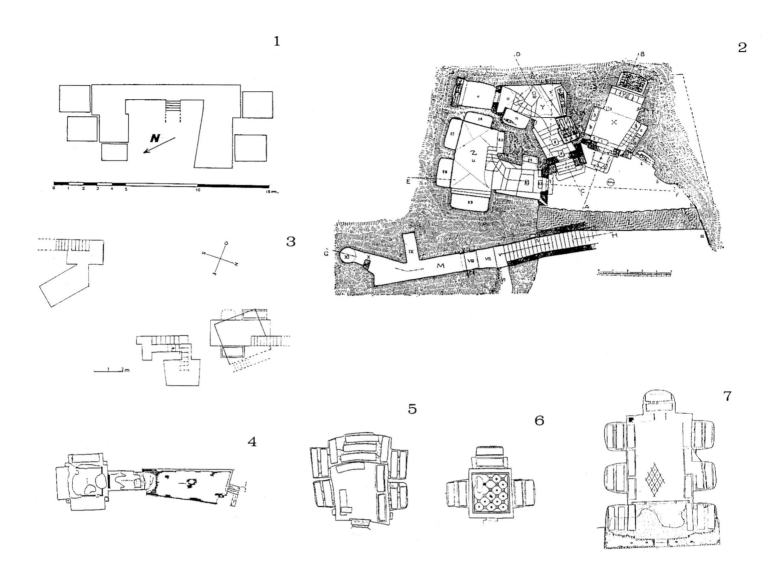

1

2

3

5

6

7

4

4 *Plans to the same scale of the pagan chamber hypogea of* Ampliatus *on Via Ardeatina (1); of the* piazzola *under S. Sebastiano (2); of the* torretta *in the complex of S. Callisto (3); of the* Octavii *on Via Trionfale (4); of "Via Ravizza" on Via Portuense (5); of the* Favilla *(6); of the* Nasoni *on Via Flaminia (7)*

urrection (John Chrys., *Coemet*. 1 = PG, 49, p. 393–394). In the *Traditio Apostolica*, Hippolytus confirms the practice of collective subsidies intended for the cemeteries and geared towards guaranteeing the burial of the most needy of the community (Hippol., *Trad. Ap.*, 40 = SC, 11bis, p. 122).

The archaeological evidence, after the critical chronological revision of the last decades, agrees with the sources in dating the origin of Christian cemeteries more or less to the last years of the second century. Before that time, as demonstrated by the archaeological data, members of the new religion buried their dead in pagan communal areas, either in individual or family tombs or in tombs belonging to funerary associations. This ancient practice is most evident in Rome. For example, the apostle Peter was buried in 64 in the existing pagan necropoli on the Vatican hill[31]. S. Paul was also buried within the Roman funerary area of Via Ostiense[32]. Perhaps already by the Trajanic period, and certainly from the second half of the second century, individual tombs of Christians were inserted into the pagan cemetery that had re-occupied the pozzolana quarries and the walls of a deep tufa crater located at the 3rd milestone of Via Appia, beneath the Basilica of S. Sebastiano (fig. 157)[33].

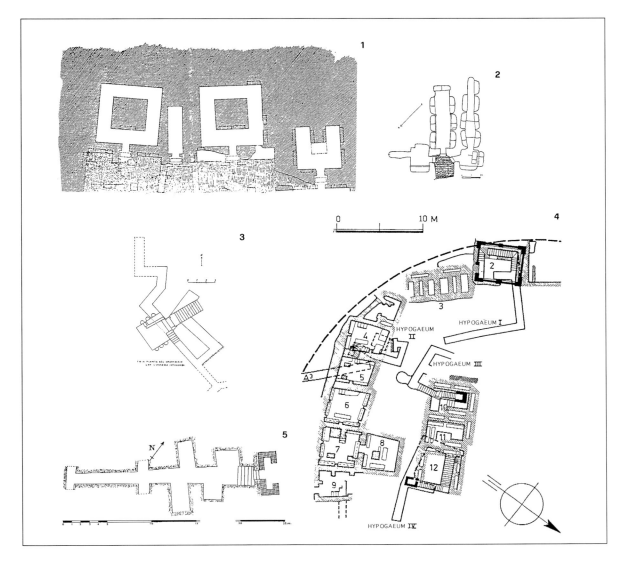

5 Plans to the same scale of pagan gallery hypogea in the necropoli of Falerii Novi (1); of Antium (2); of the Circus of Maxentius (3); of the area of Lucina in the complex of S. Callisto (4); of the Flavii on Via Ardeatina (5)

The need to create burial grounds for the exclusive use of the community must have arisen at the close of the second century. It was motivated by several factors, such as the numeric and organisational growth of the community (Hippol., *Philosoph.*, IX.12.23–4 = GCS, 26, p. 250; Tert., *Apol.*, 37.4 = CSEL, 69, p. 88), an awareness of building a compact and united religious community that would be preserved even in the repose of death (Aristides, *Apol.*, 15.5–7 = Alpigiano 1988, p. 116–121; Tert., *Apol.*, 39.1–2 = CSEL, 69, p. 91), the desire to set out proper spaces for the celebration of burial rites, in part distinctive such as the prayer for the dead, the funerary Mass, etc. (*Mart. Polycarpi*, 18–28 = SC, 10bis, pp. 230, 232; Tert., *De anim.*, 51 = CSEL, 20, p. 383, Cypr., *Ep.*, 1.2 = CSEL,3/2, pp. 466–7) and the aspiration, out of charity and solidarity, that sought to grant everyone, as has been seen, even and especially the poorest members of the community, a Christian burial (Aristides, *Apol.*, 15.6 = ed. Alpigiano 1988, pp. 118–9; Tert., *Apol.*, 39, 5–6 = CSEL, 69, p. 92; Hippol., *Trad. Ap.*, 40 = SC, 11bis, p. 122)[34]. In addition, the greater economic and organisational capacity of the community could at this point have made possible the realisation and management of burial grounds[35].

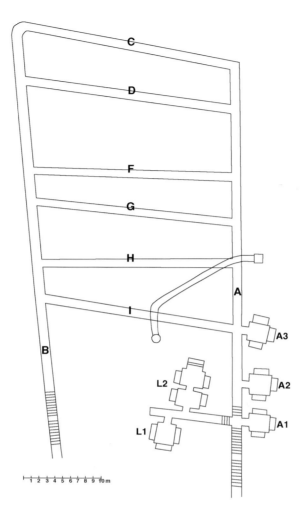

6 Plan of the so-called "Area I", Catacomb of S. Callisto (A.D. 230–240)

The practice of creating underground areas for funerary use was certainly not an invention of the earliest Christian communities of Rome. It was widespread, as is known, in various civilisations and cultures of the ancient world, especially where the type of ground permitted easy excavation and reliable support for underground structures. Within the geographical surroundings of Rome and Latium, the Etruscans, Sabines, and the Romans themselves created underground tombs, more or less vast (figs. 4–5)[36]. Underground burial in this geographical area was extraordinarily facilitated by excellent local tufa, that was easy to work and relatively reliable statically.

By the second century, a demographic increase and the predominant diffusion of the rite of inhumation must have entailed an ever-increasing demand for burial spaces in the suburbs, and a consequent, inevitable rise in the cost of land[37]. Cicero already recorded how the areas most in demand, usually around the cities or in places particularly favourable, were often too costly and subject to frequent speculation (Cic., *Att.*, XII.21.33)[38]. This phenomenon must have been accentuated in the Imperial period[39]. In order to deal with this new situation, between the end of the first century and the beginning of the second, some families and Roman funerary associations turned once more to the use of underground burial. They excavated small hypogea under mausolea above ground, individual chamber tombs, and short galleries (figs. 4–5, nos. 3–5). The exploitation of underground areas through a rational and intensive use of plots provided the possibility of considerably increasing the space for inhumations. Numerous examples of pagan funerary hypogea are attested in the suburbs, in the areas of Via Portuense, Via Trionfale, Via Flaminia, Via Latina, Via Appia, etc.[40] (figs. 4–5). They are characterised by a limited extension, probably indicative of family commissions. Not infrequently, they were entirely covered by frescoes, thus precluding the intention of the builders to later extend the burial area.

When, at the end of the second century, the Christian community in Rome also felt the need to create extended areas for communal burial for the above mentioned reasons, they naturally resorted to hypogea since this choice guaranteed the most economical solution[41]. The novelty of commissions, numerically substantial and subject to continual increases, determined the original architectural solutions, characteristic of Christian communal underground cemeteries (the catacombs), that rendered these monuments, from their first appearance, distinctive and exclusive to the Christian communities[42].

In fact, already in the oldest areas of the catacombs, completely innovative characteristics can be detected that distinguish them from non-Christian hypogea. These innovations included a much greater extension of the space, constituted by a series of interconnected galleries, generally organised according to a regular scheme. In addition, the architectural design anticipated from the very beginning the possibility of later expansion, compared to the "closed" scheme of the pagan hypogea[43] and was based on an absolutely rational and intensive use of the available space.

Such "characteristic" architectural details are evident in many of the oldest communal burial regions, datable between the end of the second and the mid-third centuries.

In the so-called "Area I" of S. Callisto (fig. 6), to which, as has been seen, the deacon and future pope of the same name was assigned at the end of the second century[44], a plot 75 x 30 m (250 x 100 ft.) was marked out by a fence. Underground, it was occupied by a system of galleries laid out in a "grid" pattern composed of two parallel main passageways (A–B), accessible through their own staircases located at the boundary of the area. The passageways were connected by a series of secondary orthogonal galleries placed at more or less regular distances (C–D, F–I)[45]. The entire complex was evidently planned from the beginning, anticipating successive extensions of the two major galleries and the opening of transversal ones. Narrow tombs in niches, the so-called *loculi*, placed in vertical *pilae*, occupied all of the available wall space. Sections of tufa were left blank at the end of the galleries to be extended and in the points in which openings of transverse galleries were planned (fig. 6, A1–A3, L1–L3). The desire on the part of the founders to produce a communal cemetery of vast dimensions in this way is clear. The catacomb was of a strongly egalitarian character, thus all the tombs share the same typology; it was capable of housing hundreds of inhumations and open to continuous enlargement. Only later, around 235, were five *cubicula* opened along one of the two principal arteries and in the first transverse gallery (fig. 6, A1–A3, L1–L2). These *cubicula* represented the first "privileged" spaces, equipped with more monumental tombs (*a*

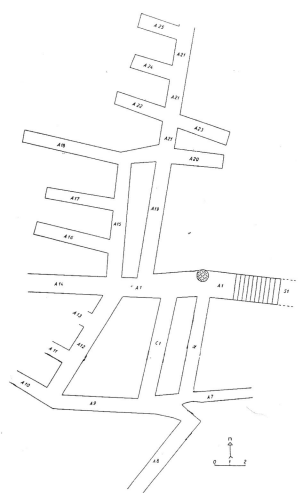

7 *Plan of the Catacomb of Calepodio in its first phase*

mensa)[46] and rich pictorial decoration (figs. 14–15). One of them, the so-called Crypt of the Popes (L2), housed the tombs of nine bishops of Rome by the end of the third century (fig. 32)[47].

The foundation of another communal Christian cemetery, that of Calepodio on Via Aurelia Vetus, must be dated to the same period as "Area I". This catacomb received the tomb of Pope Callistus in 222[48] (fig. 7). Here too, a fairly vast underground area is characterised by a multiple series of galleries mostly arranged in a "comb-like" fashion along two parallel arteries (A15, A19), that branch off from a passageway on axis with an entrance staircase (A1). As in "Area I", simple *loculi* filled the available spaces in a rational manner.

In the Catacomb of Priscilla on Via Salaria, a vast area for communal inhumations was hewn out of an abandoned poz-

17

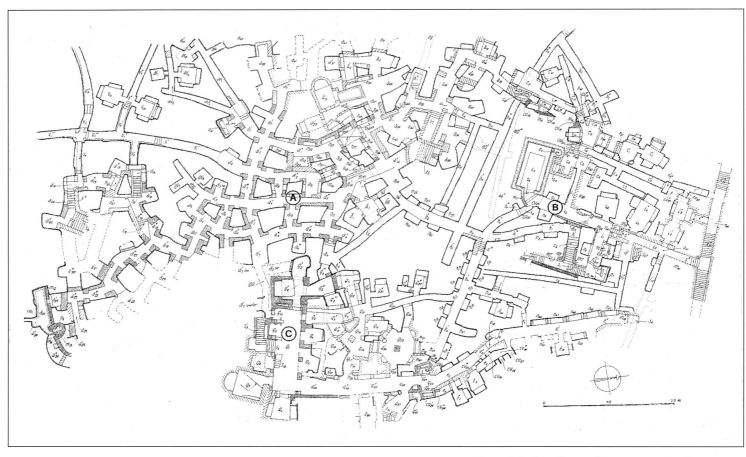

8 Plan of the first floor of the Catacomb of Priscilla

*9 Plan of the Hypogeum of
the Flavii Aurelii "A" in the
Catacomb of Domitilla*

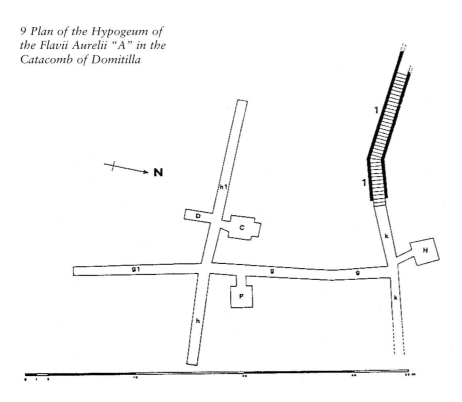

zolana quarry. The catacomb, the largest of this period, was filled with dozens of very large galleries characterised by a rough profile and irregular plan (fig 8, A)[49]. The area, precisely datable from its furnishings (inscriptions, brick stamps, paintings) to the first decades of the third century, housed thousands of *loculus* tombs (figs. 13, 81). In addition, there were several more monumental burials with large masonry niches containing marble sarcophagi, mostly located along a gallery (a1) into which the entrance staircase led (s6-s7)[50].

In one of the oldest areas of the Catacomb of Domitilla, the so-called Area of the *Flavii Aurelii* "A", the same structural characteristics are also found (fig. 9). Thus, orthogonal galleries, onto which open a few *cubicula*, were served by an entrance stair-

18

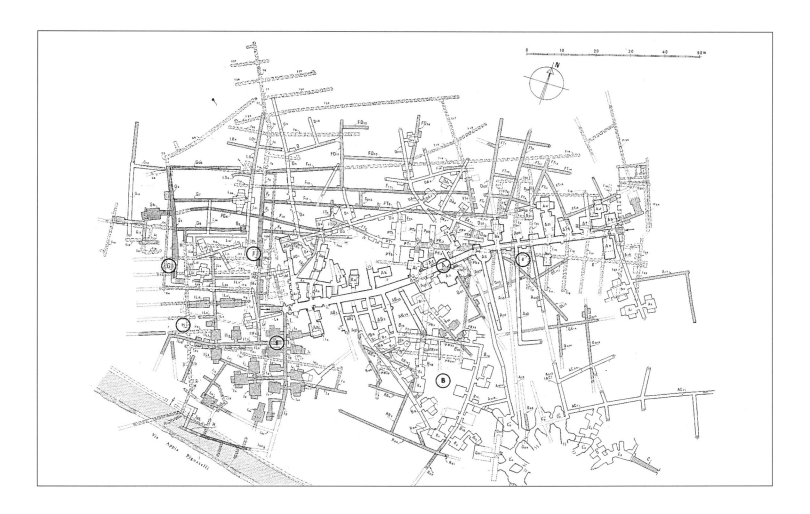

10 Plan of the Catacomb of Pretestato

case and intensively occupied by *loculus* and *a mensa* tombs[51].

Still in the first decades of the third century, the cemetery of Pretestato on Via Appia was established in an area measuring 100 x 120 ft., set off by a walled precinct. As in "Area I" at S. Callisto, two parallel galleries, accessible from two separate staircases (fig. 10, F–G), were arranged at the far ends[52]. From these two main access routes, numerous transversal passageways branched out in an orthogonal pattern. These transverse galleries eventually extended beyond the delineated area, giving rise to two distinct regions, called respectively the *Scala Maggiore* and the *Scala Minore*. Only the so-called *coronatio cubiculum* (Gb) was excavated probably at a later time in this area[53].

Yet another example of a communal area of vast extension, dated to the mid-third century, is represented by a system of galleries found on Via Tiburtina. Characterised by a mixed scheme combining the "fishbone" and "grid" patterns, it housed the tomb of the martyr Novatian, probably the schismatic who died during the Valerian persecution of 257–258 (fig. 11)[54]. The earliest development of the area can be precisely dated by five funerary inscriptions found *in situ* that refer to the years 266 and 270 (ICUR, VII, 20335–20339). All the tombs, with the exception perhaps of the martyr's tomb that is thought to have originally been of the *a mensa* type, are simple *loculi*.

In the examples cited, one can clearly see the structural novelty of the earliest Christian communal underground cemeteries: their great extent, careful planning and intensive and rational exploitation of the burial space. The tombs are characterised by a marked ty-

19

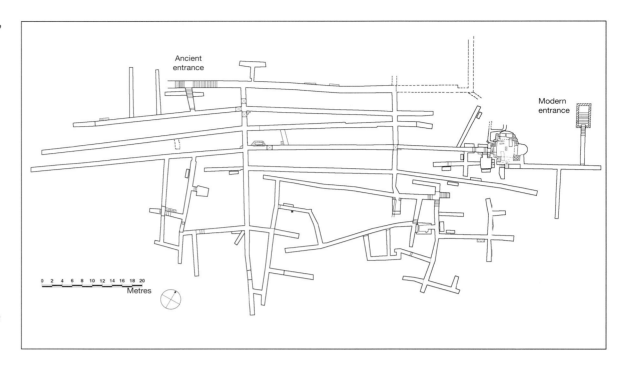

11 Plan of the Catacomb of Novaziano

12 Gallery of the earliest region of the Catacomb of Novaziano

pological uniformity that manifests itself in the systematic adoption of *loculus* tombs (figs. 12–13, 81). These *loculi* are usually very large and closed off with marble slabs or tiles. They are well aligned along the walls and alternate with wide segments of tufa (figs. 12, 13, 81). More monumental burials (niches for sarcophagi, *a mensa* type tombs) or more exclusive spaces (*cubicula*), sometimes decorated, are rather rare. As mentioned earlier[55], the marked uniformity of the tombs was evidently in agreement with the heavily egalitarian ideology of the new religion[56] It seems that the aspiration to ostentatiously commemorate one's own individuality, by "self-representation" through the funerary monument so common in the Roman world[57], was deliberately set aside.

The epigraphy of these early funerary complexes, on the other hand, conforms to the mostly undifferentiated character of the tombs. The epitaphs were normally inscribed on gravestones or painted in red lead on the tiles that closed off the *loculi* (or onto the mortar that more rarely covered their exterior) (figs. 159–161). They record only the name of the deceased, rarely accompanied by that of the dedicator or a wish that

13 Gallery in the area of the arenaria of the Catacomb of Priscilla

14 A mensa tomb in Chapels of the Sacraments A2 in "Area I" of the Catacomb of S. Callisto

15 Chapels of the Sacraments A3 in "Area I" of the Catacomb of S. Callisto

16 *The so-called Cryptoporticus of the Catacomb of Priscilla.*

the dead rest in peace. All of the retrospective biographical elements that characterise contemporary non-Christian epigraphy are omitted[58]. A conscious choice, it was a way of arranging the faithful within a unified eschatological view, and thus, according to the more genuine dictates of the "re-socialisation" advocated by Christianity[59].

Nevertheless, although rare, examples of more monumental tombs (niches for sarcophagi, *a mensa* tombs) (fig. 14) and exclusive spaces (*cubicula*) are also documented, as has been seen, in these first communal areas. Sometimes decorated, these were evidently the prerogative of commissioners of high-birth (figs. 6, 9, 10 (Gb), 15, 132).

Burial areas that can be attributed to particularly wealthy clientele are also attested in the vicinity of some communal cemeteries. These consist of family hypogea of limited extent, often richly decorated and equipped with more monumental tombs. This is the case of the Hypogea of the *Acilii* and the Cryptoporticus near the *arenarium* of Priscilla (figs. 8, B–C; 16). Another example is the group of *cubicula* of early date found in the so-called *Spelunca Magna* of the Catacomb of Pretestato (fig. 10, A), alongside the two intensively utilised regions of the *Scala Maggiore* and *Scala Minore*[60]. In the Catacomb of Domitilla, the so-called Hypogeum of the Good Shepherd,

22

dated to the first decades of the third century, demonstrates the contemporary presence of a *cubiculum* richly decorated with wall paintings (figs. 17, A; 100–101) and a series of galleries for poorer inhumations, that branch off orthogonally from the principal artery (that leads to the *cubiculum*) (fig. 17)[61].

It is likely that some of these hypogea and more monumental tombs, connected to the intensely used underground areas and the prerogative of those faithful who were evidently better off economically, belonged to the actual founders of these funerary areas. The example of the Catacomb of Priscilla seems indicative. The foundress of the cemetery, from whom it took its name[62], was with all probability a member of the *Acilii Glabriones* family. This family's funerary area can in fact be identified in the area of the more exclusive hypogeum of the same name[63].

On the other hand, the names of many of the earliest communal cemeteries in Rome (just like contemporary ones in Carthage)[64], attested by the sources from the first half of the fourth century, evidently seem to refer to private intervention in the foundation of communal cemeteries. Only the Catacomb of Callisto appears from the very beginning, as seen earlier, to have been directly administered by the ecclesiastical hierarchy[65]. The names of these early funerary complexes transmitted by the literary and epigraphic sources, Domitilla, Priscilla, Pretestato, Bassilla, and Trasone, can only be suitably explained in connection with their foundation by private individuals[66]. A member of the community must have donated his land, or furnished the necessary funding for its purchase, for the excavation of a communal funerary area. Later, his tomb and those of his family members would have been located in that place (fig. 18). In some cases, the founders belonged to rich families of senatorial rank, as the examples of the *Acilii Glabriones* and the *Flavii* who founded the Catacombs of Priscilla and Domitilla attest[67]. These were members of the Roman aristocracy who

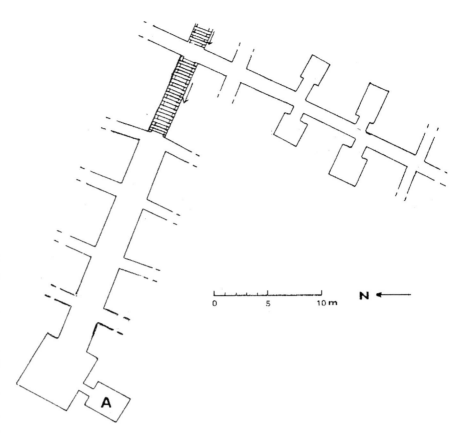

17 *Plan of the Region of the Good Shepherd in the Catacomb of Domitilla in its first phase*

18 *Inscription from the territory of Velletri (Latium) that mentions the foundation of an Early Christian cemetery by a certain* Faltonia Hilaritas

Faltoniae Hilaritati,
dominae filiae carissimae,
quae hoc coemeterium
a solo sua pecunia fecit
et huhic religioni donavit.

converted to Christianity at a very early stage, as recorded in the contemporary sources. Thanks as well to the donations of these rich proprietors, the communities could secure an adequate economic sustenance[68].

The contemporary Carthaginian burial areas of Tertullus, Faustus, Macrobius, and Candidianus also reveal by their very names, as mentioned earlier, an origin tied to private benefaction[69].

The administration of these communal cemeteries, the "*areae sepulturarum nostrarum*" of Tertullian, in fact must have been co-ordinated by the ecclesiastical authorities. The passage cited from the *Traditio Apostolica* of Hippolytus seems to attribute both the authority and the ability to supervise the cemeteries to the bishop[70].

This seems to be confirmed, several decades later, by the interventions of Pope Fabian (236–250) carried out *per cymiteria* (LP, I, p. 4) and especially by the decree of Gallienus that restored the cemeteries confiscated during the persecution of Valerian (257–258) directly to the bishops (Euseb., *Hist. eccl.*, VII.13 = GCS, 9,2, p. 666).

Ownership of a funerary area tied to a private foundation must have been guaranteed by the most basic norms of Roman funerary law[71]. The bishop probably corresponded in the eyes of the State to the communal ownership, that the community could have held due to its likely assimilation to the *collegia religionis causa*[72].

In addition to burial in the communal burial places used exclusively by the community, at any rate, the individual believers could always choose to be buried in individual or family tombs in the great pagan suburban necropoli. Burial in communal cemeteries was not required for everyone. This is confirmed by a passage of Cyprian, in which a bishop who buried his own children "*apud profana sepulcra*" is mentioned (*Ep.*, 67.6 = CSEL, 3/2, p. 740). In the third century at Rome, this is demonstrated by the tombs of faithful mixed with pagan burials in the Vatican necropoli, as well as by family hypogea in various outlying areas[73]. The latter obviously followed the structural model of the pagan examples; they were characterised by reduced dimensions and sometimes rich pictorial decoration. One of the most important of these hypogean tombs is that of the *Aurelii* on Viale Manzoni, dated to circa 230–250. It was constructed of two funerary chambers built above ground within an enclosure wall and an underground area, that also consisted of two large rooms (and a small vestibule), that housed a limited number of tombs (fig. 19)[74]. The monument is known for the important pictorial decoration that covers its entire surface (figs. 76, 98, 124, 135, 145). Alongside themes probably of Christian character, the wall painting records scenes from pagan mythology (fig. 135) as well as others of less certain meaning[75].

19 Funerary monument of the Aurelii on Viale Manzoni: plans of the rooms above ground and the hypogean areas

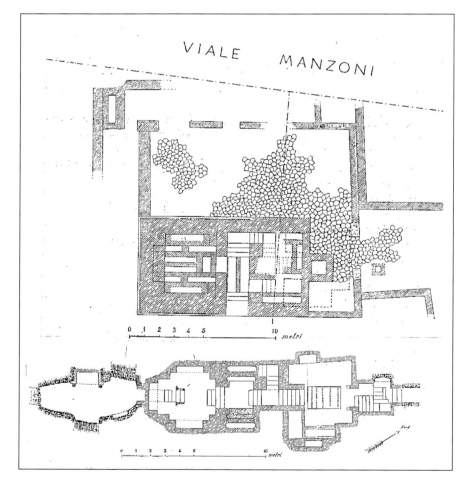

4. The Development of Underground Cemeteries in the Second Half of the Third Century

The number and extent of communal cemeteries datable to the first half of the third century provides clear evidence of the importance and size that the Christian community had achieved in Rome by around 250. In those years, the sources also confirm the numerical and organisational progression of Christianity within the city. A famous letter of Pope Cornelius (251–253) written to the bishop of Antioch, Fabius records how the Church in Rome already had numerous clergy with diversified tasks, consisting of 46 priests, 7 deacons, 7 subdeacons, 42 acolytes, 52 exorcists, various lectors and custodians of the cult sites. The same letter mentions the presence of more than 1500 widows and poor people, whose sustenance was provided for by communal charity (Euseb., *Hist. eccl.*, VI.43.11 = GCS, 9,2, p. 618). At the beginning of this century, A. von Harnack a bit audaciously deduced from this that the community could have comprised a total of c. 30,000 members in that period[76]. On the other hand, already in the period of Pope Fabian (236–250), as attested by the *Catalogus Liberianus* (LP, I, p. 4), Rome had subdivided its ecclesiastical territory into seven regions (parallel to the Augustan civil regions). This division was aimed at a more efficient and detailed capacity for assistance in urban quarters. The pope assigned jurisdiction of these areas to seven deacons[77].

The period of the Peace of the Church, that is, the period between the last general persecution in the third century of Valerian (257–258) and the persecution of Diocletian (303–304), further facilitated the numerical and organisational development of the community. Christianity penetrated in a widespread manner into many diversified social strata. It began to integrate itself always more profoundly into the managerial structures of the empire and into the ideals and culture of the Roman world[78].

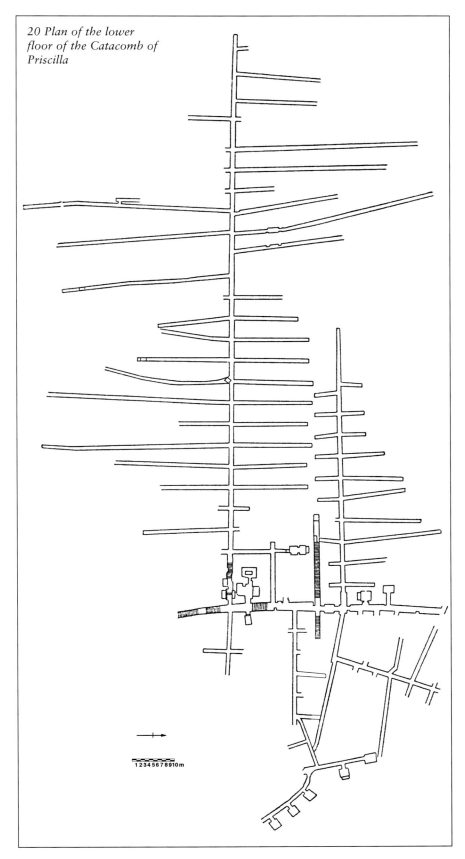

20 Plan of the lower floor of the Catacomb of Priscilla

1 2 3 4 5 6 7 8 9 10 m

21 The main gallery of
the lower floor of the
Catacomb of Priscilla

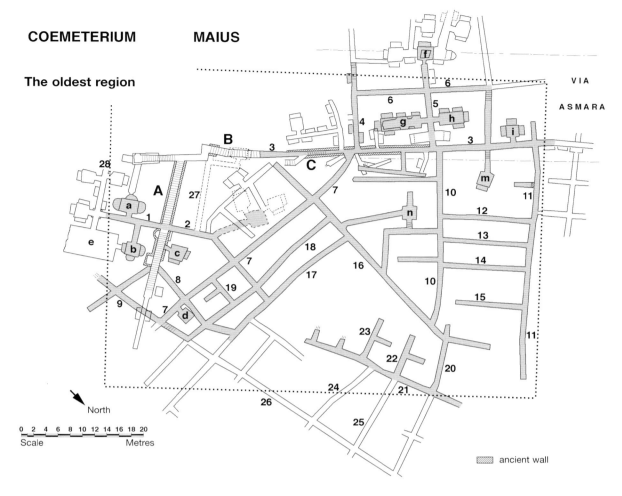

COEMETERIUM MAIUS

The oldest region

During this period, cemetery areas in the suburbs increased considerably. The catacombs established during the first half of the century grew in extent; other areas were added in the vicinity of already existing ones. New catacombs sprang up in different areas of the extra-urban territory.

The names of some of the cemeteries created in this period seem to support the hypothesis that these areas were originally founded collectively, and therefore not strictly tied to private sponsorship[79]. The names can be generic, such as the *Coemeterium Maius*, tied to a simple toponym, such as *catacumbas*, or connected exclusively with the saint buried there (*Agnetis, Laurenti, Gorgoni*)[80]. One that was an episcopal foundation was the cemetery of Novella on Via Salaria that, according to the *Liber Pontificalis*, was planned by Pope Marcellus

(308–309) (LP, I, p. 164). It probably corresponds to the large lower level of the Catacomb of Priscilla (figs. 20, 21)[81]. The cemetery of S. Callisto partially retained its ecclesiastical character, as demonstrated by the tombs of Popes Gaius (283–296), Eusebius (309–310) and Miltiades (311–314), located in a new region added alongside "Area I"[82]. Moreover, in order to be able to build a family *cubiculum* there, the deacon Severus had to ask Pope Marcellinus (296–304) for permission (ICUR IV, 10183).

The new underground areas dated to this period are characterised by the same intensive use and the same regularity and planning as the areas of the first half of the century. Around 250, a new catacomb on Via Nomentana, the so-called *Coemeterium Maius*, was constructed from two contiguous areas. The catacomb has galleries arranged

27

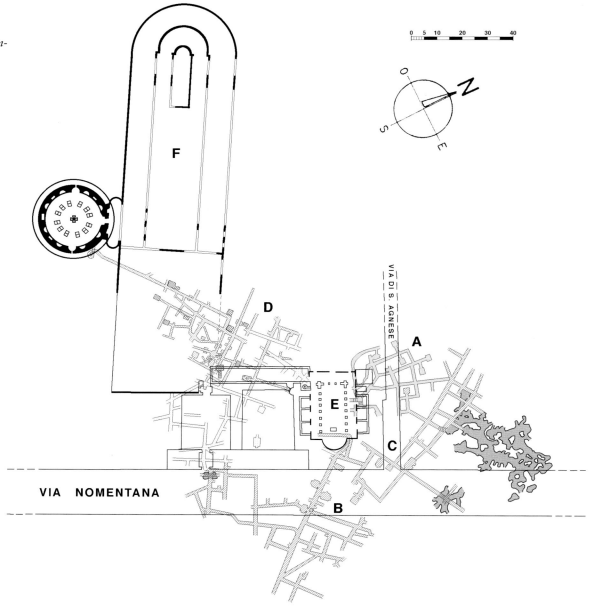

23 *Plan of the monu-
mental complex of S.
Agnese on Via Nomen-
tana*

F

D

A

VIA DI S. AGNESE

E

C

VIA   NOMENTANA

B

in a "grid" pattern, accessible from two in-
dependent staircases. These galleries were
generated out of two major arteries aligned
with the entrances (figs. 22; 6, A–B). Simple
loculus tombs occupied the area. Only in a
later phase, around 270–280, did it house
several *cubicula*, one of which was decorated
with painting[83]. The epigraphic production
of the catacomb during this phase is known
for its splendid "ostrian" inscriptions, which
were certainly produced by a specialised lapidary workshop[84].

Similar structural and epigraphic characteristics are found in the nearby, more or less
contemporary, primitive nucleus of the Catacomb of S. Agnese (the so-called "Regio I")
(fig. 23, A), at least as far as it is possible to
deduce in the area not destroyed by the later
insertion of the basilica *ad corpus* constructed on top of the martyr's tomb[85]. This
nucleus consists of a series of long galleries,
arranged in an orthogonal pattern, that were
occupied by *loculus* or *a mensa* tombs onto
which opened several *cubicula* (fig. 24)[86].

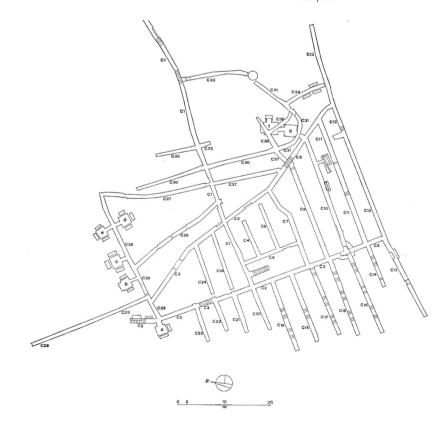

24 Cubiculum of "Regio I" of the Catacomb of S. Agnese

24 Cubiculum of "Regio I" of the Catacomb of S. Agnese

25 Plan of the lower floor of the Catacomb of Panfilo

The "ostrian" epigraphy that also characterises this area (fig. 24) reveals the presence of a workshop of craftsmen that served the cemeteries in this sector of Via Nomentana.

During the second half of the third and the beginning of the fourth centuries, the laying out of communal burial areas in the so-called "fish-bone" pattern seems to have been particularly widespread. A staircase gave access, either directly or through a transversal, to a long gallery (the "matrix" in the scheme), onto which opened a series of offshoots facing each other in an orthogonal pattern. These were placed only a few meters apart so as to occupy all of the available space. The scheme finds an impressive and spectacular application in the lower floor of the Catacomb of Panfilo on Via Salaria Vetus (figs. 25–26) and especially in the corresponding level of the Catacomb of Priscilla, whose initial stage can be dated to the beginning of the fourth century (fig. 20)[87]. On the latter, twenty-three facing offshoots open

26 Gallery of the earliest region of the lower floor of the Catacomb of Panfilo

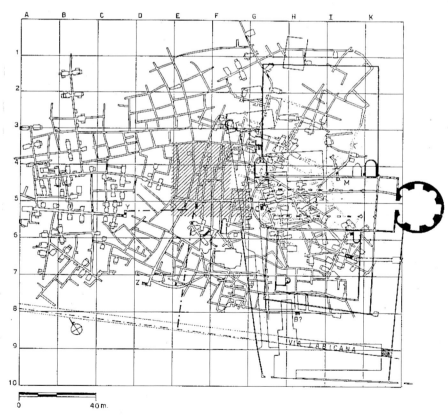

27 Plan of the Catacomb of SS. Marcellino e Pietro with "Regio X" indicated by hatched lines

onto one of the two principal galleries that is 150 meters long (fig. 21). In the cemetery of Panfilo, as already was the case in that of Novaziano, some characteristic *loculi* closed off with tiles covered externally with mortar occur. The funerary epigraph was painted in red lead or traced in charcoal on top of this mortar.

Plans of a "fish-bone" type also characterise "Regio X" of the Catacomb of SS. Marcellino e Pietro (fig. 27), the so-called area of the "Staircase of 1897" in the cemetery of Domitilla, the anonymous catacomb in the Villa Pamphilj on Via Aurelia Vetus (fig. 28)[88]. These areas, considerably extensive and capable of containing thousands of burial sites, take the form of vast funerary spaces intended for modest and undifferentiated burials. Only in "Regio X" of SS. Marcellino e Pietro, do four *cubicula* located in the southern periphery of the area (X9–X11, Xt) betray a more elevated commissioner; three of the *cubicula* are decorated with paintings[89]. In this same catacomb, characterised by communal areas intended for common burials, there are also two other sections that date to the second half of the third century (Regions "B" and "Z"). In contrast, a fourth zone (Region "Y" with its southern addition "I") displays a thick concentration of *cubicula*, often finely decorated, that suggests that this area of the catacomb was used by groups who were better off economically and of a higher social status (figs. 29, 137)[90]. According to the calculations of J. Guyon, in its poor and rich areas, the Catacomb *ad duas lauros* housed a total of 11,000 tombs in the second half of the third century[91]. Adding to these those tombs located on the surface, one can assume that the entire cemetery served a population of circa 9,000 souls (fig. 29)[92].

One must also consider those who used the so-called "Region of Gaius and Eusebius" in S. Callisto as affluent commissioners, in part ecclesiastical[93]. Established between the end of the third and the beginning of the fourth centuries near "Area I", this region was characterised by a series of monumental *cubicula* and *arcosolia* (some of

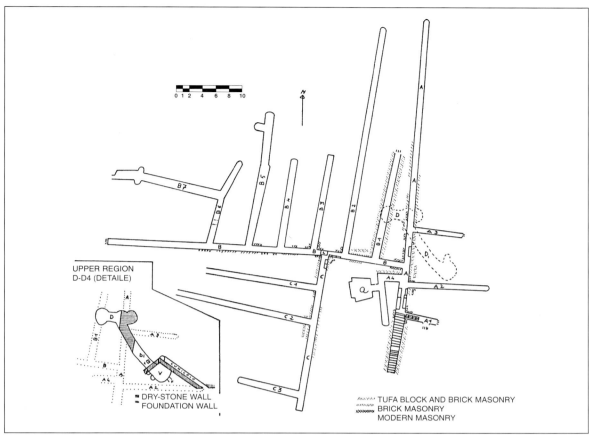

28 Plan of the Anonymous Catacomb of Villa Doria-Pamphilj

UPPER REGION
D-D4 (DETAILE)

■ DRY-STONE WALL
▬ FOUNDATION WALL

TUFA BLOCK AND BRICK MASONRY
BRICK MASONRY
MODERN MASONRY

29 Plan of the Catacomb of SS. Marcellino e Pietro with the pre-Constantinian areas indicated by hatched lines

which were painted) that opened along the principal artery (G1) and oldest offshoots (fig. 30)[94]. The same characteristics are found in the eastern development of this same area (the so-called "Region of Miltiades") (fig. 30, 105). The area in the Catacomb of Domitilla that was installed at the end of the third century on the upper floor of the Hypogeum of the Good Shepherd is also characterised by a similar construction (fig. 17)[95].

In the cemeteries of Via Anapo and of Giordani on Via Salaria Nova, more exclusive nuclei with a limited development, fitted out with *cubicula,* existed side by side with more extensive inhumations carved out in pre-existing *arenaria*[96].

In fact, the presence of monumental tombs (*arcosolia,* large niches) and reserved spaces (*cubicula*) becomes more intensive in this period. The *cubicula* in particular show an evolution towards more complex forms.

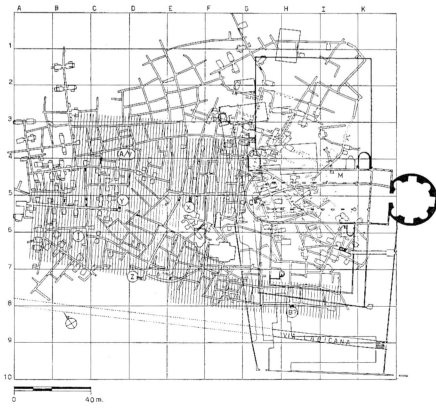

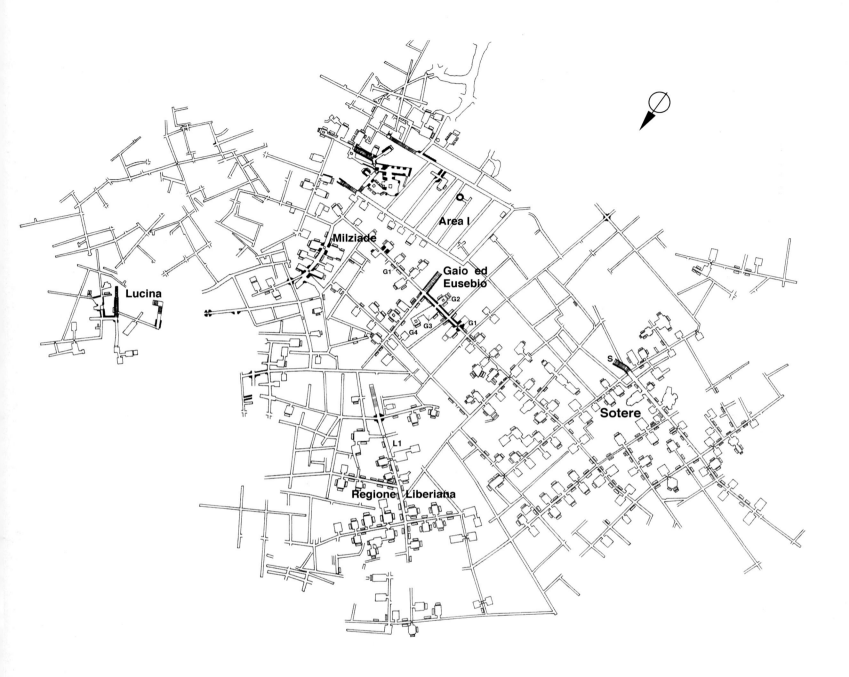

Milziade

Area I

Lucina

G1

Gaio ed
Eusebio

G2

G3
G4

G1

S

Sotere

L1

Regione Liberiana

30 Plan of the Catacomb of S. Callisto

31 Cubiculum with benches and cattedrae in the Coemeterium Maius

In the oldest examples, just as in the areas of the first half of the century, the *cubicula* are of modest proportions with a flat roof and contain *loculi* or *a mensa* tombs (fig. 15)[97]. In the last decades of the third and the beginning of the fourth centuries, the rooms assume greater proportions and are not infrequently covered by barrel vaults and lit by large skylights. *Arcosolium* tombs are positioned along the walls (fig. 33)[98]. In "Regio I" of S. Agnese, there are some remarkable *cubicula* with real *dromoi* leading into them. Superimposed *arcosolia* with apses or reduced arches, *a mensa* tombs and *loculi* with an arched upper profile are hewn out of the walls (fig. 24)[99]. A room exhibiting similar characteristics is also found in the oldest section of the nearby *Coemeterium Maius*[100]. In the expansions of the end of the third and the beginning of the fourth centuries, this ceme-

tery was also fitted out with several extremely remarkable rooms of great height. These rooms were ennobled by the presence of benches, stools, niches and various architectural elements, all carved out of the rock (fig. 31)[101]. The structural similarity between the *Coemeterium Maius* and the adjoining Catacomb of S. Agnese, as already mentioned earlier, and confirmed in glaring fashion by the parallel production of "ostrian" epitaphs[102], proves the existence of specialised workshops of *fossores* operating within the same territory.

In the second half of the third century, epigraphy reveals progress towards the evolution of more specifically Christian formulae[103]. The repertoire of paintings that decorate the *arcosolia* and *cubicula* is enriched with new themes[104].

The cult of the tombs of the martyrs and bishops does not yet seem to have resulted in significant monumental work during this period. The tombs of the nine Popes that from 235–236 to 283 occupied the crypt of the same name in "Area I" of S. Callisto[105] were composed of simple *loculi* (fig. 32). Only the bishop and martyr Sixtus († 258) was probably interred in an *a mensa* tomb that stood alone on the back wall of the room[106]. The tomb of Pope Cornelius, who died in exile at Centumcellae in 253 and whose remains were later transferred to the nearby Crypts of Lucina, was also an *a mensa* tomb. It was set under a skylight, on a wall next to the entrance into a kind of double *cubiculum* with a vestibule[107].

The tomb of Bishop Gaius (283–296) was also composed of a simple *loculus*. Nevertheless, it was particularly large and placed in a dominant position on the back wall of a monumental *cubiculum* plastered in white and lit by a large skylight (fig. 33)[108]. Gaius was the first bishop who was not placed in the already full Crypt of the Popes of "Area I"; rather his tomb was located in the nearby region created in the closing years of the third century (fig. 30, G3)[109]. Not much is known about the original arrangement of the tomb of Pope Eusebius (309–310) due to modifications that it

underwent in later periods. At any rate, the tomb was perhaps an *a mensa* tomb on the west wall of a *cubiculum* that faced that of Gaius (fig. 30, G2)[110].

Especially from the second half of the fourth century onwards, the transformations that the tombs of the martyrs underwent following the development of their cult[111] make possible the appreciation of their original structures only in exceptional cases. For example, simple *loculi* set in galleries or *cubicula* housed the tombs of SS. Callistus († 222), Januarius († 258?), Calogerus and Parthenius, Marcellinus and Peter (the last four were martyrs of the

33 Cubiculum of Pope Gaius of the Catacomb of S. Callisto

32 The Crypt of the Popes in "Area I" of the Catacomb of S. Callisto

34 *Loculus tombs of SS.*
Peter and Marcellinus in
the Catacomb of SS.
Marcellino e Pietro

35 *Section of the rooms*
of the Catacomb of S.
Ermete that contain the
tombs of the martyrs
Protus and Hyacinth

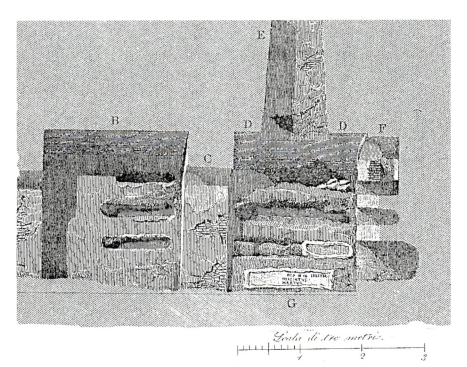

Scala di tre metri.

Diocletian persecution), respectively in the Catacombs of Calepodio, Pretestato, S. Callisto and *ad duas lauros*[112]. Perhaps a tomb of *a mensa* type held the remains of the schismatic Novatian († 258) in a gallery of the Catacomb of the same name[113]. In only one case has archaeological investigation allowed the recovery of an intact burial of a martyr, that of S. Hyacinth in the Catacomb of Bassilla on Via Salaria Vetus. Here, it has been verified that the tomb of the martyr was composed of a simple small niche carved out of the tufa that housed the burned bones of the martyr. To endow it with dignity, the *loculus* was closed off with a large rectangular marble slab inscribed with an epitaph in which the name, the title of martyr and the date of the interment of Hyacinth[114] was recorded (fig. 35). The tomb was positioned in the lower part of one of the walls of a short gallery.

5. The Development of Catacombs during the Reign of Constantine and the Pontificates of Julius (337–352) and Liberius (352–366)

The religious peace of 312, as is well known, marked a decisive stage in the history of Christianity. With Constantine, it could rely on a completely exceptional type of protection in the person of the Emperor himself. A whole series of legislative measures and material donations promoted by the sovereign allowed the Church to have at her disposal for the first time the proper means for complete fulfilment of her mission. This "shift" had enormous consequences on the objectives of the new religion of the masses to gain ever-increasing numbers of faithful[115]. With regard to catacombs as well, the Constantinian period marked a decisive shift. Underground cemeteries considerably increased their dimensions in line with the ever-growing rate of conversions fostered by this religious peace.

Significant enlargements within the first quarter of the fourth century are recorded in the peripheral areas of the *arenaria*, the lower level and other areas of the Catacomb of Priscilla[116], the eastern section of the "Catacomba Anonima" of Via Anapo[117] and the Catacomb of SS. Marcellino e Pietro. In the latter, to the north and south of the pre-Constantinian regions "X" and "Y", a vast area of galleries was carved out, equipped with numerous *cubicula*, in which the majority of the most famous pictorial decoration of the catacomb is found (fig. 29)[118].

New extensive regions for generally "poor" and undifferentiated inhumations in simple *loculi*, characterised by areas laid out in a "fish-bone" pattern with a dense series of galleries capable of containing thousands of tombs, were created during the Constantinian period in various suburban areas. Examples of these new areas include the lower levels of the regions of the *Scala Maggiore*, and *Scala Minore* and the Region of the "*Pistores*" in the Catacomb of Pretestato

(fig. 10, F3–F8, F14–27, H, E). Other new areas were constructed on the lower floor of the area of the "Staircase of 1897" in the Catacomb of Domitilla and the lowest level of the Catacomb of S. Ermete[119]. The lower level of the Catacomb of the Giordani consisted in this period of an extended network of galleries, with broad links laid out along two long parallel principal passageways[120]. In the Catacomb of S. Agnese, two vast regions formed by orthogonal galleries that branched off from the axial main arteries with entrance staircases, equipped with a few *cubicula*, were built behind the site in which the tomb of the martyr was located (fig. 23, B–C)[121]. The more peripheral sections of the two areas were systematically used for common burials in simple *loculi*.

In this same period, other regions also display more monumental characteristics. This is true of an area south of the *Spelunca Magna* in the cemetery of Pretestato (the so-called "Regio B"), dated to the beginning of the fourth century. It is composed of a few galleries into which *arcosolia* and *cubicula* are set in a regular fashion; some are frescoed as well (fig. 10.B)[122]. The elitist character of some areas in the Catacomb of Pretestato, alongside the more modest character of the areas discussed above, is demonstrated not only by the luxurious painted *cubicula* along the *Spelunca Magna* (fig. 10, A)[123], but also by one of the less monumental ones, that as the epigraphy testifies was occupied by members of the senatorial aristocracy (ICUR V, 14016, 14132, 14155, 14445). Among the *clarissimi* of the families of the *Annii*, *Postumii* and *Insteii*, two were buried in decorated marble sarcophagi, datable to the first quarter of the fourth century[124].

Spaces reserved for elite commissioners can be seen as well in the early expansions in the "Region of Gaius and Eusebius", the complex of S. Callisto and the *Coemeterium Maius*. In the latter, to the west of the oldest network of tombs, a region was created on a slightly higher level with a series of galleries in an orthogonal pattern; the galleries were fitted out with a large number of *cubicula*

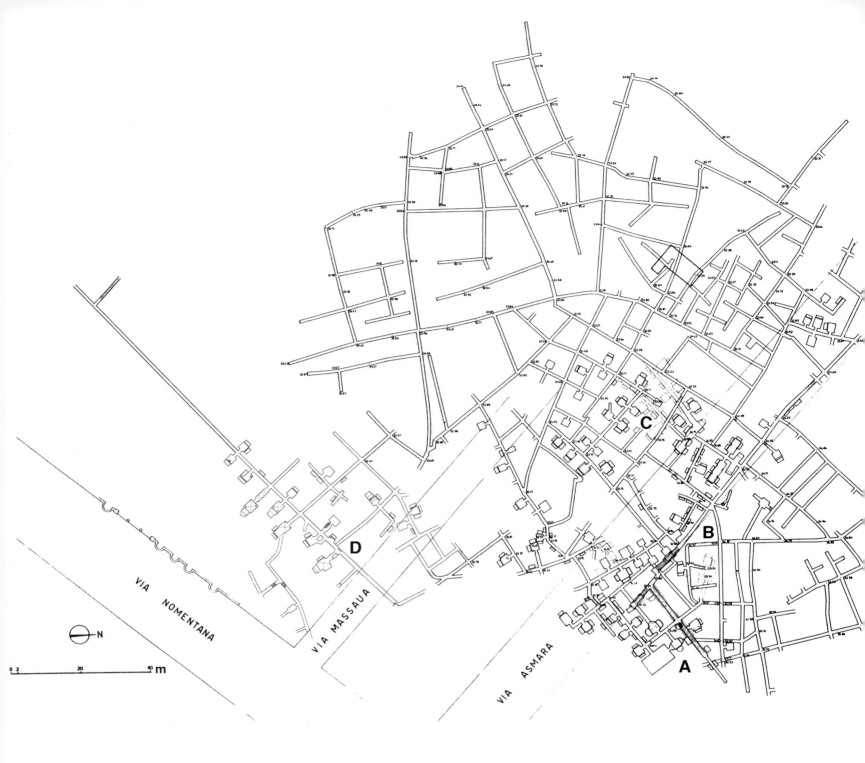

36 Plan of the Coeme-
terium Maius

and *arcosolia*, not infrequently decorated[125]. The monumental character of this area contrasts with the more peripheral sections of the catacomb that were also the result of subsequent expansion. These peripheral areas were equipped exclusively with simple galleries (fig. 36)[126].

In the 330s and 340s and in the first decades after the middle of the century, the development of catacombs continued in a substantial manner. In comparison with the preceding period, the new regions seem generally to reveal a more marked presence of monumental areas. This phenomenon manifests itself essentially and especially by the ever more widespread adoption of family *cubicula* whose architecture assumed increasingly grandiose and elaborate forms

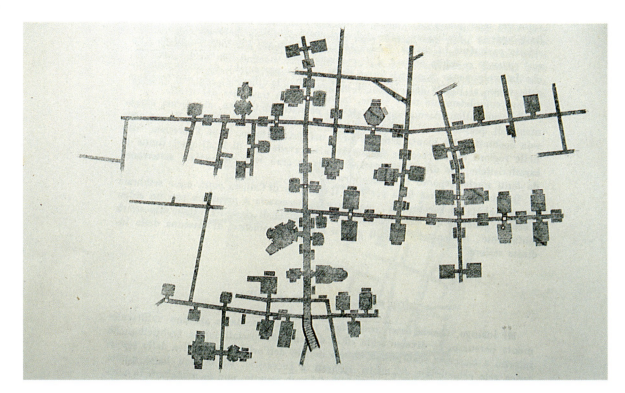

37 Plan of a sector of
the so-called "Regione di
Sotere" of the Catacomb
of S. Callisto

38 Plan of the Catacomb
of SS. Marcellino e
Pietro, with the regions
which developed under
and alongside the Con-
stantinian Basilica (after
A.D. 325) indicated by
hatched lines

(figs. 39–45)[127]. The layout of these plans also seems at times subordinate to the placement of the rooms. The links of the network of galleries become larger to allow the systematic opening of *cubicula* (fig. 29, 37). Family tombs reappear conspicuously. The monumentality and decoration of the *cubicula* in many cases points to affluent commissioners, who can be associated at least in part with the richest ranks of the Roman aristocracy. The increasing conversion of this class in precisely this period is attested to by the literary sources[128]. On the other hand, in this same period, areas just as vast with networks of galleries containing simple *loculi* show characteristics that point to more modest commissioners (fig. 47), thus revealing the coexistence of specialised areas with differentiated use within single funerary complexes (fig. 36)[129].

The basilicas in honour of the most important martyrs of the city built during the Constantinian period in suburban Rome, themselves funerary spaces of considerable

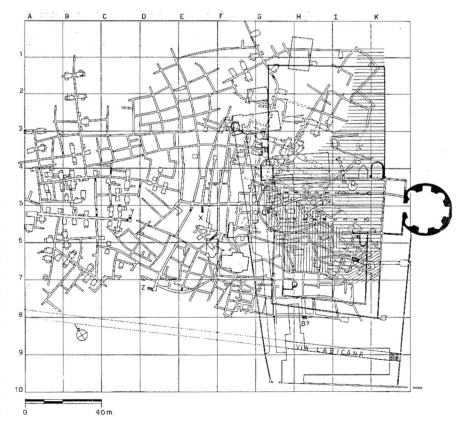

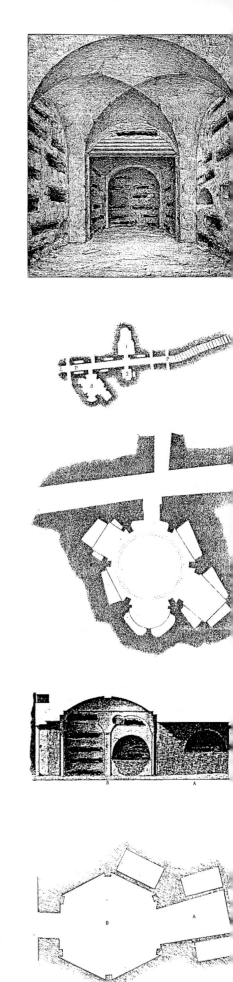

extent[130], became centres of attraction for underground necropoli. Three new regions were dug out beneath and behind the Basilica of SS. Marcellino e Pietro on Via Labicana. Two were directly accessible from the church, the third from one wing of the porticoed structure that flanked the building to the south (fig. 38, M, S, C)[131]. The area that developed under the basilica reveals in particular the presence of a considerable number of monumental *cubicula*[132]. Characteristics more or less similar are found in "Regio X", in the contemporary extension of the lower floor and in the more peripheral sections (fig. 144). In total, during the second quarter of the fourth century, according to the calculations of J. Guyon, about 8,000 new tombs were added to the catacomb *ad duas lauros*[133].

The ambulatory Basilicas of S. Sebastiano on Via Appia and S. Agnese on the Nomentana also constituted fulcrum points of new underground areas. In the first, clusters of regions were created on different levels starting from access staircases located outside the building, near the façade and the north side. The network of galleries on the second floor, fitted out with numerous *cubicula*, was accessible directly from the church through at least three staircases[134]. The new regions were particularly used from the 340s onwards. On Via Nomentana, the construction of an ambulatory basilica dedicated to S. Agnese, commissioned by the daughter of the emperor, Constantina, led to the creation of a vast new region, the so-called "Regio IV" from the 340s onwards (fig. 23, D). This area had its entrance just to the north of the

40 The so-called "Pantheon" of the "Regione di Sotere" in the Catacomb of S. Callisto

39 Plans and drawings of several "architectural" cubicula of the "Regione di Sotere" in the Catacomb of S. Callisto

41

41 *"Architectural" cubiculum of the "Regione di Sotere" in the Catacomb of S. Callisto*

quadriporticus of the church; it developed in part precisely under that structure[135], with galleries intended primarily for communal burials.

During the pontificates of Popes Julius (337–352) and Liberius (352–366), vast and important underground regions were added to the cemetery of S. Callisto. Further development to the west of the principal gallery of the "Region of Gaius and Eusebius" (fig. 30, G1) became the cardinal point of an extensive and extremely regular "quarter" for aristocratic tombs, the so-called "Regione di Sotere" (fig. 30). It was organised according to a network of orthogonal corridors onto which opened *arcosolia* and monumental *cubicula*, usually facing each other (fig. 37). During the second half of the fourth century,

this region was equipped with a second entrance staircase that facilitated visits. The dimensions of the *cubicula* in some cases were truly exceptional. Lit by large skylights, these *cubicula* often assumed complex and spectacular architectural forms, imitative of the architecture of the rich mausolea above ground (figs. 39–41)[136].

Around 330, a new catacomb was created just a little more than 100 meters north of the "Regione di Sotere", in an area perhaps associated with the above ground cemetery that housed the tombs of the martyrs Marcus and Marcellianus. A large number of inscriptions testify to the use of the area by members of the Church hierarchy (priests, lectors, acolytes, exorcists, *fossores*), public officials, craftsmen and mer-

42

chants[137]. The mostly affluent commissioners, also probably connected to the presence of the sanctuary of the martyrs above ground, would explain the strong monumental connotations of the area. The area closest to the entrance staircase is characterised by a considerable number of *cubicula*, often richly decorated with wall revetment in *opus sectile* and mosaics; the *cubicula* housed a great number of sculpted sarcophagi as well[138]. The area also preserved its elitist character in its earliest extensions that are characterised by the presence of many *cubicula* of grand dimensions with sometimes elaborate plans. Only a few galleries in the most peripheral sector seem to have been intended to house communal burials[139].

The ecclesiastical "vocation" of the cemetery of S. Callisto was also maintained in the so-called "Regione Liberiana", created near the "Regione di Sotere" during the period of the episcopate of Liberius. The numerous dated inscriptions found there reveal the chronology of the area. Several record its use by members of the clergy, such as priests, deacons and lectors[140]. The unusual status of the users of this region is indicated, also in this case, by the area's monumental characteristics. *Cubicula* and *arcosolia* regularly open along the main artery of the area, located on axis with the entrance staircase (L1), and in the network of transversal galleries that originates from it. The chambers, as in the nearby "Regione di Sotere" and the adjoining Catacomb of SS. Marco e Mar-

42 Cubiculum with large niches in the Catacomb of Marco, Marcelliano e Damaso celliano, are sometimes of grandiose dimensions, richly decorated with marble and paintings[141]. This area for privileged inhumations distinguishes itself from another contiguous area, situated more to the east, that is characterised by galleries occupied by simple *loculi* (fig. 30)[142].

During the last decades of the fourth century, characteristics of considerable monumentality are also found in other regions of Roman catacombs. Examples include a section of the upper floor of the Catacomb of Panfilo, an area of the cemetery of S. Ippolito (fig. 43), and "Regio I" of the Catacomb of Pretestato (fig. 10)[143]. The so-called "Regione delle cattedre" in the *Coemeterium Maius* (fig. 36, D), whose origin is perhaps datable to the last years of the first half of the fourth century, also displays a series of noteworthy *cubicula* in the very long gallery that constitutes its main axis. The principal characteristics of these *cubicula* are the grandiose size of the tombs (large niches, *arcosolia a tribuna*) and the presence of architectonic decoration carved from the rock, particularly numerous funerary *cattedrae* (thrones) carved out of the tufa (figs. 44, 45)[144].

During this period, in fact, *cubicula* greatly increase in number and monumentality. They are characterised, as mentioned earlier, by often grandiose forms and elaborate layouts (polygonal, cruciform, circular, rec-

tangular, apsidal, etc.) and more complex architectural structures that sometimes include columns, pilasters, architraves, cornices, brackets, arches, niches or other architectural elements carved directly out of the rock (figs. 39–44, 46). The rooms were not infrequently lit by large skylights and decorated with frescoes, marble revetment and mosaics (figs. 39, 41, 144, 148)[145]. As already mentioned, there was a clear desire to reproduce the forms of the rich mausolea, that in this period began to crowd the necropoli above ground, in these underground areas. These mausolea were often related to and strictly adjacent to the great basilicas of the martyrs[146]. Towards the mid-fourth century, *cubicula* covered by a simple layer of white plaster were also frequent[147].

In the areas that were most intensively used and undifferentiated, the *loculi* were usually of more moderate dimensions. They were placed closer to each other along the

walls, sometimes in a disorderly fashion, so that they completely occupied the available surfaces in response to the increasing need for space (fig. 47). The *arcosolia* assumed more monumental forms. Their niches could take an apsidal form while the façades could be further enriched with architectural elements (fig. 48). Not infrequently, the arched niches were also used for burials by closing the entrance with small vertical walls or *transennae*. Monumental funerary niches were opened in galleries and *cubicula* (figs. 39–42).

From the Constantinian period onwards, functional structures used for the rite of the *refrigerium* (the funerary meal) were always more frequently set in the tombs, especially in the *cubicula*. Benches, stools, *cattedrae* that perhaps symbolise the invisible presence of the deceased during the banquets (figs. 31, 44–45, 97), wells, and especially tables, usually composed of cylindrical or square blocks of masonry that supported marble or ceramic plates (figs.43, 46, 49) all appear.

These *mensae* most likely held offerings of food for the deceased or the food consumed by the participants in the rite (figs. 126, 130, 175)[148]. Several areas containing benches and richly decorated with marble revetments that are devoid of tombs could perhaps have

45 Cubiculum with a cattedra and an a kline tomb in the Coemeterium Maius

46 Cubiculum with an arcosolium closed off with a transenna and a cylindrical mensa in the Catacomb of Marco, Marcelliano e Damaso

47 Gallery with funerary gifts "displayed" in the Catacomb of Commodilla

been used as communal banquet halls (fig. 94)[149]. The presence of these structures confirms the diffusion of banqueting in Christian communities, especially from the late Constantinian period onwards, as is attested by the literary sources[150].

Particularly in those catacomb areas with simple *loculi* tombs, the fashion for the placement of small objects in the plaster that closed off the tombs, already evident in the third century, becomes always more widespread. The variety of objects (lamps, personal belongings, bracelets, rings, necklaces, toys, coins, glass or ceramic containers, simple marble slabs, glass paste, etc.) suggests diverse interpretations of this "display". It certainly served in part to identify and characterise the more anonymous tombs, or per-

haps partially to decorate them in a simple way. However, the glass or ceramic containers in particular could possibly refer to the *refrigerium* rite and to the relevant libations and food offered to the deceased (figs. 84, 88)[151]. In any case, it is clear that the originality of this phenomenon, that might be called an "explosion" of the funerary display from the interior to the exterior, was strictly connected with the conditions for conservation peculiar to the monumental space, that is, the hypogean environment[152].

The impressive excavation of the catacombs for the construction of burial sites and the interment of corpses, as in the preceding period, was carried out by the *fossores*, specialised workers who by the fourth century had become assimilated as members of the ecclesiastical hierarchy. During the Constantinian period, the *fossores* are increasingly represented in iconographic evidence and inscriptions (figs. 50, 134, 164)[153].

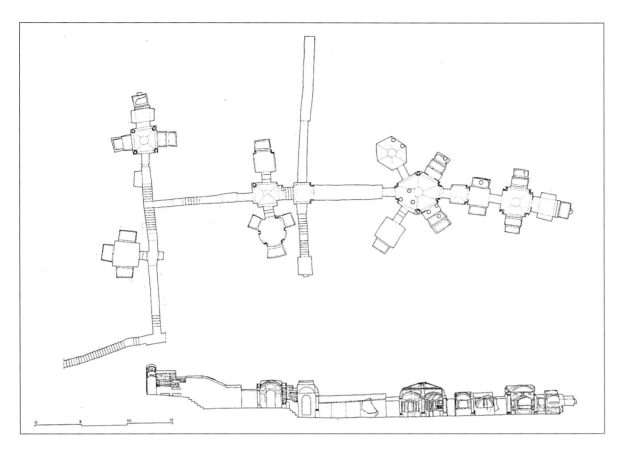

Throughout the entire fourth century, the custom of some families to equip burial hypogea outside the communal areas (hypogea "of private law") continues. These family burial sites are usually characterised by their limited extension, scarcity of tombs, architectural elegance, and the richness and originality of their painted decoration[154]. The most famous of these private hypogea is that of Via Dino Compagni on Via Latina, dated circa 320–370. It was composed of a very limited number of galleries that gave access to a series of funerary chambers, sometimes of elaborate plan. The rooms had cross or pavilion vaults as well as architectural elements such as columns, cornices, brackets, gables, arches, etc. (figs. 51–52)[155]. Almost all of these rooms were decorated with frescoes of high quality (figs. 104, 108, 113–115, 117, 134)[156]. Alongside biblical themes sometimes with unusual iconography, these frescoes represent entirely new themes, at times also dealing with the pagan mythological repertoire. These representations document the presence in this hypogeum, alongside completely Christian family groups, of groups not yet converted to the new religion. This phenomenon is also attested in other private areas, such as in the small Catacomb of Vibia on Via Appia that houses not only Christian tombs, but also the burials of several followers of the cults of Mithras and Sabazius (fig. 53)[157]. Justification for this mixture is to be found precisely in the family character of these areas. A particularly affluent commissioner, detached from any type of conditioning, explains the quality and originality of the decoration, verifiable as well in other private cemeteries such as those of Trebius Justus, the *Cacciatori* and Villa Cellere[158].

In the first half of the fourth century, the tombs of martyrs still seem to have received a moderate amount of care. Only the tomb of S. Lawrence, one of the most venerated saints in the city, had already been subjected to a series of important

47

52 *Cubiculum of the Catacomb of Via Dino Compagni*

53 *Female figure from the Catacomb of Vibia*

structural work during the reign of Constantine, aimed at embellishing its appearance and facilitating visits by devotees. As recorded in the *Liber Pontificalis*, "*gradus ascensionis et descensionis*", that is, descending and ascending staircases, were created, at the beginning and end of the underground passage that led to the tomb of the martyr to make the journey of the faithful more rational and fluid. The tomb itself was fenced off with *plutei*, decorated with marble, lit by lamps and candelabra and further emphasised by an apsidal structure (LP, I, p. 181)[159]. Elsewhere, before the radical and systematic endeavours of Damasus[160], the tombs of martyrs and bishops were subject to works of a more modest nature. Near the burial sites of the Popes Callistus and Cornelius and the martyrs Felicissimus and Agapitus, simple tables were built[161]. In the Catacomb of SS. Marcellino e Pietro, the *cubiculum* that housed the tombs of the two saints was equipped with an arched entranceway supported by columns. The room was widened by linking it with other nearby chambers to create more space for the visits and burials of the faithful (fig. 54.C–D)[162]. At S. Callisto, a *retro sanctos* room for more privileged burials was created behind the Crypt of the Popes[163]. The tomb of S. Agnes was fenced off by a series of *plutei*, donated by Pope Liberius; one of the *plutei* depicted the figure of the young martyr in relief[164].

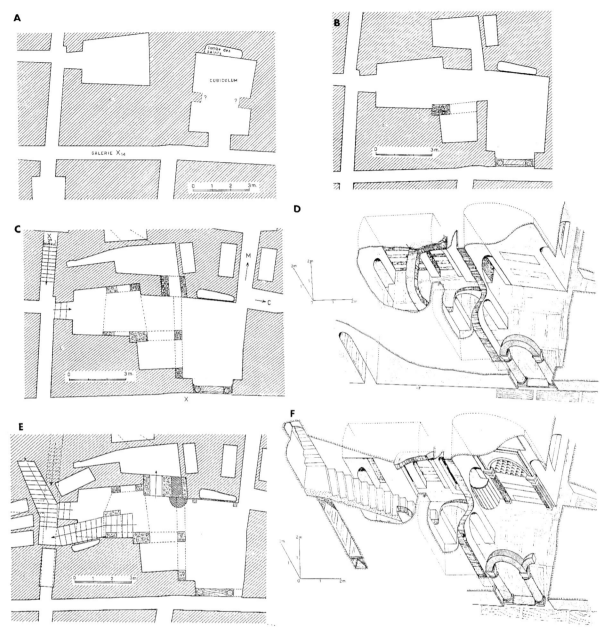

A

B

C

D

E

F

54 Plans and axonometric reconstructions of the transformations of the crypt of SS. Peter and Marcellinus in the Catacomb of SS. Marcellino e Pietro

In the Catacomb of S. Tecla on Via Ostiense, a *retro sanctos* area was created behind the presumed tomb of the martyr that was housed in a small irregular underground basilica probably already in the first half of the fourth century. This area was characterised by the presence of large rooms used intensively with *loculi* along the walls and a series of *a cappuccina* tombs organised in several layers on the interior of the chambers (fig. 55)[165].

6. THE PONTIFICATE OF DAMASUS AND THE CULT OF THE SAINTS

In the 360s, the golden age of the construction of catacombs seemed to decline. In the underground cemeteries, the pontificate of Damasus (366–384) was characterised primarily by the Pope's monumental modifications to the tombs of the martyrs that aimed at fostering their cult and devotion.

49

the *Depositio Martyrum* and *Depositio Episcoporum* record the feasts of 46 martyrs and bishops. By the first decades of the fifth century, more than 150 celebrations were noted in the *Martyrologium Hieronymianum*[168].

In the second half of the fourth century, the promotion of the cult of the saints also entailed an increase in pilgrimages and devotional visits, already manifested in an embryonic state in the course of the second half of the third century[169]. This phenomenon is testified to not only by the monuments[170], but also by various literary sources. The most significant of these sources is that of S. Jerome. As a young man around the 360's, he made systematic "tours" of visits to the burial sites of the apostles and martyrs in Rome on Sundays (*"solebam...diebus Dominicis, sepulcra apostolorum et martyrum circuire"*) (*In Ezech.*, XII.40 = PL, 25, col. 375)[171].

With regard to the monuments, the work of Damasus is shown especially, as mentioned earlier, in his work of restructuring the venerated burial places and the areas which contained them. The grand metrical commemorative inscriptions, incised on the large marble slabs in splendid capital letters by the calligrapher and friend of the Pope, Furius Dionysius Philocalus (fig. 174), were placed in "closed" architectural perspectives, squeezed onto the walls into which the tombs were cut (figs. 56–57)[172]. Their placement can be reconstructed from the best preserved examples, such as the tombs of Popes Sixtus II and Cornelius at S. Callisto, of the martyrs Januarius and Felicissimus and Agapitus in the Catacomb of Pretestato and of Peter and Marcellinus in the Catacomb of the same name. Columns or small pilasters that supported arches and architraves often delineated these perspectives. Within they sometimes included, in addition to the epigraphic slabs, openwork *transennae* that both protected and allowed glimpses of the venerated tombs[173]. The remaining wall surfaces of these rooms were covered with marble slabs or more simply with white plaster to stress these completely singular spaces within the cemetery. The luminosity of the

The desire to quickly mend the rifts produced within the community as a result of his troubled election must have prompted Damasus to reconstruct unity under the highly significant patronage of the early witnesses of the faith[166]. The more than sixty metrical inscriptions that he composed for the martyrs of the city, and had placed beside their tombs, praised the deeds of those heroes. Thus, they assumed a clear catechetic value of support for the pastoral mission. On the other hand, the marble slabs "signed" by the Pope and the concomitant structural interventions in the tombs constituted a clear official sanctioning of the cult of the saints by the Roman Church, with her subsequent claim to the control and management of popular devotion[167]. The consequences of this papal policy in favour of the cult of the martyrs was also evident in the development of the Roman religious calendar as recorded by the hagiographic sources. In the late Constantinian period, the calendars contained in

50

marble revetment, that sometimes included the pavement, must have increased the dim light that penetrated the crypt from the skylights that were installed or widened at this time[174]. Square or circular tables were set up near the tombs to hold lamps or the offerings of the worshippers (figs. 54, E–F)[175]. An altar table supported by four small pilasters was placed in the Crypt of the Popes of the cemetery of S. Callisto (fig. 32)[176]. An enclosure, probably covered by a *ciborium* with small columns with relief representations of the life of the martyr, was installed above the tombs of SS. Nereus and Achilleus in the Catacomb of Domitilla (fig. 120)[177]. Painted or mosaic decoration does not appear to have been very frequent in the building projects of this period[178]. Only above the burial site of the martyrs Felix and Adauctus in the Catacomb of Commodilla do the papal interventions perhaps include a painted representation of the two saints[179].

To facilitate devotional visits, in some cases the rooms that housed the venerated tombs were enlarged. The attribution to Damasus of true underground basilicas *ad corpus*, such as those that sprung up in the fourth century within the hypogea, remains doubtful however[180]. Nevertheless, the transformations attested in the tombs of SS. Nereus and Achilleus in the Catacomb of Domitilla and in that of S. Hermes in the underground cemetery of S. Ermete reveal the creation of spaces, if not yet "basilican", still of not insignificant proportions[181]. In some cases, even the underground passageways that led to the sanctuaries were developed by papal intervention. New stairs were added to already existing ones to create itineraries that rapidly and directly carried the worshipers to the tombs. Together with the existing staircases, they provided a system of *gradus ascensionis et descensionis*[182] that allowed an easy "one-way" route and avoided slowing down the "bustle" of people that, as the poet Prudentius recorded at the beginning of the fifth century in connection with visits to the tomb of the martyr Hippolytus on Via Tiburtina (*Perist.*, XI, 190 = CSEL, 61, p. 418), crowded the most venerated sanctua-

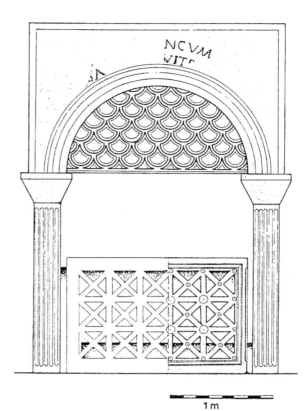

56 Reconstruction of the Damasan systemisation of the tombs of SS. Peter and Marcellino in the Catacomb of SS. Marcellino e Pietro

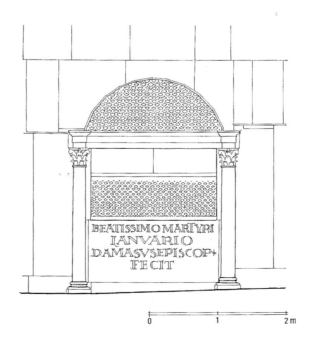

57 Reconstruction of the Damasan systemisation of the tomb of the martyr Januarius in the Catacomb of Pretestato

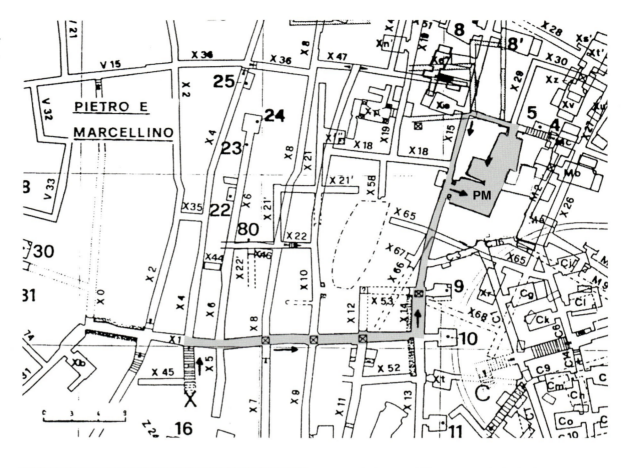

58 Plan of the route set up by Pope Damasus for visits to the tombs of SS. Peter and Marcellinus in the Catacomb of SS. Marcellino e Pietro

59 Gallery with plastered walls along the route set up by Pope Damasus for visits to the tombs of SS. Peter and Marcellinus

ries of the city[183]. Series of skylights and masonry structures leaning against the walls of the galleries, sometimes covered with white plaster (fig. 59), emphasised these underground *itinera* and indicated the path to the visitors. These structures created an emotive setting of light and shadow that even contemporaries found extremely striking, as recorded by both Jerome and Prudentius (Jer., *In Ezech.*, XII.40 = PL, 25, col. 375; Prudent, *Perist.*, XI.159–168 = CSEL, 61, pp. 417–418).

In carrying out this vast development of the sanctuaries of the martyrs in the catacombs, Damasus was sometimes helped, as attested by inscriptions, by the priests of his "entourage", who probably also had to contribute financially[184]. Analogous financial support was provided by the rich Roman lay aristocracy, that according to the sources, was increasingly involved in the construction of urban cult buildings or in increasing the patrimony of the Roman Church through be-

60 Plan of the retro sanctos region located behind the Basilica of SS. Nereo ed Achilleo in the Catacomb of Domitilla

quests and oblations in precisely this period[185]. Several monumental tombs located near the burial sites of the martyrs and planned at the same time as the papal restructuring should probably be connected to these lay or ecclesiastical benefactors. The generosity of their donation assured them at least a "privileged" tomb near the remains of the saint[186].

The promotion of the cult of the martyrs by Damasus contributed in effect to an increase in the phenomenon of burials *ad sanctos*, that was already found in a moder-

ate form in the preceding decades[187]. During the pontificate of Damascus, this practice assumed ever greater significance. The belief that proximity to a martyr's burial place conveyed some benefit for the deceased thanks to the saint's intercession towards eternal reward (August., *Cur. Mort.*, 5 = CSEL, 41, p. 631; CIL V, p. 617, n. 5) incited a real "contest" amongst the faithful to obtain these privileged spaces near venerated tombs[188]. The role of prayer, as emphasised by Augustine (ibid., 4–5.18 = CSEL, 41, pp. 629–631, 658–659), that the de-

53

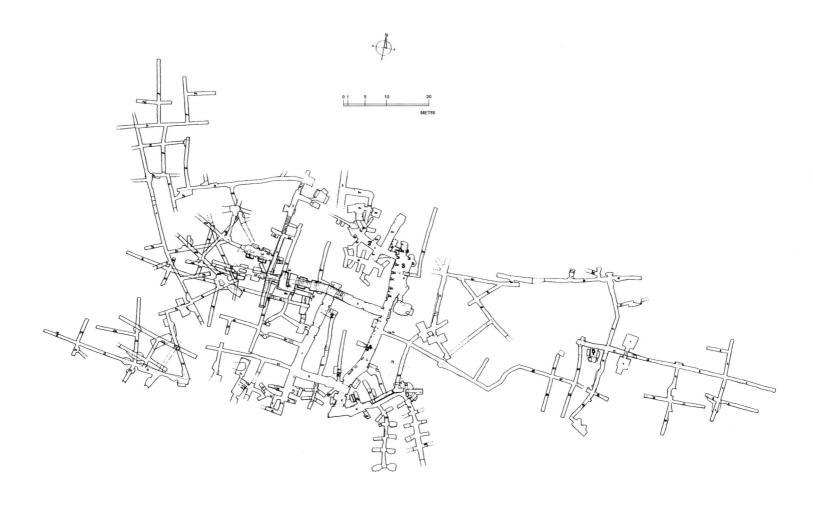

61 Plan of the Catacomb of Commodilla

ceased received in the orations that recommended him to the martyr, must have constituted a key element in the choice of a burial *ad sanctos*[189].

The development of several underground cemeteries in this period, precisely where the cult of local martyrs had been "launched" by the Pope, can be also considered from the point of view of this search for privileged funerary spaces. In the Catacomb of Domitilla, near the tombs of SS. Nereus and Achilleus subject to the attention of Damasus[190], three new regions were created on the lower level. These burial areas were accessible from as many large staircases[191]. A vast network of galleries with monumental *cubicula*, already begun towards the middle of the fourth century, developed as well behind the papal sanctu-

ary, thus assuming the characteristics of a true, vast *retro sanctos* (fig. 60)[192]. Monumental characteristics were also found in some sections of new regions nearby in which *cubicula* and *arcosolia* appear, not infrequently decorated.

In the Catacomb of Commodilla near Via Ostiense, a kind of *inventio* of the tombs of the local martyrs, Felix and Adauctus by Damasus[193] and the subsequent development of their cult, led the rather modest funerary area already on this site to assume the dimensions of a vast cemetery. The numerous dated inscriptions make possible the assignment of almost the entire development of this cemetery around an earlier nucleus[194] to the years of the pontificate of Damasus and the successive period down to the first decade of the fifth century. The importance

of the cult of the eponymous martyrs in the catacomb is revealed by abundant iconographic evidence and by the very fact that they gave their name to the area (ICUR III, 8669)[195]. The cemetery contains funerary occupation that betrays its use by a generally modest level of society[196]. Exceptions to the rule are several privileged spaces *retro sanctos*[197] and rare *cubicula*, including the richly frescoed one of *Leo officialis annonae*[198] (pl. I, p. 8).

The most peripheral of the regions of S. Sebastiano, situated to the north of the Basilica and known as the Catacomb of the ex-Vigna Chiaraviglio, was also created beginning in the pontificate of Damasus. Its foundation was related to the "launching" of the cult of

the martyr Eutychian, whose tomb, located in the area, was subject to a true *inventio* by the Pope (ICUR V, 13274). Based on the most recent research, this sector seems to represent one of the latest examples of communal catacomb regions. The numerous dated inscriptions found *in situ* and several frescoes testify to its use up until the first decades of the fifth century[199]. The region displays intensive funerary use and a modest number of *cubicula* and *arcosolia*, including decorated examples.

The development of the cult of a group of martyrs, perhaps the so-called "Greek Martyrs" recorded in ancient historical-topographical sources, buried in a cemetery on Via Ardeatina resulted in the enlargement

62 *Room with* opus sectile *decoration behind the cubiculum of Pope Gaius in the Catacomb of Commodilla*

63 Shaft tomb in the Catacomb of Commodilla

sites[202]. These privileged sectors, composed of galleries and *cubicula*, were often inserted forcibly into the already existing network of corridors. Examples include that behind the Crypt of the Popes and the tombs of Cornelius and Gaius in the Catacomb of S. Callisto (figs. 30, G4; 62), the area that housed the tombs of SS. Felix and Adauctus in the Catacomb of Commodilla (fig. 65), of S. Callistus in the Catacomb of Calepodio, of S. Alexander in the cemetery of the Giordani and in the small and unique "sub-hypogea" created in the central region of the Catacomb of SS. Marco, Marcelliano e Damaso[203].

The monumentality of these *retro sanctos* sites reveals their use by extremely wealthy individuals. This is particularly evident in the *cubiculum* created behind the tomb of Pope Gaius at S. Callisto, splendidly decorated with marbles and mosaics (fig. 62)[204]. The same phenomenon is attested in the *ad arcosolio* tombs in the cemetery of Priscilla, equally richly decorated with mosaic and *opus sectile* revetment. These *arcosolia* filled the two L-shaped galleries of the Hypogeum of the *Acilii* beneath the basilica that contained the tombs of the martyrs Felix, Philip and Pope Sylvester (fig. 8, B)[205]. Nevertheless, the privilege of being buried near the saints ("*quod multi cupiunt et rari accipiunt*" (ICUR I, 3127)) was also obtained by faithful of a more modest level. This is shown conspicuously by the "intact gallery" inserted forcibly under the staircase that led to the burials of Felix and Adauctus in the Catacomb of Commodilla (fig. 64). This gallery was occupied by simple *loculi* that were individualised only by the "displayed" funerary gifts and some epitaphs[206]. In this same catacomb, poor characteristics are displayed by the tombs inserted in unique funerary devices for multiple burials composed of deep wells excavated under the floor of the galleries. These were occupied in an intensive manner with *loculi* in the walls and *a cappuccina* tombs stacked up in the openings of the shafts[207]. As in the case of the large rooms used for multiple burials of the Catacomb of S. Tecla, to benefit from

of this underground area. This "Catacomba Anonima" of Via Ardeatina was constructed as an appendix to the large ambulatory basilica recently discovered a few meters away[200]. The dated inscriptions, elaborate architecture of the *cubicula* and pictorial decoration (fig. 136) can be dated to between 370 and the first decade of the fifth century[201].

The promotion of the cult of the martyrs by Damasus also entailed ever more frequently the creation of small areas *retro sanctos* in proximity to venerated burial

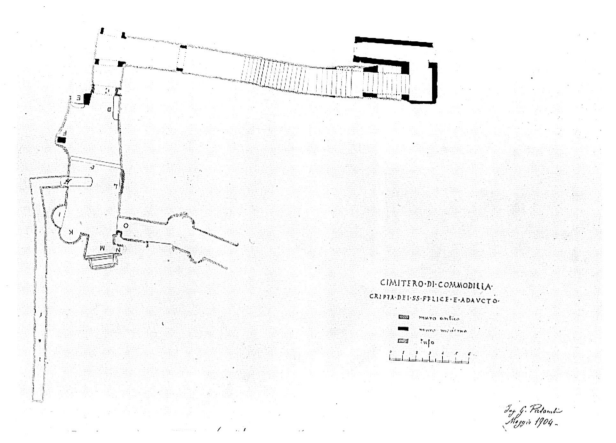

proximity to a venerated tomb, the faithful were willing to renounce individual burial and to condemn their own tomb to anonymity[208].

After 360–370 A.D, with the exception of the vast areas recorded above and the more limited *retro sanctos* sites, the catacombs do not seem to have undergone an increase equal to that which characterised the preceding decades. Sectors used in this period are certainly attested in various cemeteries such as, for example, S. Pancrazio, S. Ippolito, the Catacombs of SS. Marcellino e Pietro, Gordiano ed Epimaco, Aproniano, Pretestato, S. Callisto, Marco e Marcelliano. Extensions through to new areas were, however, limited[209]. In the Catacomb of Domitilla, some regions of monumental type containing *cubicula* with elaborate architecture that were sometimes frescoed, such as the so-called Region of the "*Pistores*" (figs. 95–96)

can be dated to the last decades of the fourth century. Other contemporary areas in the same catacomb were composed of simple, poor galleries used exclusively for *loculi* tombs[210]. On Via Appia, a hypogeum of a very late period had a very limited development; it was located behind the southern offshoots of the Catacomb of S. Callisto[211].

Certainly in this period the majority of communal graves must have been placed in the large funerary basilicas and adjacent areas created above ground towards the middle of the century. Examples include the Basilicas of St. Peter, S. Sebastiano, SS. Marcellino e Pietro (fig. 38), S. Agnese (fig. 23, F), S. Lorenzo, the new ambulatory basilica on Via Ardeatina, the basilicas of Pope Julius on the Via Flaminia (S. Valentino), Via Aurelia (S. Callisto) and Via Portuense (S. Felix?) and the church of S. Felix II (355–358) on Via Aurelia[212]. In many cases,

the evidence of dated inscriptions as well as the chronology of the sarcophagi that belong to these monumental structures explicitly attest to this[213].

On the other hand, Damasus gave another funerary basilica on Via Ardeatina to the community. It was here that he himself was later buried[214]. At the end of his pontificate, the construction of a new extremely grandiose basilica on Via Ostiense dedicated to the apostle Paul was launched thanks to the direct initiatives of three emperors, Valentinian II, Theodosius and Arcadius[215]. This basilica provided further burial space for thousands of people. Pope Siricius (384–399) was perhaps the creator of the semi-interred church with three naves built on top of the tombs of SS. Nereus and Achilleus in the Catacomb of Domitilla (figs. 72–73). He also seems to have been responsible for the underground basilica built above the tomb of the martyr Silanus in the cemetery of Felicita on Via Salaria Nova[216].

According to the explicit testimony of Prudentius (*Perist.*, XI.215–226 = CSEL, 61, p. 419)[217], a basilica with three naves must also have existed above the Catacomb of S. Ippolito on Via Tiburtina at the beginning of the fifth century.

In effect, the option of being buried within these churches and in the surrounding areas must have slowly provoked the abandonment of inhumation in the catacombs. The prayer that took place in the buildings and the "protection" offered by their sacredness must have played a key role in this choice[218].

The dated inscriptions discovered in the catacombs do not seem to support a continuity of use after the first decades of the fifth century. The singular and extremely limited spaces associated with the tombs of martyrs are an exception[219]. The last dated inscription found *in situ* refers to an ordinary tomb in an underground cemetery at S. Pancrazio in 454 (ICUR, II, 4277).

65 Hypogean Basilica of SS. Felice ed Adautto in the Catacomb of Commodilla

66 Plan of the hypogean Basilica of S. Ippolito in the Catacomb of S. Ippolito

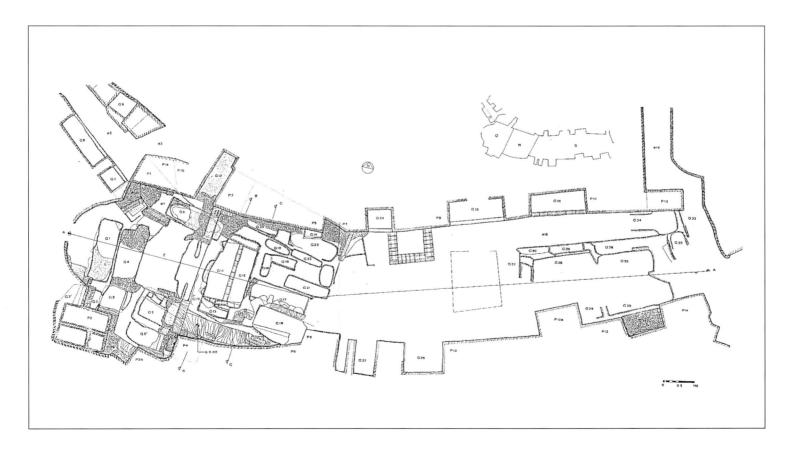

67 *Hypogean Basilica of S. Ippolito in the Catacomb of S. Ippolito*

7. LATEST USE AND SUBSEQUENT ABANDONMENT OF THE CATACOMBS

During the fifth and sixth centuries the catacombs were used almost exclusively for devotional reasons in those very limited areas, the underground sanctuaries, where the tombs of martyrs were loctated. The routes to the venerated tombs that had already been established in the fourth century were restored and enlarged with structures that made the journey more secure. New *itinera ad sanctos* (ICUR II, 4753) were created in other catacombs. These itineraries were set in galleries whose walls were reinforced with masonry and sometimes covered with plaster. The corridors were often lit by skylights located in strategic points that suggested the path to the worshipers through a sort of "light and shadow effect". Walls not infrequently blocked off access to other sur-rounding galleries now out of use, thus creating "fixed routes" that facilitated visits[220]. Examples of these underground circuits are recorded near the tomb of the martyr Alexander in the cemetery of the Giordani, in the vicinity of the sanctuary of the "Quattro Coronati" in the Catacomb of SS. Marcellino e Pietro, beside the tombs of the martyrs of the cemetery of Generosa on Via Portuense and in the area adjacent to the tomb of S. Hippolytus on Via Tiburtina[221].

From the first half of the sixth century onwards, the practice of having the altar used for Eucharistic celebrations coincide with the tomb of the martyr[222], already seen sporadically in the fourth century[223], resulted in the creation of real basilicas *ad corpus* within the setting of the underground cemeteries. Such cult environments were normally of rather modest dimensions and irregular shape, produced by the labourious transfor-

mation of pre-existing underground areas.
This is demonstrated by the examples constructed by Pope John I (523–526) near the
tombs of SS. Felix and Adauctus in the Catacomb of Commodilla (fig. 64, 65, cf. fig. 61)
and by Vigilius (537–555) near the tomb
of Ippolito on Via Tiburtina (figs. 66, 67).
Pope Honourius I (625–638) was responsible
for similar construction over the tombs of
Peter and Marcellinus on Via Labicana (LP I,
pp. 276, 324; ICUR VII, 19937) (figs.
68–69). These cult places were completely
underground and accessible through large
staircases that led directly into the rooms or
close to them[224]. Large skylights chiefly provided their lighting. Greater size and regularity is found in the basilicas *ad corpus* built
over the tombs of a group of anonymous

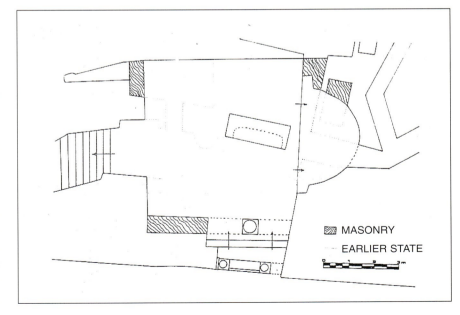

MASONRY

EARLIER STATE

70 Anonymous hypogean Basilica of Via Ardeatina

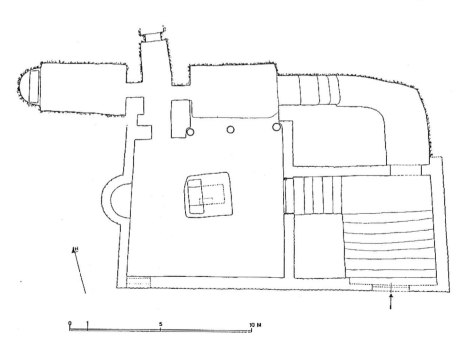

71 Plan of the anonymous hypogean Basilica of Via Ardeatina

0 ___ 1 ___ 5 ___ 10 M

martyrs on Via Ardeatina of the first half of the sixth century[225](fig. 70, 71), the burial site of S. Hermes in the Catacomb of the same name, probably by Pelagius II (579–590) (LP I, p. 309)[226] and the tombs of Nereus and Achilleus at Domitilla (figs. 72, 73). The chronology of the latter building os-

cillates between the second half of the fourth century, that is, the period of Pope John I (523–526) (LP, I, p. 276: "*refecit cymiterium beatorum martyrum Nerei et Achillei*") and the beginning of the seventh century[227]. In these cases, the buildings assume the form of standard basilicas of grand dimensions accessible through long staircases that led into a vestibule or sort of narthex. The roofs must have projected above ground, giving these constructions a characteristic semi-hypogean form.

These "catacomb" basilicas, as far as is known, normally received rather sombre decoration. Only the basilica built above the tombs of SS. Felix and Adauctus was decorated with a series of paintings and some mosaics that covered the walls and apses that closed the room (fig. 65)[228]. In these buildings, as a rule the altars coincided with the tombs of the martyrs. The altar could even consist of the same stone block, expressly recut, that contained their remains (figs. 68–71), or else in a structure built on top or in proximity to them. *Ciboria* and enclosures (figs. 70–73) conferred on these churches an appearance and internal division similar to

72 *Basilica of SS. Nereo ed Achilleo in the Catacomb of Domitilla*

that of buildings regularly constructed on the surface.

The building of these underground martyr basilicas, as far as can be reconstructed from the sources, was the responsibility of the Popes. The contribution of a lay sponsor can however be supposed in the case of the small Basilica of SS. Felice e Adautto. The privilege obtained by the widow *Turtura* to be buried in this building just after its construction and especially the fact that her image was immortalised beside that of the Virgin and saints in the grandiose panel that occupies part of one of the long walls of the basilica (figs. 65, 121), could be justified by some participation of this pious woman in the work[229].

The series of basilicas *ad corpus* built above the tombs of the martyrs housed in the

73 *Plan of the Basilica of SS. Nereo ed Achilleo in the Catacomb of Domitilla,*

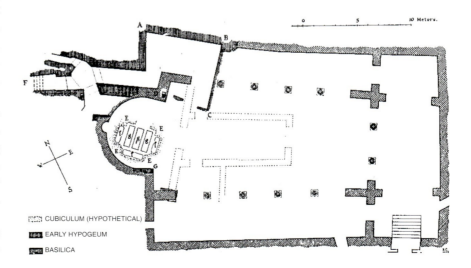

CUBICULUM (HYPOTHETICAL)
EARLY HYPOGEUM
BASILICA

63

74 Basilica of S. Lorenzo fuori le mura (built under Pope Pelagius)

catacombs was completed between the end of the sixth century and the first decades of the seventh by Popes Pelagius II (579–590) and Honourius I (625–638) with the construction of the monumental churches of S. Lorenzo on Via Tiburtina (fig. 74) and S. Agnese on Via Nomentana (fig. 23.E)[230]. Such buildings assumed the form of regular basilicas with elaborate architecture. Their peculiarity consisted in their partial construction within the hills that housed the funerary areas containing the tombs of SS. Lawrence and Agnes. The buildings were articulated on two superimposed levels (fig. 74). The lower level with three naves and a narthex that contained the tombs of the two saints was below ground; the upper level, above ground and open to the sky, consisted of a U-turn of the *matronei* accessible from the summit of the hill. One reached the lower level at S. Agnese through a long staircase from the surface level (fig. 23). At S. Lorenzo, one entered an entrance on the level of one of the long sides of the church, the only one not set against the rock.

Sometimes the martyr sanctuaries of the catacombs were subject to more modest endeavours, consisting of simple pictorial decoration that embellished but did not alter the spaces that housed the venerated tombs. These paintings often depicted the eponymous martyrs or other saints connected to the cult (fig. 75)[231]. In the *cubiculum* that housed the remains of the martyr Panfilus in the cemetery of the same name on Via Salaria Vetus, a small block altar was set up for the liturgical celebrations that took place there (fig. 177)[232]. An analogous marble altar is found in the area that housed the tombs of SS. Peter and Hyacinth in the Catacomb of S. Ermete[233].

The intensive devotional use of these underground sanctuaries is recorded by hundreds of graffiti traced by visitors on the walls of the underground basilicas, in the more modest areas that contained venerated remains (fig. 178), or else in the *itinera ad sanctos* that led to them[234].

During the fifth and sixth centuries, as has been pointed out, the use of catacombs for burials continued only sporadically and exclusively in the areas marked by the presence of venerated tombs. This is proven by the dated funerary inscriptions found in the underground Basilicas and the surrounding areas of SS. Felice e Adautto, SS. Marcellino e Pietro, S. Ippolito, S. Felicita, in the "Catacomba Anonima" of Via Ardeatina, as well as those found *in situ* in the crypt of S. Sebastian on Via Appia and near the tomb of S. Alexander in the Catacomb of the Giordani[235]. In the proximity of the underground Basilica of SS. Felice e Adautto, the pictorial decoration of a *loculus a forno* inserted in the wall of an earlier gallery at a later period, dates this burial site to the second half of the

seventh century[236]. In all these cases, the vicinity of the venerated tombs makes it possible to attribute to these burial sites the character of privileged tombs *ad sanctos*.

Moreover, locations for ordinary burial, as has been seen, had already been definitively transferred to sites on ground level[237]. From the middle of the sixth century onwards, as a result of the instability caused by the Graeco-Gothic War (536–553) and an evident change of mentality, burials within the city began, thus violating a tradition consolidated by the centuries[238].

As documented by a few inscriptions and references recorded in the *Liber Pontificalis*[239], the damage caused to the underground sanctuaries by the Graeco-Gothic War were systematically repaired by Popes Vigilius (537–555) and John III (561–574). But the invasions of the Longobards in the middle of the eighth century and those of the Saracens in 846 must have inflicted a mortal blow to the latest frequentation of the cata-

65

combs. The terrible devastation of Astolfo in the year 756, in particular, as mentioned in a letter of Pope Paul I, reduced some underground sanctuaries into stalls for animals[240]. The very serious damage caused by these last sacks again led to interventions by Popes Hadrian I (772–795) and Leo III (795–816). Hadrian was particularly involved in this restoration work[241].

But already by the mid-seventh century, the impossibility of maintaining the sanctuaries in an adequate way had sporadically suggested a more radical solution to save the venerated bodies, that of transfering them within the city, into the urban churches. These tranferrals were still episodic during the pontificates of Theodorus (642–649) and Leo II (682–683) and especially targeted the further away and less protected sanctuaries.

They became systematic under Paul I (756–767) and the Popes of the first half of the ninth century, Pasquale I (817–824), Sergius II (844–847) and Leo IV (847–855)[242].

Stripped of their primary function of visitation, the sanctuaries of catacombs fell into oblivion. Only a few survived some time after the transferral of the bodies of their martyrs, as demonstrated by the archaeological evidence and a few literary sources[243]. Only those sections of the catacombs connected with a few basilicas of the martyrs that still jealously preserved the remains of the eponymous martyrs *in situ*, remained accessible throughout the entire Medieval period[244] (fig. 1). The remainder were abandoned and forgotten until their "renaissance" at the end of the sixteenth century.

NOTES

1 Allodi-Levi 1885, p. 28, n.12.
2 *Gesta Episcoporum*, p. 404.
3 See Valentini-Zucchetti 1940, p. 280; Luiselli 1986, pp. 852–854.
4 Valentini-Zucchetti 1942, pp. 19, 62.
5 ILCV, 2128, 2149, 2152–2154, 3334; Nestori 1971, p. 270; see also LP, I, p. 161.
6 See below, p. 65.
7 Reekmans 1984, p. 244.
8 See de Rossi 1864–1877, I, pp. 9–10; Armellini 1880, p. 9.
9 For examples of these signatures: de Rossi 1864–1877, I, pp. 2–8; II, pp. 5–7, 70–71, 83.
10 See de Rossi 1864–1877, I, pp. 3–8; Lumbroso 1889, pp. 215–239; de Rossi 1891, pp. 81–94; Ferretto 1942, pp. 74–80.
11 Panvinio 1568, pp. 18–22; on Panvinio's work: de Rossi 1864–1877, I, pp. 9–10; Fremiotti 1926, pp. 28–41; Ferretto 1942, pp. 91–99; Ferrary 1996.
12 Fiocchi Nicolai 1991, pp. 3–4 (with biblio.); Deichmann 1993, pp. 28–29; Frend 1996, pp. 12ff., Fiocchi Nicolai (in press).
13 Cecchelli 1929, pp. 105–112; *idem* 1938; Fiocchi Nicolai (in press).
14 On the discovery, most recently see Fiocchi Nicolai 1991, pp. 3–4.
15 L'Heureux 1856, pp. 2–4; see Fiocchi Nicolai 1991, p. 4; *idem*

(in press). On the figures of these three scholars, see primarily: de Rossi 1864–1877, I, pp. 14–19; Ferretto 1942, pp. 115–125; Recio Veganzones 1968; *idem* 1974, pp. 295–297; Brandenburg 1983, cols. 319–320; Schuddeboom 1996.
16 Ugonio 1588; cf. de Rossi 1864–1877, I, pp. 15, 19–20; Ferretto 1942, pp. 120–124; Josi 1954, cols. 715–716; Fiocchi Nicolai (in press).
17 Bosio 1632; on Bosio's work, see esp. de Rossi 1864–1877, I, pp. 26–46; Valeri 1900; Ferretto 1942, pp. 132–161; Ferrua 1949, cols. 1943–1944; Testini 1966, pp. 19–21; Parise 1971, pp. 257–259; Spigno 1975, pp. 281–311; *idem* 1976, pp. 277–301; Wataghin Cantino 1980, pp. 10–11; Brandenburg 1983, cols. 319–320; Deichmann 1993, pp. 28–29; Finocchiaro 1995, pp. 189–193; Fiocchi Nicolai (in press).
18 Cf. de Rossi 1864–1877, I, pp. 46–51; Testini 1966, pp. 21–22; Brandenburg 1983, cols. 321–322; Deichmann 1993, pp. 29–31.
19 Ferretto 1942, pp. 201–268; Testini 1966, pp. 21–26; de Rossi-Ferrua 1944.
20 De Rossi-Ferrua 1944, pp. XVIII–XIX.
21 Cf. de Rossi 1864–1877, I, pp. 51–56; Ferretto 1942, pp.

167–173, 201–222; Testini 1966, pp. 22–24; Parise 1969, pp. 247–249; Brandenburg 1983, cols. 321–322. Boldetti 1720 is particularly important for much information concerning monumental sites now lost.
22 Marchi 1844; on the activity of this scholar: Ferretto 1942, pp. 312–318; Testini 1966, pp. 25–26; Deichmann 1993, p. 32.
23 Ferrua 1968, pp. 251–278.
24 On the multifaceted work of de Rossi, see most recently, Deichmann 1993, pp. 32–34; Baruffa 1994; Giovanni Battista de Rossi 1994 (with an extensive biblio.); Fiocchi Nicolai (in press). Fundamental for the study of catacombs are especially the dozens of articles published by de Rossi in *Bullettino di Archeologia Cristiana* 1864–1894 and the volumes, de Rossi 1864–1877 (a complete bibliography of the scholar appears in Leclercq 1950, cols. 93–99).
25 Armellini 1893; Marucchi 1933; for the activity of these three scholars, see Ferretto 1942, pp. 349–357; Testini 1966, pp. 30–32.
26 Wilpert 1903; *idem* 1916; *idem* 1929–1936; on the scholar: Ferretto 1942, pp. 362–365; Testini 1966, pp. 34–35; Brandenburg 1983, col. 325; Deichmann 1993, p. 39; Bisconti 1998, p. 33.
27 On the activity of E. Josi: Fasola 1975–1976, pp. 3–9.

28 Styger 1933; *idem* 1935; cf. Testini 1966, p. 33; Fasola-Testini 1978, p. 138; Pergola-Barbini 1997, p. 43.

29 See Brandenburg 1984, pp. 11–12.

30 Brandenburg 1984, p. 47.

31 Apollonj Ghetti-Ferrua-Josi-Kischbaum 1951, pp. 107–144.

32 Cf. Kirschbaum 1957, pp. 176–184; Tolotti 1983, pp. 117–132.

33 Tolotti 1953, pp. 87–153; Carletti 1981, pp. 302–307; Fiocchi Nicolai 1997, p. 121.

34 Cf. Brandenburg 1984, pp. 47–49; *idem* 1994, pp. 223–224. Reference to an already well-established custom of burying members of the community in funerary areas separate from pagan ones is alluded to in a letter of Cyprian written around 250: *Ep.*, 67.6 = CSEL, 3/2, p. 740 (cf. Brandenburg 1994, p. 222). The importance of the burial service, addressed especially to the poorest of the community, is recorded by Lactantius at the beginning of the fourth century (*Div. inst.*, VI, 12 = CSEL, 19, pp. 529–530). Still in the 360s, the emperor Julian must have noted bitterly how precisely "solicitude for the burials of the deceased" constituted one of the winning cards for the affirmation of Christianity (*Epist.*, 80 = ed. Bidez 1924, p. 144).

35 Mazzarino 1973, II, pp. 454–469; *idem* 1974, pp. 57–73.

36 Toynbee 1993 [1971], pp. 9–16, 86–88, 110–111, 162–215; Steingräber 1981, pp. 28–30 and *passim*; Brandenburg 1984, pp. 12–30; Reekmans 1986, pp. 11–37; von Hesberg 1992, pp. 100–112.

37 Cf. Reekmans 1986, pp. 35–36; Pergola 1986, p. 340; Brandenburg 1994, p. 220.

38 Cf. von Hesberg 1992, p. 14.

39 Purcell 1987, pp. 32–34.

40 See Brandenburg 1984, pp. 19–28; Cianfriglia-Filippini 1985, pp. 217–234.

41 Cf. Brandenburg 1984, pp. 43–49; Reekmans 1986, pp. 35–36; Pergola 1986, pp. 339–344.

42 Deichmann 1993 [1983], p. 53; Brandenburg 1984, pp. 43–49; *idem* 1994, pp. 225–226.

43 Pergola 1979, pp. 332–335; Pergola-Barbini 1997, pp. 60–62.

44 See above, p. 13

45 Styger 1925–1926, pp. 112–119; Brandenburg 1984, pp. 31–32.

46 These are casket tombs hewn into the walls about a meter from the ground, preceded by a parapet. They are closed by a horizontal slab (*a mensa*) and crowned by a niche (de Rossi 1864–1877, III, pp. 418–419; Reekmans 1964, p. 63; Pergola 1983, pp. 216–217).

47 Styger 1925–1926, pp. 119–153.

48 Nestori 1971, pp. 169–278.

49 Tolotti 1970, pp. 63–106, 171–189.

50 Spera (in press).

51 Pergola 1983, pp. 201–207, 214–245.

52 Tolotti 1978a, pp. 160–165, 170.

53 Styger 1933, pp. 148–149; Bisconti 1997a, pp. 7–49.

54 Ferrua 1944, pp. 232–239; Fasola-Testini 1978, pp. 109, 191–194 (with earlier biblio.).

55 Carletti 1988, pp. 134–135; *idem* 1997, pp. 145–148.

56 See Brown 1974, pp. 51–52; Meeks 1992, pp. 291–295, 301.

57 Cf. von Hesberg 1992, 9. 20; Toynbee 1993, pp. X–XI.

58 Carletti 1988, pp. 128–131; Petrucci 1995, pp. 35–37; Carletti 1997, p. 148.

59 Meeks 1992, pp. 294–295, 301.

60 Tolotti 1970, pp. 135–170, 213–236; *idem* 1977, 15–58; *idem* 1978, pp. 171–181.

61 Pergola 1975, pp. 77–93; *idem* 1979, pp. 332–333.

62 Valentini-Zucchetti 1942, pp. 13–14, 20; de Rossi 1888–1889, pp. 15–30, 37–57, 115–120; Tolotti 1970, pp. 165–170.

63 See below, p. 23.

64 See above, p. 13.

65 Valentini-Zucchetti 1942, pp. 12–28.

66 Particularly indicative of this practice is an inscription from an Early Christian cemetery located around Velletri (fig. 18) that records the donation of a funerary area (*hoc coemeterium*) by a member of the aristocratic senatorial *gens Faltonia, Faltonia Hilaritas*, to the confraternity of the Christian community (*huic religioni*). The woman built this area *sua pecunia* and she was probably buried there (ILCV, 3681A; see Fiocchi Nicolai 1994, pp. 243–245, with further biblio.).

67 See above, n. 62 and Pergola 1978, pp. 407–423.

68 Mazzarino 1973, II, pp. 463–469; 478–490; *idem* 1974, pp. 72–73; Sordi 1984, pp. 83–85; Dal Covolo 1989, pp. 30–31; Meeks 1992, p. 308.

69 Mercati 1937, p. 180; *Acta Cypr.*, 5 = ed. Saxer 1984, p. 191.

70 See above, p. 13

71 De Visscher 1951, pp. 39–54; Sordi 1965, pp. 468–470.

72 Mazzarino 1974, pp. 70–71; Sordi 1965, pp. 470–473; Pietri (L.) 1995, p. 170.

73 Apollonj Ghetti-Ferrua-Josi-Kirschbaum 1951, pp. 38–42; Kirschbaum 1957, pp. 28–38; Reekmans 1986, pp. 15–16; 21–22, 25–28.

74 Bendinelli 1922.

75 Bisconti 1985, pp. 889–903; *idem* 1998, p. 39.

76 Von Harnack 1924, II, p. 806; cf. L. Pietri 1995, p. 134.

77 Pietri 1976, pp. 134–136.

78 Daniélou-Marrou 1970, pp. 269–273; Brown 1974, pp. 54–67; Pietri (L.) 1995, pp. 171–172.

79 Cf. Pietri 1976, p. 565, for analogous views in relation to the foundation of urban parish churches ("*tituli*").

80 Valentini-Zucchetti 1942, pp. 17, 19, 23, 25; ICUR VIII, 21590.

81 See below, p. 29

82 See below, p. 30

83 Fasola 1954–1955, pp. 80–82; *idem* 1956, pp. 140–143; Fasola-Testini 1978, pp. 110–112; Fasola, ibid., pp. 195–196.

84 Carletti 1997, p. 186.

85 See below, p. 62

86 Armellini 1880, pp. 78–147; Fasola-Testini 1978, pp. 121–122, n. 26.

87 Josi 1924, pp. 54–86; *idem* 1926, pp. 51–106; Styger 1933, pp. 229–237; Tolotti 1970, pp. 322–340.

88 Nestori 1959, pp. 5–47; Pergola 1985–1986, pp. 52–60; Guyon 1987, pp. 62–66; 94–96.

89 Guyon 1987, pp. 64–65; Deckers-Seeliger-Mietke 1987, nn. 10–12.

90 Guyon 1987, pp. 71–89, 94–96, 192; Deckers-Seeliger-Mietke 1987, nn. 54ff.

91 Février 1983, pp. 33–34.

92 Guyon 1987, p. 101.

93 See above, pp. 25–7.

94 De Rossi 1864–1877, III, pp. 42ff.; Reekmans 1988.

95 De Rossi (M.S.) 1864–1877, II, pp. 62–67; Pergola 1975, pp. 70–71, 76, 90; Fasola-Testini 1978, pp. 113–114, 154–155; Reekmans 1988, pp. 6, 20; Carletti 1992, pp. 141–168; Baruffa 1992, pp. 106–117.

96 Fasola 1972, pp. 275–276, 293, 296–297; Fasola-Testini 1978, pp. 122–123; Fiocchi Nicolai 1991, pp. 7–12, 17–19. The re-utilisation of older *arenariae*, just like that of obsolete water shafts, is very widespread in the catacombs: Testini 1966, p. 124; Tolotti 1980, pp. 7–48; Fiocchi Nicolai, *et al*

1992, pp. 13–22; Pergola-Barbini 1997, pp. 62–64.

97 Reekmans 1964, pp. 53–54, 56, 70; Guyon 1987, pp. 64–65, 136; Styger 1925–1926, pp. 124, 129–145.

98 Cf. Guyon 1987, p. 66, 141–142; see above, p. 30–31, for the examples attested in the "Region of Gaius and Eusebius" in S. Callisto, in the upper floor of the Region of the Good Shepherd in the Catacomb of Domitilla and in the oldest nuclei of the Catacombs of the Giordani and Via Anapo.

99 Armellini 1880, pp. 100–110, 112–116.

100 Fasola 1954–1955, pp. 80–81.

101 Marchi 1844, pls. 17, 19, 25, 28, 35–37; Fasola 1956, pp. 140–143; Testini 1966, 137–138, 163; Fasola-Testini 1978, pp. 195–196.

102 See above, p. 27.

103 Carletti 1988, p. 129; idem 1997, pp. 149–150.

104 Bisconti 1998, pp. 49–51.

105 See above, p. 17

106 Styger 1925–1926, pp. 128–139; Wilpert 1910, pp. 10–15.

107 Reekmans 1960, pp. 109–166.

108 Reekmans 1988, pp. 39–77, 208–212.

109 See above, p. 30

110 Idid., pp. 143–148; 212–218.

111 See below, p. 48ff.

112 Nestori 1971, pp. 197–200; Tolotti 1977, pp. 58–71; Reekmans 1988, pp. 218–223; Guyon 1987, pp. 104–121.

113 Ferrua 1994, pp. 236–237.

114 Marchi 1844, pp. 263–268; ICUR X, 26662.

115 Mac Mullen 1989, pp. 51–68; Pietri 1993, pp. 699–705; idem 1995, pp. 189–225.

116 Tolotti 1970, pp. 190–212, 283–304, 322–340.

117 Fiocchi Nicolai 1991, p. 18–19.

118 Guyon 1987, pp. 78–80, 135–203; Deckers-Seeliger-Mietke 1987, nn. 28ff.; 65ff.

119 Styger 1933, p. 246, fig. 90; Tolotti 1978a, pp. 167–170, 180, 187; Pergola 1985–1986, pp. 56–57.

120 Fasola 1972, pp. 276–277, 297.

121 Armellini 1880, pp. 189ff.; Frutaz 1976, pl. f.t.

122 Tolotti 1978a, pp. 183–184; Nr, p. 95, nn. 15–18.

123 Nr, p. 92, nn. 7–8.

124 Deichmann-Bovini-Brandenburg 1967, nn. 557, 564.

125 De Rossi 1864–1877, III, pp. 49–77; Fasola 1956, pp. 143–147; Nr, pp. 34–36; nn. 15–20.

126 Fasola-Fiocchi Nicolai 1989, p. 1187.

127 On the function of the cubicula: Février 1983, pp. 33–34; Carletti 1989, p. 212.

128 Mac Mullen 1989, pp. 79ff.; Pietri 1993, p. 706; De Francesco (in press). On the limitations of a purely sociological interpretation of the various typologies of tombs and funerary spaces in the catacombs, see especially the important observations of Reekmans 1986a, pp. 245–246.

129 Reekmans 1986a, p. 248.

130 On these basilicas, see Brandenburg 1979, pp. 61–154; Fiocchi Nicolai 1997, pp. 127–128 (with further biblio.).

131 Guyon 1987, pp. 288–300.

132 Ibid., pp. 294–298; Fasola 1982–1984, pp. 341–359.

133 Guyon 1987, pp. 288–303, 321.

134 Fornari 1932, pp. 201–213; Prandi 1949–1951, pp. 139–152; Tolotti 1953, pp. 228–231.

135 Fasola 1974, pp. 175–205.

136 De Rossi 1864–1877, III, pp. 77–96; Baruffa 1992, pp. 147–148. See also below, pp. 43–44.

137 Saint-Roch 1983, pp. 411–423.

138 R, pp. 249–257; Saint-Roch 1981, pp. 213–247; idem 1986, pp. 189–190.

139 Saint-Roch 1981, pp. 213–214, 219–247.

140 De Rossi 1864–1877, III, pp. 236–246, 268–271; Fasola 1980, pp. 235–254; Baruffa 1992, pp. 158–160, 175.

141 De Rossi 1864–1877, III, pp. 246–260; Baruffa 1992, pp. 158–159.

142 Cf. de Rossi 1864–1877, III, pls. XLII–XLV.

143 Josi 1926, pp. 154–211; Tolotti 1978a, pp. 184–185; Fasola 1987, pp. 209–230.

144 Fasola 1961, pp. 237–267.

145 De Rossi 1864–1877, III, pp. 77–96, 246–260, 488, 492; Guyon 1987, pp. 336–340; Spera 1992, pp. 300–307; Camiruaga, et al 1994, pp. 47–48; Spera 1995, pp. 433–446.

146 For these mausolea, see Fiocchi Nicolai 1997, p. 132 (with biblio.).

147 Guyon 1987, pp. 340–343; Saint-Roch 1981, p. 212; Février 1983, pp. 28–31; idem 1983a, pp. 39–41; Bisconti 1998, p. 35.

148 On this, see Février 1978, pp. 228–255; Guyon 1987, pp. 330–336.

149 Cf. Guyon 1987, p. 336; Spera 1995, pp. 441–442.

150 Saxer 1980, pp. 148–149.

151 On these funerary gifts: Février 1978, pp. 261–263; De Santis

1994, pp. 23–51; Felle-Del Moro-Nuzzo 1994, pp. 111–158; Bisconti 1996, pp. 101–103; cf. also Armellini 1880, pp. 349–350.

152 De Rossi 1864–1877, III, p. 574.

153 Guyon 1974, pp. 551–578; Conde Guerri 1979; Guyon 1987, pp. 98–100; Carletti 1997, pp. 156–157.

154 Ferrua 1960, pp. 473–480, Testini 1966, pp. 141–143; Reekmans 1986, pp. 11–32.

155 Ferrua 1960a, pp. 15–37; Camiruaga, et al 1994, pp. 44–49.

156 Ferrua 1960, pp. 38–102; Kotzsche Breitenbruch 1976, Tronzo 1986.

157 Ferrua 1971, pp. 7–62.

158 Reekmans 1986, pp. 16–19 (with biblio.); Vitale 1995, pp. 395–402.

159 Cf. Geertman 1995, pp. 125–155.

160 See below, pp. 48–53.

161 Reekmans 1964, pp. 151–153, 228, Nestori 1971, pp. 195, 274–275; Tolotti 1977, p. 74.

162 Guyon 1987, pp. 363–381.

163 Wilpert 1910, pp. 5, 8–11; Styger 1925–1926, pp. 135–138; Testini 1966, pp. 133–135.

164 LP, I, p. 208; Broccoli 1981, pp. 150–155, nn. 106–108.

165 Fasola 1970, pp. 238–252.

166 Duchesne 1907, p. 483, Février 1992, pp. 497–506.

167 Ferrua 1942; Pietri 1976, pp. 607–617; Brown 1983, pp. 51–53; Guyon 1995, pp. 783–784.

168 Cf. Saxer 1989, pp. 922–923, 987–988, 990–993.

169 Fiocchi Nicolai 1995, p. 763.

170 See below, pp. 50–51.

171 See Pietri 1976, pp. 623–624; Fiocchi Nicolai 1995, pp. 765, 769 for other literary evidence.

172 Spera 1994, pp. 112–113.

173 Reekmans 1964, pp. 161–172, 229; Tolotti 1977, pp. 58–87; Augenti 1991, p. 48; Spera 1994, pp. 112–113.

174 Reekmans 1964, pp. 128–130, 166–172, 229; Nestori 1971, p. 195; Weiland 1994, pp. 643–645; Spera 1994, pp. 112–113.

175 Fasola 1972, pp. 287, 291; Tolotti 1977, p. 74; Guyon 1987, pp. 381–382, 385–386.

176 Spera (in press).

177 Bisconti 1995, pp. 276–279.

178 Cf. however Fasola 1972, p. 287; J. Guyon 1987, p. 389.

179 Weiland 1994, pp. 633–643.

180 For the problematic examples of the churches of SS. Nereo ed Achilleo at the Catacomb of Domitilla and S. Ermete on Via Salaria Vetus, cf. Krautheimer

1937–1980, I, pp. 195–208; III, pp. 129–135; Pergola 1986a, pp. 203–218; Tolotti 1985, pp. 374, 376–378; Spera 1997, pp. 196–207.

181 See the bibliographical sources cited in the previous note. See also Bertonière 1985, pp. 142–143, 184, for a possible Damasan contribution to the construction of the crypt of S. Hippolytus on Via Tiburtina.

182 See above, pp. 47.

183 Fiocchi Nicolai 1995, pp. 765–768.

184 Spera 1994, pp. 115–118.

185 Cf. Pietri 1976, pp. 434–436, 447–452, 558–562, 648–649; idem 1993, pp. 706–709; Salmito 1995, pp. 678–679, 695–700.

186 Spera 1994, pp. 111–127.

187 See above, p. 48.

188 For a summary of this phenomenon: Brown 1983, pp. 40ff.; Duval 1988, pp. 51ff.; eadem 1991, pp. 333–351.

189 Picard 1992, pp. 8–9, 21–22, 33–34.

190 See above, pp. 50–51.

191 Ferrua 1961, pp. 209–214; Fasola 1965, p. 23; Pergola 1986a, pp. 213–215; Pergola-Barbini 1997, p. 214.

192 Marucchi 1914, pp. 238–259.

193 Ferrua 1938, pp. 406–412.

194 Bagatti 1936; Ferrua 1957, pp. 7–43; idem 1958, pp. 5–56; Carletti 1994b, pp. 5–10.

195 Bagatti 1936, pp. 9–11; Deckers-Mietke-Weiland 1994, pp. 4–104.

196 See below, p. 56.

197 See below, pp. 55–56.

198 Ferrua 1958, pp. 7–45.

199 Carletti 1994, pp. 111–126; idem 1994a, pp. 29–41; Bisconti 1995c, pp. 71–93; Giuliani 1998, pp. 375–397.

200 Fiocchi Nicolai 1995a, pp. 776–786; Fiocchi Nicolai 1997a, pp. 78–83; Fiocchi Nicolai-Del Moro-Nuzzo-Spera (in press).

201 ICUR IV, 12242–12252A; Nestori 1990, pp. 55–60, 119–120; Nr, pp. 118–119; Fiocchi Nicolai 1995, pp. 783–784, n. 30.

202 Reekmans 1986, p. 247; see above, pp. 47–48.

203 Saint-Roch 1981, pp. 214, 217, 246; Spera 1994, pp. 119–120.

204 Reekmans 1988, pp. 95–109; Spera 1994, p. 120.

205 Tolotti 1970, pp. 161–165.

206 Bagatti 1937, pp. 40, 59–67; De Santis 1994, pp. 23–51.

207 Bagatti 1937, pp. 33–34.

208 See above, p. 48.

209 Cf. Guyon 1987, pp. 325–326, 329 on Peter and Marcellinus.

210 Cf. Reekmans 1986, p. 246; Pergola 1990, p. 168.

211 Fasola 1985, pp. 13–22.

212 Cf. Fiocchi Nicolai 1997, pp. 127–129 (see biblio.) and above, pp. 38–41.

213 Cf. ICUR II, pp. 30–32; V, pp. 77–94; VII, pp. 12–56; VIII, pp. 21–36; X, pp. 165–182; R, passim, Fiocchi Nicolai 1997a, p. 82.

214 LP, I, p. 212; the building has not yet been certainly identified: Fiocchi Nicolai 1995a, pp. 783–784.

215 Avell., 3 = CSEL, 35/1, pp. 46–47; Krautheimer 1937–1980, V, pp. 97–169; idem 1980–1982, pp. 207–220.

216 De Rossi 1874, pp. 5–33; idem 1884–1885, pp. 149–184; cf. above, p. 50–51.

217 Bertonière 1985, pp. 39–41.

218 Picard 1992, pp. 8–9, 21–22, 33–34.

219 See below, pp. 64–65.

220 Cf. Fiocchi Nicolai 1995, pp. 769–775.

221 Ibid., pp. 769–775; Spera 1997, pp. 211–224.

222 Deichmann-Tschira 1957, pp. 92–109; Deichmann 1970, pp. 144–169.

223 See above, pp. 48, 50–51, 57.

224 Bagatti 1936, pp. 37–58, 101–120; Bertonière 1985, pp. 145–165, 176–181; Guyon 1986, pp. 439–455; Spera 1994a, pp. 39–42; Spera 1997, pp. 217–231.

225 Nestori 1990.

226 Krautheimer 1937–1980, I, pp. 195–208; Spera 1997, pp. 196–207.

227 Krautheimer 1937–1980, III, pp. 129–135; Tolotti 1985, pp. 374, 376–378; Pergola 1986a,

pp. 203–218; cf. above, pp. 50–51, 57.

228 Deckers-Mietke-Weiland 1994, pp. 48–86.

229 Cf. Fiocchi Nicolai 1997, p. 139; on the wall painting and its dating: Russo 1979–1981, pp. 35–49; Minasi 1998, pp. 296–298.

230 LP, I, pp. 309, 323; Krautheimer 1937–1980, I, pp. 14–39; II, pp. 1–94, 125–129.

231 Farioli 1963, pp. 10–13, 19–29; Osborne 1985, pp. 317–322; Bisconti 1995, pp. 286–289; idem 1997a, pp. 307–339.

232 Josi 1924, pp. 86–97; Mazzoleni 1993, pp. 95–113.

233 Marchi 1844, pp. 237–238, pls. 47–48.

234 Carletti 1995, pp. 197–225; Eck 1996, pp. 107–123.

235 Bagatti 1936, pp. 41–56, 77–80, 98, 103; Bertonière 1985, pp. 43–48; Guyon 1987, pp. 318–319; Nestori 1990, pp. 101, 120; ICUR II, pp. 324–328; IV, pp. 432–433; V, 13123; VI, pp. 99–101; VII, pp. 426–429; VII, pp. 422–424; IX, 24316.

236 Deckers-Mietke-Weiland 1994, pp. 87–89, n. 4.

237 See above, p. 57.

238 Meneghini-Santangeli Valenzani 1993, pp. 89–111; eidem 1995, pp. 283–290; Fiocchi Nicolai 1997, p. 141.

239 LP, I, p. 305; ICUR VII,19937; IX, 24313; cf. Fasola 1972, pp. 289–291; Dulaey 1977, pp. 13–15; Bertonière 1985, pp. 49–51; Spera 1994a, pp. 39–51; Spera 1997, pp. 210–224.

240 Mansi 1766, col. 646.

241 Cf. primarily Osborne 1985, pp. 291–292; Spera 1997, pp. 185–241.

242 See Testini 1966, pp. 240–242; Osborne 1985, pp. 286–296; Spera 1997, pp. 188–189, 239.

243 Cf. Osborne 1985, pp. 310–312; Spera 1994a, pp. 47–49; Fiocchi Nicolai 1998, p. 313.

244 See above, p. 9.

II. THE DECORATION OF ROMAN CATACOMBS

Fabrizio Bisconti

1. THE ATMOSPHERE

Two patristic sources provide an equal number of views of "Christian underground Rome", that correspond to two antithetical but partially complimentary ways of conceiving and experiencing the catacombs. They both date to the very end of the fourth century and the beginning of the fifth, precisely the time in which Roman catacombs reached the apex of their development, yet also began to show the first explicit signs of decline that foreshadowed their progressive abandonment.

The first passage refers to S. Jerome's stay at Rome. While he was still a student, Jerome went on Sundays to visit the tombs of the apostles and martyrs, along with his fellow students. "We would enter into the galleries, carved out from the depths of the earth, completely covered by burials and so dark that it seemed to actualise the prophetic motto: 'They descend alive into hell' (*Psalm* 54.16). Occasionally lights, coming from above ground, softened the shadows a little, but the dim light was so faint that it seemed to originate from a mere crack rather than the skylight. We proceeded slowly, one step at a time, so completely surrounded by darkness that the Virgilian passage came to mind: 'The souls are frightened by the horror and the silence' (*Aeneid* II, 755)"[1].

The other source also records a visit to the Roman catacombs, that which the Spanish poet Prudentius, presumably at first hand, made to the cemetery of S. Ippolito on Via Tiburtina at the beginning of the fifth century[2]. According to this poetic description, Prudentius arrived in Rome to look for epigraphic material to show to a certain bishop Valerian. During his search, he came across the sanctuary on Via Tiburtina that held the remains of the martyr Hippolytus in an underground area. The catacomb that Prudentius visited can be identified with the monumental complex still accessible today[3]. Prudentius retraced the route followed by the pilgrims coming both from the Roman hinterland and nearby regions on the feast day of the martyr. This itinerary started off from the wall and then, by means of a tortuous staircase and a path lit by faint light from skylights, arrived at a dark "crypt", the tomb of the martyr[4]. The description of a painting that evoked in a dramatic crescendo, typical of legendary fables, the trial and cruel execution of the martyr[5] enriched his very detailed chronicle. In his description, Prudentius follows a dynamic iconographic typology rather unlikely for such an early period[6].

The two passages, for diverse motives, document a literary attitude that emphasises tones and images. The passage by S. Jerome seems to recall the typical dramatisation of childhood memories. The vision that emerges must accurately reflect the conception that was developing in those years of these singular underground cemeteries as obscure, silent and rather sad places. In other words, one of the innumerable commonly held beliefs concerning catacombs was being formed, generated in every period through to the present day. According to this interpretation, the catacombs were considered at one

Pl. II
"Catacomba Anonima
of Via Anapo: two
niches with loculi

71

76 Hypogeum of the Aurelii on Viale Manzoni, vault of a cubiculum with a skylight

The *carmen* of Prudentius, although characterised by an emphasis on digressions and literary compromises typical of poetic compositions, offers a less apocalyptic interpretation of the catacombs[9]. At the same time, by relying on romanticised narratives of the epic passions, it sublimates the cult to a popular hagiographic manifestation, with the entirely folk vitality of a pious ballad. Here the play of shadows is softened by the impromptu light from the skylights; darkness is as if fought and conquered by the figurative decoration of the hagiographic cycle[10].

Thus, these patristic passages offer two different perspectives, two points of view that coincide and are distant at the same time. The first describes a more typical "dark" vision of the catacombs, whereas the second is more sensitive to the rays of light, colour schemes, and presents a less "infernal" concept of these singular underground places.

Their coincidence resides in their consideration of darkness as an entity to fight and conquer, an element to eliminate through technical and structural means, and finally, through the more subtle instruments of decoration

It is not by chance that the custom of equipping these underground cemeteries with "wells of light", the so-called skylights[11] was introduced when they were just conceived. Skylights are already found in the earliest nuclei, or even in private tombs not yet fully Christianised, such as the Hypogeum of the *Aurelii* on Viale Manzoni (fig. 76)[12]. With the passage of time and the structural evolution of catacombs, these features became a sign of privilege, since their creation always entailed extra effort in construction and thus a considerable economic strain[13]. Skylights were built to mark out monuments that were particularly important or decorated, so that the light could emphasise their architectural features, the iconographic programmes of the frescoes and placements of marble or mosaic furnishings[14]. These skylights, as is well known, also functioned as ventilation shafts and wells for the removal of soil[15]. In a later period of the

moment as secure places of refuge during the persecutions, the next as unsettling and dismal stages for martyrdoms, at another as the site of religious rites that verged on the illicit and blasphemous[7]. This interpretation manifested itself first in patristic literature, contemporary with the utilisation of the catacombs as cemeteries. During the early Medieval period, the *topos* was further refined, as many legendary passions were set in these dark hypogean ambiences. The historical establishment of this commonly held belief occurs in the romantic literature of the nineteenth century, and more precisely in novels such as *Fabiola*. These later inspired the popular colossal films of our century, such as *The Robe, Ben Hur,* and *Quo Vadis?*[8].

use of the catacombs and especially when they became sites heavily visited in connection with the cult of the martyrs, skylights became salient signals of the *itinera ad sanctos*[16].

The skylights, but also the use of white plaster along these passageways, represented extremely useful, even indispensable, tools to mark out the path that the pilgrims had to follow in order to come into contact with the "sacred tombs"[17]. But, at the same time, they created an evocative atmosphere, in which the darkness of the galleries was slashed by bands of light, strengthened, in fact, by the whiteness of the walls.

The search for light, at first discreet and later systematic, led to the opening of skylights that were always more substantial in proportions and more audacious in architectural terms. One might think, for example, of the one that links the two levels in the Catacomb of Priscilla (fig. 77), or that which connects the *cubicula* of Miltiades and that of the Seasons at S. Callisto. This play of lights and shadows or, better yet, this never placated desire to conquer darkness with points of light, is also reflected in the epigraphic formulae. In the inscriptions, in evocations of paradise or more generally the other-worldly condition, continuous reference is made to the afterlife as *coelistia regna, regna beata poli, sidera onnipotens aula, lux, lumen*, and *astra*[18]. Painted decorations, with a more are less explicit reference to the celestial firmament are not absent, as seen in the Catacombs of Priscilla, the ex-Vigna Chiaraviglio, SS. Marcellino e Pietro, and S. Ermete[19].

Skylights were located strategically to dispel darkness and to illuminate the decorations and monuments that, as a result of their composition, could capture light, such as those partially or completely covered with marble[20] or with rare mosaic decoration[21]. The particularly humid *habitat* of Roman catacombs did not encourage decorators to choose mosaic technique for their iconographic schemes. While the Neapolitan[22] and Sicilian[23] complexes preserve monuments and complexes decorated in mosaics, this decorative device did not enjoy great popularity at Rome[24]. The unusual case of a mosaic pavement in the Hypogeum of Villa Cellere[25], and the even more unique example of two "mosaic slabs" with scenes inspired by the cycle of Jonah from the cemetery of Aproniano, are exceptions to the rule. In addition, elaborate mosaic decorations can be found in an *arcosolium* near the tomb of SS. Protus and Hyacinth in the cemetery of S. Ermete, in the crypt of S. Eusebius in the cemetery of S. Callisto, in several niches in the

77 *Catacomb of Priscilla: skylight between the first and second floors*

Hypogeum of the *Acilii*, in an *arcosolium* on the second floor of the Catacomb of Priscilla and in a famous *arcosolium* in the Catacomb of Domitilla[26].

These last two monuments, together with other sporadic examples of minor fig-urative significance[27], contain true complex decorative programmes. Recent ultra-violet analysis of the *arcosolium* of Priscilla[28] has revealed an iconographic programme cen-tred on the orant image of the deceased in the peak of the *intrados*. An adoration of the Magi is represented on the right and on the left, a judgement scene, perhaps the

episode of the accusation of Susanna by the elders.

More complex from the point of view of colour and symbolism, is the famous *arco-solium*, already seen in 1742 by Maran-goni, near a staircase in the Catacomb of Domitilla, and rediscovered by Ferrua in 1960[29]. The lunette on the back wall depicts an evocative scene of *maiestas Domini* with Christ enthroned between the two princes of the apostles, in front of a *capsa* of volumes (fig. 78). A mandorla of light, composed of glass paste tesserae of brilliant green, sets the representation within a visionary state, alluding to the epiphany of the *Logos* in reference to *Apoc.* 4.2–3. In the *intrados* of the *arcosolium*, scenes of the resurrection of Lazarus (fig. 79), the three youths in the furnace and the sacrifice of Isaac can be identified. An inscription that seems to allude to the consubstantiality of Father and Son, an orthodox answer to Christological controversies that emerged from the spread of Arianism, can be deciphered on the arch[30].

These monuments and decoration that, more than others, capture the light of the lamps and torches for illumination and the skylights, bring us down to the second half of the fourth century. This represents the most mature moment of the catacombs and at the same time, the epilogue of decorative activity in these underground settings, when they seem to give way to buildings above ground. But the evocative atmosphere that must have been felt in the catacomb setting was composed precisely through this play of light and dark. It was also characterised by other features, perhaps less striking but equally functional, that defined the borderline that distinguished the world of darkness from the one of sudden illumination. All of these elements were found in less advanced periods, less aristocratic zones and areas destined for a broader and more modest level of the *societas christiana*.

Namely, in those areas of the catacombs that were characterised by undifferentiated funerary systems, where the norms of equality and extreme simplicity regulated the origin of the *coemeteria* as communal dormitories in which brothers in faith rested, in anticipation of the Resurrection[31]. In this sober and basic *habitat*, funerary morphologies represented especially by the *loculus* designed as a sort of primitive cell, a type of unit of measurement that could be repeated

79 Catacomb of Domitilla: arcosolium with mosaic decoration, detail of the scene of the resurrection of Lazarus

were entombed in anticipation of a better systemisation, the definitive one that Christians awaited at the end of time (fig. 80).

The *loculi* were closed off carelessly, using marble fragments or tiles joined by unsightly joints of mortar that also ran along the perimeter of the tomb. The systemisation of the *loculi* always and invariably indicates the rapidity of execution, with an almost complete absence of a preliminary plan and a procedure marked by urgency. Everything was done quickly with the complicity of the *fossores* and the relatives of the deceased. All was aimed at an immediate, summary and provisional placement of the tomb, as if the corpse awaited a final and more dignified burial[32].

The *loculus*, in its essential nature, represents, as already mentioned, the basic element of common burial in the catacombs. It offered the most coherent answer to the law of equality that characterised the mentality and culture of the Early Christian world. Yet, it was a difficult law to follow for a people that was accustomed to the monumentalisation or dignified decoration of the tombs of their dear ones.

It is this sense of community spirit and law of equality that, acting in tandem, produced the endless galleries of *loculi* whose decoration, as might be expected, reflects clear improvisation. Even the material used to close off the tombs, the result of the most ordinary economy of reuse, without recourse to overly careful selection, demonstrates this phenomenon. Sometimes, terracotta fragments were juxtaposed with marble pieces, rendering difficult any uniform epigraphic scheme or forcing the writer of the text to opt for painting in red lead rather than writing in charcoal or lime.

At other times, as mentioned, the epigraphic text was entirely eliminated or relegated to the mortar of the borders or joints, offering the extreme solution of difficult, narrow supports, not at all amenable and welcoming, for the display of funerary equipment. This last detail also demonstrates the rapidity and improvisations within which the dynamic of the systemisation of the tomb

80 Catacomb of Priscilla: gallery with loculus tombs

and multiplied *ad infinitum*, held remains. Sometimes they even lack the minimum amount of furnishing or any form of epitaph. Even when the latter appears, it very often consists only of the name of the deceased. Glancing at the galleries still intact, one gets a sense of the provisional character of these vast burial deposits, consisting of simple spaces carved in the tufa, stacked up in piles, sometimes even on a very high level as if they were shelves of large closets. Here the bodies evolved. It is precisely this timeliness that produced the galleries cum dormitories, where the interminable "pigeon-holes" of *loculi*, either anonymous or barely identified with only the essential onomastic references, sometimes reduced to the *cognomina singula*, seem a visual response to a need of this period[33].

The laws of equality and sobriety were rigorously respected in several of the very early Roman catacombs, therefore ascribable to the first decades of the third century. These include the central *arenaria* of the Catacomb of Priscilla (fig. 81)[34], "Region I" and the Crypts of Lucina in S. Callisto, and several sections of the cemeteries of Calepodio, Novaziano and Maggiore[35]. Immediately, these rules were broken, always by the use of essential but barely visible devices, however, these were symptomatic of a tendency to emulate the privileged and decorated tombs of notable figures of the community.

Thus began a "figurative period" in the Roman catacombs that could be called alternative or substitutive of the major arts. Poor and fragmentary materials, displaced in a disorganised and sparse manner, were used to imitate the decoration of the grand *cubicula*, paved in *opus sectile*[36], decorated with mosaics[37], equipped with tables carved out according to daring architectural schemes and embellished with the presence of sculpted marble sarcophagi.

The first symptoms of these infractions and imitations can be found in several barely coherent and almost insignificant signs traced directly onto the plaster, either beside the funerary text or in an isolated manner as the sole decorative expression of the *loculus*. These take the form of dashes or letters, often indecipherable, at least in the global sense. Imitating ordinary epitaphs, they reproduced their graphic form, thereby imparting to the tomb a generic and approximate sense of decorum and respect. They could also have taken on an apotropaic value. These alphabetic sequences and inscriptions and ingenious pseudo-graphic tricks employed by semi-literate commis-

sioners, decorators and readers, nevertheless endowed a certain dignity on the burial[38].

These signs rotated primarily around the orbit of elaborate threats to protect the tomb, of the type seen in the text of epitaphs that contain promises of fines, curses, and declarations of inviolability. Sometimes, actual seals[39] or Christological signs impressed into the mortar that sealed the tomb[40] reinforced them. At the same time, these symbols also assumed a figurative value when they

81 Catacomb of Priscilla: loculi in the area of the arenaria

82 *Catacomb of Priscilla: representation of a moray eel in glass paste*

83 *Catacomb of S. Felicita: tusk of a wild boar*

entered into an intimate and ambiguous relationship with the decorative elements. Often the letters of these sequences alternated haphazardly with crosses, Christograms and palmettes, creating a sort of graphic and semantic equivalence between the various signs.

Even in coherent texts with a complete and perfectly comprehensible significance, such as the famous epitaph of *Filomena* in the Catacomb of Priscilla[41], punctuation marks and purely decorative elements assume the same proportions as the letters of the text. Thus an equal relationship is created between the text, its punctuation and its figurative commentary.

These phenomena also document a shift in the concept of funerary decoration. The text of the inscriptions, including its complementary and pseudo-figurative accessories, as a whole and assuming increasing proportions, performed the function of protecting and decorating the burial site, occupying it completely as if to respond to the precept of *horror vacui*, so dear to the culture of this period[42].

84 *Catacomb of Panfilo: glass perfume bottle*

85 *Catacomb of Panfilo: bone statuette fixed in the mortar of a loculus*

These details led to a more mature period of art in the catacombs, when material, at times of minimal proportions and of little value, appears in the sealing mortar of the *loculi*. These additions can take the form of fragments of coloured marble, pieces of glass paste (fig. 82), shells, animal teeth (fig. 83), glass and ceramic containers (fig. 84), lamps, dolls and statuettes in bone (fig. 85) and ivory, buttons, fibulae, *armillae*, necklaces, small metal bells (fig. 86), coins, gems, lamps and gilded bases of glass containers.

Giovanni Battista de Rossi attributed only a "mnemonic" significance to this material. In his opinion, they represent efficient compositions for the recognition of the tomb, within the context of the packed walls of galleries, studded with *loculi* otherwise completely the same and difficult to identify. This was particularly the case when the tombs lacked even an epigraphic sign. Nevertheless, considering the level of literacy of the Christian population connected with these sections of the catacombs, epigraphy

did not always in itself represent a discriminating element for the identification of the tombs of loved ones[43].

But de Rossi had a very partial idea of the phenomenon, since he knew only a few rare intact areas of the Roman catacombs that escaped the spoliation of the past. Recent discoveries, first in the complexes of S. Agnese[44], Panfilo[45], Commodilla[46], and later in the more recent archaeological investigations in the cemeteries of SS. Marcellino e Pietro[47], S. Ippolito[48] and the ex-Vigna Chiaraviglio[49], have contributed substantially to a broader understanding of the panorama of *loculi* decoration.

The first observation that can be deduced from these recent findings is the significance of the fact that the materials deposited around the tombs are repeated both in variety and placement. The suggestive interpretation of de Rossi must therefore be abandoned. In fact, it would have been very difficult to recognise the tombs through the presence of very similar materials, often placed in the margins of rather high tombs, and located so that they would have been almost invisible from the gallery level[50].

In the last few years, other meanings have been proposed. In my opinion, there must have existed, first of all, a profound and fundamental reason that governed each intervention that took place within these very simple and extremely anonymous burials. This must even have been true for those who could not permit themselves more complex decorative programmes for economic reasons or religious convictions. The systemisation of these burials is the answer, certainly less striking and more subdued, to the law of equality that was responded to in a much more significant manner by the frescoed *cubicula* and sarcophagi[51].

In precisely the moment in which communal galleries were invented, the mechanism for infractions of the law of equality was triggered. These breaches took several forms, but always sought to create some minimal decorative furnishing around these humble tombs that emulated, even if on a basic level, the major arts.

86 Catacomb of S. Felicita: small bronze bell

79

This was an "alternative' art, a substitute for the great decorative programmes that, as already mentioned, were used in the *cubicula* of Christians of high social status, high economic potential or an important hierarchical level within the community. In the galleries, an attempt was made to copy these decorative schemes in very reduced spaces and with little means. As mentioned, everything was done rapidly with the compliance of the *fossores* who satisfied the *desiderata* of the relatives of the deceased, fixing the small amount of coloured and luminescent material that they had to hand within the lime. This material was juxtaposed with the true burial equipment that, in fact, was removed from the interior of the *loculus* in order to be displayed on its exterior.

During these operations, urgent but targeted selections of materials were made. Alongside objects dear to the deceased and therefore more true to the concept of "funerary equipment", a selection was made of materials considered to be the most decorative and aesthetically pleasing and appealing to the viewer, and most functional in terms of an immediate visual impact.

Thus, the "funerary equipment on display", represented by toys and statuettes, was flanked by so-called "gilded glass", or rather the bases of glass containers decorated in thin gold leaf with different iconographic themes and inscriptions that were largely good wishes. In placing these unusual glass elements, the worker in charge of the systemisation of the *loculus*, systematically broke the bases of the containers to isolate and display the decorated part, that which was most important iconographically. It is precisely this last practice, of breaking the container to isolate and display the decorative element, which leads to a still unresolved debate. This concerns the primary function of these special containers whose use was so widespread in the catacombs. At least 500 examples, 200 of which are preserved in the Museo della Biblioteca Apostolica Vaticana, are known to date[52]. It is clear that these containers had a daily use not strictly tied to the world of catacombs, since they have also

been found in other contexts. And yet, in the past, an exclusively Christian liturgical role was attributed to these containers[53], even if an alternative, vaguely domestic function was also proposed[54]. Only at the end of the last century was the multi-functional role of these containers recognised, in which, however, the concrete and convivial use was predominant as indicated by the repeated invitation in the inscriptions that accompany the decoration: *pie zeses*[55]. These cups, used also by the pagans, most probably served as gifts that carried good wishes on the occasion of wedding anniversaries and other family feasts[56] or as good wishes for the New Year[57]. The contexts in which they were found and the themes that they expound, often inspired by genre scenes, mythology, divinities, or portraits of the deceased, document this usage.

These unusual funerary gifts had in the first place a concrete function, whereas in their secondary use, they served as decorative elements and funerary equipment. As F. W. Deichmann has pointed out in recent years[58], however, they could also have had another role more or less involved in the practices related to funerary ritual. Deichmann suggests that they were specifically connected to the funerary rites of ritual meals, both the classic type of libations and the more typically Christian one of the *refrigerium*[59]. We cannot exclude, in fact, that breaking the body of the glass containers and their deliberate elimination could have been directly connected to the ritual gesture of a mystical and apotropaic breakage of the food container used for the funerary meal[60].

In addition to these diverse layers of use, the decorative function of this material remained essential, that bears, as has already been mentioned, an impact both luminescent and strongly tied to iconographic meaning. In fact, it should not be forgotten, concerning the themes selected for the gilded bases, that the most popular biblical scenes of the Early Christian repertoire, the symbols and images of the saints and martyrs were very quickly added to the neutral images, portraits and genre scenes[61]. It should also be noted that the gilded bases also depicted the figures of the martyrs most loved by the Early Christians in Rome: from S. Agnes, whose image appears on a glass still *in situ* in the cemetery of Panfilo (fig. 87), to S. Lawrence, S. Hippolytus and S. Timothy and Pope Damasus[62]. These iconographic choices demonstrate how the glass vessels became true protective objects for the Christians, a type of support for the images of saints as intercessors[63], whom the faithful selected as companions in life on earth and as guides in the afterlife[64].

Glass vessels with a gilded base, but also other glass or ceramic containers, according to some scholars, could also have performed a specifically funerary role when they were placed in a specific manner so that they could hold liquids or solids[65]. This particularity, so rare and difficult to prove except by hypothesising a "symbolic meal" extremely limited in proportions and diffusion, does not represent the most convincing meaning of the employment of these elements within the *loculus*. Rather, as already mentioned several times, their significance resided in their ambivalent and multivalent role that oscillated between decoration and funerary

equipment. In the same way, after the intensive and yet heavily opposed studies by de Rossi[66], the idea that some of these glass vessels should be considered the "blood vases" of the early champions of the faith must also be rejected (fig. 88)[67]. Nevertheless, this has also become a commonly held belief and a means of identifying the tombs of martyrs.

The insuppressible desire to attract attention to the tomb, with bright materials that captured the light of the pilgrims' lamps was added to the decorative intent of these objects placed around the *loculus* was added, as has been observed. This made the visitors direct their glance towards these multi-

87 Catacomb of Panfilo: gilded glass with a representation of S. Agnes

88 Catacomb of S. Felicita: small glass vessel

81

89 Catacomb of No-vaziano: ceramic lamp

coloured "flashes". Among other things, it also fed and enriched the symbolic tension with respect to light that accompanied the Christian belief in the evocative concept of illumination seen by the believer involved in a spiritual journey that led from baptism to the final resurrection[68].

A concept and tension that, in the dark *habitat* of catacombs, resulted in the multiplication of the use of lamps until they became a fixed feature of the decoration of the *loculi*. At times the lamps, like all the other objects, were immersed in the closing mortar; at others, they were placed on small marble or ceramic shelves on the sides of the tomb (fig. 89)[69]. These lamps form part of the most common production of the late Antique period, especially in the local or African typologies attested between the fourth and fifth centuries. These examples present a round or oval profile, a pearl decoration around the shoulders, or an elongated channel[70], with the shoulders and disc decorated with plants and animals or biblical scenes[71].

The concept of light, intended as a force that suppressed darkness, was recorded in scripture[72] and by the Church Fathers[73]. This concept is defined precisely by the popular belief that saw the flame of lamps as an alternative to or substitutes for the light of day that the deceased could no longer enjoy. That light, radiating from the lit candles around the bier, or from the torches used during the funerary procession, served to dispel the shadows and demons, but also to symbolise the eternal light illuminating paradise[74].

An epitaph in the cemetery of Panfilo of a *Lucernius servus Christi*[75] provides a sense of the role attributed to light in the underground cemeteries, in that the significance of the onomastic form was figuratively commented on by a candle and a lamp incised in the centre of the slab. Thus, this demonstrates on the one hand the simple equation of image equals name, and on the other hand an evocative symbolic cue. And again, in an inscription dedicated to *Ianuaria* in the complex of S. Callisto[76], a small series of objects is represented, namely, a small amphora, a large lamp and a glass. In this example, containers used for the *refrigerium* and therefore for the fundamental funeral practice for the Early Christians are also connected to the sense of the *lux aeterna,* to which the lamp alludes, essentially recording the concept of baptismal illumination, as the link between this world and the next[77].

2. THE CONTEXTS

The communal galleries of catacombs, in light of what has been pointed out, offered the visitor an extremely evocative atmosphere, even though produced using very simple materials. The entire funerary equipment of the deceased was located on the exterior of the tomb, so as to share even these poor objects, that the ancient mentality in contrast would have jealously enclosed within the tomb together with the body of the deceased. Within the interior of the *loculi* in the catacomb, rather, were preserved a few, humble personal objects: small rings (fig. 90), earrings (fig. 91), bone bracelets (fig. 92), the remains of the clothing or shrouds with which the dead bodies were wrapped.

90 Catacomb of the ex-Vigna Chiaraviglio: silver ring

92 Catacomb of S. Felicita: ivory bracelet

In a few rare cases, a small pile of coins was associated with the burials, demonstrating how the funerary practice of the "obol for Charon", was also followed by Christians[78]. However, more frequently, the coins were also displayed on the exterior of the *loculus* (fig. 93).

All of the observations proposed so far suggest the development of a great revolution in the conception of death and funerary equipment by the Early Christians. This new conception broke down the intimate link between individual burials and funerary goods directly managed by the survivors, and

91 Catacomb of the ex-Vigna Chiaraviglio: gold earrings

93 Catacomb of Panfilo: coins fixed in the mortar of a loculus

94 Catacomb of SS.
Pietro e Marcellino: marble revetment covering
the walls and pavement
of a cubiculum

opened out to a broader, common view. As mentioned earlier, the objects usually preserved within the individual tombs were placed at the disposal of the entire community of the living and the dead.

Walking through the galleries of catacombs provides only a very approximate idea of the contexts, funerary equipment and ancient layout of different regions of the underground cemeteries. The more or less traumatic decline of the catacombs at the end of the late Antique period, the isolation of vast areas at the time of the great early Medieval

pilgrimages, the removal of numerous objects in later periods, the chaos and systematic plundering by the "*corpisantari*" and the uncontrolled excavations of the recent past have all taken their toll on the catacombs. Now, they are just mute and empty containers, deprived of their decoration, that, although not always rich, was often complex and diversified, and at any rate symptomatic of a changing mentality.

While objects of the funerary equipment were removed, dispersed or amassed in private collections[79], other elements that served

to decorate the catacomb settings of both the communal regions and the family *cubicula* or the areas of the martyrs have been completely lost. In particular, the marble decoration, when not reused, often became material for limestone or construction. And yet, in antiquity, many rooms of the catacombs must have contained marble elements, both pavements and socles, and constructions related to the monumentalisation of the tombs of the martyrs or in the architecture and sarcophagi of special and privileged tombs. The surviving traces of the mortar used for attachment, several slabs found *in situ* and several exceptional monuments found intact demonstrate that the decoration of domestic, funerary and civil buildings above ground was imitated in these underground settings[80].

The contexts present, above all, revetment using large marble plaques, mostly of light colour, always to reflect the light of the skylights, torches and lamps. Such decoration covered the walls in particular, but could also cover those elements used for the funerary rites, such as the benches and tables for the communal meal[81]. Sometimes marble also covered the pavements, using the sought-after and rather costly technique of *opus sectile*. Thus, in the Chapels of the Sacraments A4 in the earliest area of the Catacomb of S. Callisto, the pavement is decorated with an inlay of white and grey marble that forms square motifs enclosed diagonally within other squares[82]. In a *cubiculum* of the Catacomb of SS. Marcellino e Pietro, dated to the fourth century, is found a complex pavement with flowers with four petals in red porphyry and serpentine on a background of pavonazzeto (fig. 94)[83].

Traces of very complex marble decoration are not lacking, such as in a *cubiculum* of the Catacomb of SS. Marco e Marcelliano, in which even the corner columns are covered in *opus sectile*[84]. Another example is provided by an area of the Catacomb of Pretestato near the *spelunca magna* in which *opus sectile* alternates with mosaic decoration[85].

Marble, in all its forms, was the preferred material for the systemisation of the tombs of the martyrs. Solid slabs, *transennae*, *plutei*, pergolas, pseudo-ciboria, façades set against the tufa walls, structures within which were set monumental inscriptions, particularly of the Damasan period all are found. This can be seen first in the Crypt of the Popes in the Catacomb of S. Callisto[86], and later in the tomb of S. Januarius in the Catacomb of Pretestato[87], the tombs of SS. Peter and Marcellinus in the cemetery of Via Labicana[88] and the tomb of S. Alexander in the Catacomb of the Giordani on Via Salaria, in which white marble is used alongside green marble from Greece[89].

In all these examples, marble represents the only decorative feature of the monumentalisation, emphasised only by the authentic pontifical inscriptions by Damasus, and sometimes, although much more rarely, by fresco decorations. For example, in the tomb of SS. Felix and Adauctus in the Catacomb of Commodilla, the marble *ciborium* must have framed the lunette representing the two saints pointing to a Christogram and a *cista*[90].

Very often the use of marble was imitated through painting, with the creation of painted imitation marbles, both to decorate architectural features and to replicate *opus sectile*. The triumph of marble imitation, in the form of architraves, columns, façades, tables and capitals can be abundantly observed in the rich rooms of the Hypogeum of Via Dino Compagni, where these imitations of marble were also associated with the presence of fake fronts of sarcophagi and stuccoes. With regard to the last, the presence of stucco decoration, either isolated or associated with frescoes, in the underground cemeteries was rare, perhaps as a result of their deterioration in the excessively humid *habitat* of the catacombs[91].

Returning to marble imitations, it should be noted that painted imitations were particularly used for the decoration of the socles of *cubicula*, respecting Roman architectural canons that entailed a tripartite division of spaces. Just as in the mausolea, in the *cubicula* of catacombs, there was an attempt to recreate the atmosphere and settings of the

domus aeterna; thus, the conventional divisions that characterised domestic buildings were also replicated.

As mentioned earlier, the room was also organised in three principal registers. The lowest, that which ran along the pavement, was decorated with more or less complex marble work. The middle register, in contrast, displayed a figurative frieze, while the vault contained a more ethereal and symbolic decoration, entirely crossed by geometric figures or vegetable patterns.

This organisation of the parts, that ultimately offers an overlay of registers, suggests, from the semantic point of view, an important crescendo. The lower section sometimes displays a simple marble revetment, more or less complex and more or less attentive to the imitation of the socles of the *domus*, civil buildings and Christian basilicas. Alternatively, it can engage itself in the reproduction of railings, *transennae*, perspectives of *viridaria*, fountains and views of a generic and neutral otherworld.

In the middle register, the figurative discourse becomes more penetrating and often narrative. For example, in the *cubiculum* of the *Pistores* in the Catacomb of Domitilla, dated to the very end of the fourth century, a fake marble socle[92] is overlaid by a long cycle of the activity of *pistores* or *mensores*[93]. The interior of the apsidal calottes and the *arcosolia* space is reserved for biblical themes (the Jonah cycle) and theophanies (the Apostolic College, and the Good Shepherd amongst the Seasons) (figs. 95 and 96).

95 *Catacomb of Domitilla: cubiculum of the* Pistores, *view of the apse depicting the Apostolic College*

96 *Catacomb of Domitilla: cubiculum of the* Pistores, *view of the apse depicting the Good Shepherd*

The outermost room of the *Cappella Graeca* in the Catacomb of Priscilla, of the late Gallienic period, demonstrates, more than any other monument of the late Antique period, the superimposition of registers and the semantic crescendo mentioned earlier. Above a socle in fake marble appears the cycle of Susanna depicted in megalographic proportions. The vault, largely lost, seems to have displayed, within a complex linear framework, cosmic themes and signs interpreted according from a Christian perspective (fig. 97)[94].

In some cases, the wall divisions were simplified, corrected, and or rather, rendered original by several iconographic inversions and the merging of diverse sections within the spaces reserved for other registers. The decorative scheme of one of the two under-ground rooms of the Hypogeum of the *Aurelii* on Viale Manzoni is quite original in this sense. It displays a high socle occupied by a procession of standing philosophers, who articulate the space with their rhythmic verticality and significant proportions, suggesting a sequence of figurative orthostats. The middle frieze is also treated in an unusual fashion, at times flowing in a naturally horizontal pattern, at others insinuating itself in the space reserved for the vault with lunette fields (fig. 98)[95].

If some *cubicula* reflected, therefore, the canonical division of superimposed registers, more often catacomb rooms contain wall surfaces that are completely whitewashed. Yet, even these walls are crossed by a system of divisions, adopted to emphasise the decorative fields, that betrays, very generically a

88

dependence on "Pompeian" wall painting, with extreme simplification of the architectural imitation[96].

Thus, a decorative system emerges, based on geometric patterns created by lines more or less thin, predominantly in red and green, which characterised "catacomb art" for many decades of its evolution. The red and green linearity in diverse syntactic forms and the more or less organic strings of panels that divide the fields of a neutral, mostly white, background, seem to synthesise the element most dear to this wall decoration, that of the imitation of architecture[97].

This evolutionary process transformed the rich and complex wall decorations of domestic settings into more simple geometric patterns, in which the light backgrounds emerge almost to reflect, as has been mentioned several times, the small amount of light available in these underground environments.

The first symptoms of a transformation in the organisational conception of pictorial decoration can already be seen in domestic buildings of the late Antique period. Of particular interest are several *domus* in Ostia, in which a new decorative period was inaugurated that recalls the architectural imitations of the Pompeian styles[98].

The most significant examples come from the houses of the *aurighi* (charioteers), that of Temistoche and the house of *Annius*, the houses "of the painted vault" and "of the yellow walls", the "*caupona* of the peacock" and the House of the Muses[99]. In the decoration of all of these houses, a progressive impoverishment of the fundamental structures of the architectural scheme can be detected. They are dated to between the late Antonine and the mature Severan periods, in perfect chronological harmony with the earliest pictorial examples in the catacombs The architectural elements are reduced to ethereal and thin pavilions that recall the so-called fourth Pompeian style[100].

The Severan period sees the definition of the wall surface as a chromatic unity, no longer intended as a space open towards an illusionary depth, but rather as a solid and substantial surface to be articulated with panels. The convention of the organisation of the wall as a theatre backdrop is thus broken. In addition, the individual pavilions expand to receive broader, uniform and monochrome panels, at one time painted in with *pinakes* with genre scenes, at another with elements suspended in mid-air, or again, with figures looking out of doors and windows.

The decoration of the buildings beneath the complex of S. Giovanni in Laterano and those of the "villa piccola" under S. Sebastiano (fig. 99) are usually considered typical examples of the transition from the "architectural style" to the "red and green linear style". Similarly, the Chapels of the Sacraments and the Crypts of Lucina in the Cata-

98 Hypogeum of the Aurelii on Viale Manzoni: entrance to a cubiculum

comb of S. Callisto, and the *cubiculum* of the *coronatio* in the Catacomb of S. Pretestato serve as Christian examples[101].

Thus the range of funerary monuments and dwellings of the late Antique period that stand at the confines and junction with catacomb decoration is expanding. At the same time, the funerary monuments seem to include a conspicuous number of examples of this transition. These include the Hypogeum of the *Aurelii* in Viale Manzoni[102], the Cryptoporticus[103] and the sarcophagus gallery in the Hypogeum of the *Acilii*[104] in the Catacomb of Priscilla.

Both groups of pictorial examples introduce a simplification of the already evolved partitioning system and display always less reference to the architecture[105].

Walking through the galleries of Roman catacombs, some extraordinary monuments still articulate clearly the delicate passage from architectural decoration to red and green linearity. A good example is the *cubiculum* of the Good Shepherd in the Catacomb of Domitilla[106] in which two different and inverted phases suggest the coexistence of the framing style and a true linear style[107], still in the course of the third century (figs. 100, 101). But even in a more mature period of catacomb art, the structural organisation, always mindful of its origins and still characterised by true architectural elements, continues to survive. For example, in the *cubiculum* of Ampliatus, also in the Catacomb of Domitilla, a complex succession of decorative phases is represented, in the sense that the architectonic divisions were later painted in with bucolic scenes (figs. 102, 103)[108].

The *arcosolium* of Orpheus in the Catacomb of SS. Marcellino e Pietro, dated to the end of the fourth century, seems to me to be more typical in this regard. Here, in the area above the arch, several biblical scenes seem to be trapped between colonnaded doors and a socle that imitates the fake marble pattern of *opus sectile*[109].

This fresco alludes to a domestic version of the paradisial *habitat*, sometimes referred to by views of dwellings, at another time by isolated features such as doors and windows that only allow one to glimpse or imagine the Eden-like setting[110]. A clear allusion, in this sense, is represented by the massive half-open portals in the circular *cubiculum* of Via

Dino Compagni (fig. 104)[111]. Another example is the later decorative phase of the gallery of the *Acilii* in the Catacomb of Priscilla. Here, a string of portals and pilasters along the walls is just barely outlined. In the vault unfolds an innovative and unusual starry sky, as if to propose two versions of paradise, to be understood as either a sumptuous *domus aeterna* or a luminous firmament[112].

An interesting example of an architectural background is also found in a niche of the "Catacomba Anonima" of Via Anapo, dated to the late Constantinian period. The architectural background moves, in a scenographic manner, creating an evocative paradisial stage setting for the figure of the deceased, portrayed in the afterlife in a characteristic orant stance[113].

100 Catacomb of Domitilla: cubiculum of the Good Shepherd

101 *Catacomb of Domitilla: vault of the cubiculum of the Good Shepherd*

102 *Catacomb of Domitilla: cubiculum of Ampliatus*

103 *Catacomb of Domitilla: cubiculum of Ampliatus*

104 Hypogeum of Via Dino Compagni: entrance to the cubiculum of Samson

tectural *pendant* of the *cubiculum* of the Seasons (fig. 106)[115], and also in the *cubiculum* of Oceanus[116], one can observe the same decorative layout and perhaps the activity of the same pictorial workshop.

Having considered the precedents of these linear schemes, one should now ask what the motives were behind this evolution and its consequent important developments. The progressive attenuation and dematerialisation of painted architecture seems to express and reflect a tendency towards the irrational, the abbreviation, the synthetic and a symbolic language[117]. The result is the construction of a grid pattern, a light and ethereal network, that just barely sketches a scheme of partitions against a vast expanse of monochrome background within which isolated figures, extracted from Hellenistic imagery, float freely.

For the phases of this simplification, it is still useful to refer to the periodisation proposed by Wirth in the 1930's[118]. Wirth recognised a first phase in the framed panels, a second characterised by emphasis on the wall and a last phase, of greatest interest, in the linearity of the so-called illusionistic style. The last style developed between 220 to 260, at the same time as the decoration of catacombs became more original and autonomous. The three types of articulation, in reality, could also coexist and did not always indicate an incontrovertible chronological progression. In fact, these various schemes often intertwined and superimposed each other in the course of the years, giving birth to hybrid and mixed forms, including numerous revivals, even in later periods, of the ancient decorative manner.

The linear style is represented in all the decorative sites found in catacomb settings. However, it is especially predominant in the vaults of the *cubicula*, where it developed centralised schemes, with a central medallion around which diagonal and cruciform systems were organised that delineated semi-lunettes and trapezoidal, elliptical or oblong areas[119].

These linear systems perhaps wished to imitate the covering of a tent, obtained from pieces of cloth carefully cut and sown to-

But, especially the decoration of the vault and skylight of the *cubiculum* of Miltiades at S. Callisto, in the early Constantinian period, provides indispensable evidence for understanding not only the phenomenon of continuity of the architectural style, but also its relationship to the red and green linear style. The decorative scheme of the vault and skylight show a haphazard geometric inlay with red and green lines, alternating with cornices, garlands and false perspectives that open up to backgrounds painted with Dionysiac figures that seem to be suspended in an illusionistic and rarefied atmosphere (fig. 105)[114].

This does not seem to be an isolated case, if already in the recently restored archi-

gether. Sometimes the geometric partition seems to precisely reproduce extremely light constructions composed of thin poles, flexible arches, curtains, cordons and T-shaped rods. The allusion to the cosmos seems evident, taking up a metaphor that in the late Antique period linked the general concept of time to the symbolic one of eternity[120].

In Roman funerary painting, the cosmic material is referred to by very fundamental,

and yet explicit, symbols in the vaults of the *cubicula*. Thus, on the ceiling of the *cubiculum* of the *velatio* in the Catacomb of Priscilla, a couple of quails (birds of the earth) alternated with a pair of peacocks (celestial birds) in an elementary sequence, that rotated around the driving force of the Good Shepherd (fig. 107)[121].

Leaving aside the decoration of communal catacombs to concentrate on the private

105 Catacomb of S. Callisto: skylight in the cubiculum of Miltiades

106 Catacomb of S. Callisto: skylight of the cubiculum of the Seasons

hypogea, such as that of Via Dino Compagni, one finds that cosmic symbolism was expressed in the most coherent and complex way surviving by the figurative culture of the late fourth century. In the so-called *cubiculum* of Cleopatra[122], the famous personification of *Tellus* was placed so as to play a central role of a decorative programme that spread out over the walls, the vault and even the connecting chamber with the adjacent circular *cubiculum*. The decoration revolved around the cosmic theme in all its aspects, involving the planets, elements, time and the seasons, at times with personifications of the winds and fire, at others with more generic and traditional allusions to the earth (hoofed animals, vines) and the sky (winged animals) (fig. 108)[123].

The theme of the Seasons occurs in the catacombs not only in wall painting, but also in marble reliefs, especially on sarcophagus fronts and lids, as well as on the closing slabs of *loculi*. Examples include a marble piece found *in situ* in the "Catacomba Anonima" of Via Anapo[124] and a sarcophagus from the Catacomb of Novaziano[125]. Such themes, however, underwent more coherent development in fresco decorations, beginning with the recently restored fresco in the famous *cubiculum* of the Seasons in the Catacomb of SS. Marcellino e Pietro[126]. Dated to between the third and fourth centuries, the ceiling contains splendid protomes of the Seasons at the corners of a delicate setting within which the Good Shepherd is surrounded by four orant images and four scenes inspired by the story of Jonah (fig. 109).

The most eloquent monument in this regard seems to me to be that of the *Cappella Graeca* in the Catacomb of Priscilla (fig. 110)[127]. This *cubiculum*, as is well known, displays a rich decorative programme. The theme of the *convivium*, that perhaps exceptionally evokes the New Testament model[128], is the centre from which emanated the most famous episodes of the biblical repertoire that have as protagonists Moses, Noah, Abraham, Susanna, Daniel, the three Babylonian youths, the Magi, the paralytic and Lazarus. And yet the very fragmentary ceiling of the first room contains the bust of Summer, one of the four elements that, in Classical culture, served to indicate the concept of cyclical and continuous recurrence of time. Moreover, on the right wall of the first chamber is painted a phoenix amongst the flames, to reassert and stress the idea of the resurrection of the flesh. In the *Cappella Graeca* of Priscilla, the symbol maintains its Hellenistic iconographic prototype, just as is

the case with the bust of Summer, demonstrating how these ancient symbols entered into the sphere of catacomb art and came into close contact with the new Christian figurative imagery[129].

Alongside the linear scheme, Roman catacomb painting also includes another iconographic model inspired by the simpler paradisial world, that of the representation of a garden in bloom[130]. The floral elements come, as is evident, from the Classical *amoena virecta* of the Virgilian tradition that

107 Catacomb of Priscilla: vault of the cubiculum of the velatio

108 Hypogeum of Via Dino Compagni: cubiculum of Tellus

97

had already found well-defined expression in Roman pagan funerary painting. Examples include the tomb of Via Trionfale, the grave chamber on Via Portuense, the Hypogeum of "Via Ravizza". In the so-called "Scarpone" Hypogeum near Porta San Pancrazio, the floral theme becomes the only decorative feature, repeated *ad infinitum*[131].

The leitmotif of floral tapestry also appears in Jewish catacombs, as well as, significantly, in the double *cubiculum* of the Catacomb of Vigna Randanini[132] that displays this theme alternating with images and signs of the more popular cosmic repertoire. Thus, this decoration provides a useful indication of how much the common significance of the floral motif was relevant to different religious cultures. It could suggest a fertile and happy world, a vegetable garden, the Garden of Eden inspired by *Gen* 2.8–10, understood as a park, perfumed by an everlasting spring.

109 Catacomb of SS. Pietro and Marcellino: detail of the cubiculum of the Seasons

110 Catacomb of Priscilla: Cappella Graeca

111 Catacomb of Priscilla: vault of the cubiculum of the Annunciation

3. THE THEMES

Different figurative themes were also grafted onto the atmosphere and contexts just described. Some of these are original and directly inspired by the Holy Scriptures or at any rate match the new way of receiving and conceiving the Christian message, while still others are derived from the profane figurative repertoire, sometimes just barely modified in its composition, but immediately differentiated by its meanings.

In this regard, it must be remembered that a good part of "catacomb art" is the immediate result of an extremely systematic and ordered economy of reuse. Thus, one finds that many forms of pavement and *loculi* were closed off with re-utilised elements, such as architraves, *plutei*, stelai and pagan inscriptions. On the other hand, many Christian burials had sarcophagi and sculpted slabs, either produced in response to orders by the commissioner or available as stock pieces in the workshops. Some of these marbles display neutral themes. Thus, on the closing slab of a *loculus* on Via Anapo, two putti carved in low relief and decorated in red, light blue and gold, hold up the *tabula* of young *Procla*[137]. Alternatively, one might cite the monumental sarcophagus with hunting scenes used in the "Regione delle cattedre" at the *Coemeterium Maius* on Via Nomentana[138]. Reliefs are also represented. Their themes can be inspired by the myth of Amor and Psyche (for example, in the cemetery of S. Callisto[139]), marine imagery (for example, the sarcophagus from Pretestato[140]), rites of initiation (for example, the famous lid of *Aelia Afanasia* also from Pretestato (fig. 112)[141], or bucolic scenes (for example, from S. Callisto[142] and Domitilla[143])

Strictly pictorial decoration, the most prevalent catacomb decoration, undergoes a slow and progressive figurative journey that passes from neutral or poly-semantic themes to a true Christian repertoire.

Some themes drafted in the pagan tradition also continue in catacomb art, by

In many *cubicula* of Roman catacombs, monochrome walls alternate with marble imitations, such as fences, *transennae*, and gates, but the garden theme is depicted in a thousand other ways. In some *cubicula*, it takes the form of megalographic representations in which groups of more or less numerous deceased are gathered in luxuriant flower beds, such as in the so-called *cubiculum* of the Five Saints at S. Callisto[133]. Or in others, with more discreet indications, that allude to the afterlife with petals, flower buds, garlands strewn everywhere, such as in the decoration of the *cubiculum* of Amor and Psyche in the Catacomb of Domitilla, dated to the second half of the third century[134]. In the slightly later one of the Annunciation in the Catacomb of Priscilla, the floral motifs are inserted amidst biblical scenes (fig. 111)[135]. Finally, floral motifs also appear in several rooms of the "Catacomba Anonima" of Via Anapo, and especially in the scene with Daniel in the lions' den that is curiously set on a bed of roses and in the representation of the *fossor Trofimus* in the midst of a luxurious paradisial garden[136].

112 Complex of
Pretestato: Musei delle
sculture, relief of Aelia
Afanacia

113 Hypogeum of Via
Dino Compagni: cubiculum of Samson, socle
with bucolic scenes

strengthening or changing their essential meaning, or adjusting some nuances. The graphic nature and symbolic aspects of certain pictorial decorations are maintained intact. Thus, in the Hypogeum of the adherent of the cult of Sabazios, *Vibia*, the famous *arcosolium* represents the deceased being kidnapped by the quadriga of Pluto, Mercury psychopompus and a banquet of priests in which *Vincentius* participates[144].

Even more famous is Via Dino Compagni, where, as is well known, some areas display entire figurative schemes inspired by the myth of Admetus and Alcestes and the Herculean Labours. Imagery from the Hellenistic tradition pervades every corner of this unique hypogeum. Sometimes, it appears along the socles with idyllic, bucolic and zoomorphic scenes (fig. 113), at another, along the wall with chthonic, cosmic and seasonal personifications (figs. 114 and 115)

114 and 115 Hypogeum of Via Dino Compagni: cubiculum of Samson, small zoomorphic scenes in the Hellenistic tradition

that reach an *apex* with representations of abundance and *Tellus*[145].

Other images of clear pagan derivation show clear corrections. Thus, the myth of the phoenix, mentioned earlier, was adjusted to depict not the moment of its dramatic death by burning, but rather the positive, triumphal aspect of its rebirth from the ashes, more appropriate to the concept of the Resurrection of the flesh. This version occurs on a marble slab at S. Callisto and one from the Catacomb of Priscilla[146].

This alteration was based solely on the choice of different episodes from the Eastern tradition of images of the bird. In other examples, censorship of the material betrays a more dramatic debate within the Christian community or individual groups. For example, the snaky endings of the Gorgons were painted over in the vault of the Mausoleum of *Clodius Hermes* in S. Sebastiano[147] (fig. 116) and in the ceiling of the *cubiculum* of Tellus in the Hypogeum of Via Dino Compagni[148] (fig. 117). Actions such as these, that reveal second thoughts either immediately after or a little later than the first version of the images, demonstrate the hesitation and fear connected with the adoption of strong apotropaic symbols, that obviously was scarcely compatible with the free thought of private individuals.

Turning from the private hypogea to the communal cemeteries, it is not difficult to find themes and myths that were particularly popular in the pagan tradition. First among these is that of the bard Orpheus, who appears in a handful of catacomb frescoes. The earliest occurs in the *cubiculum* of the same name in S. Callisto, located in the earliest area and still datable to the third century[149]. The theme is taken up again in an *arcosolium* in the cemetery of SS. Marcellino e Pietro of the end of the fourth century. The fresco depicts the mythical bard in Oriental dress, while he prepares to play the lyre with the *plectrum*, surrounded by trees and an eagle in flight[150] (fig. 118).

In these frescoes, the mythical figure assumes the iconographic traits of the Good Shepherd, as if to stress the Christological meaning of the image. This occurs even more explicitly in two examples in the Catacomb of Domitilla. In the first example, Christ/Orpheus appears among a flock of sheep[151]. In the second, in a *cubiculum* dated to the mid-fourth century, the figure of the Thracian bard stands in the centre of the ceiling; David appears with his sling in a lateral scene, between other Old and New Testament stories[152]. This monument, now heavily damaged by eighteenth-century plundering, suggests the desire of the painter to establish a link between Orpheus and David, both characterised by the ability to soothe the most reluctant hearts with singing and playing, just like Christ/Logos[153]. But the monument that best documents the semantic transformation between the image of Orpheus and that of Christ the Shepherd is found on the entrance wall of a *cubiculum* in the cemetery *ad duas lauros*. Here, the figure of Orpheus amongst the animals represents the unifying junction of a group of four New and Old Testament scenes that alternate in a criss-cross fashion[154].

116 Complex of S. Sebastiano: mausoleum of Clodius Hermes, *detail of the Gorgon on the ceiling*

117 Hypogeum of Via Dino Compagni: vault of the cubiculum of Tellus

103

118 Catacomb of SS. Pietro e Marcellino: arcosolium with representation of the bard Orpheus

From the more traditional Roman figurative tradition, catacomb art derived some elements inspired by a repertoire that drew on the daily lives of contemporaries, and that explains some of the salient figurative themes. It is clear that this realistic imagery did not assume a predominant role, as compared with the more popular symbolic and biblical repertoire. Yet, it is not rare to find amongst catacomb imagery some explicit allusions to the life and earthly experiences of the living and the dead.

Rare, but typical, are historical representations inspired by the acts of martyrdom that were normally avoided to respect the optimism that seems to pervade Early Christian art of the first centuries[155]. Nevertheless, these violent situations of execution are perhaps alluded to in a fresco from the cemetery of S. Tecla[156] (fig. 119); in addition, on a small marble sculpted column in the Basilica of SS. Nereo ed Achilleo at Domitilla, Achilleus is led to death by his executioner[157] (fig. 120). Otherwise, the deeds of the martyrs are exalted in rather late devotional images, as direct expressions of early Medieval cult, as seen in the cemeteries of Generosa, Commodilla (fig. 121), Ponziano, Felicita, S. Ermete, S. Callisto, S. Valentino, and Calepodio (fig. 122), where true icons of martyrs appear[158].

119 Catacomb of S. Tecla: fresco with a presumed scene of martyrdom

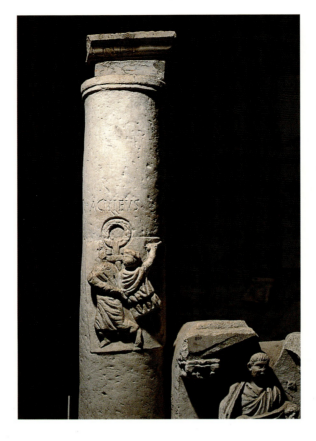

120 Complex of Domitilla: Basilica of SS. Nereo and Achilleo, small column with sculpted scene of the martyrdom of Achilleus

Portraits of the deceased only furnish weak links to the iconography of their actual appearance, since they align themselves with the "spiritual" conception of the physiognomic reconstruction of the human image. Spirituality infuses these facial expressions so that they are so detached from reality that the psychological level seems to prevail, denoting a perfect spiritual appearance[159]. In addition to these inspired, concentrated looks, the orant stance seen in the majority of these images and the heavenly settings in which the figures are almost always set contribute a great deal to this concept.

A heavenly atmosphere is alluded to in the famous trilogy of the *velatio* in the Catacomb of Priscilla, that, while maintaining a certain level of realistic imagery in the scenes of maternity and marriage, is elevated to paradise with the central portrait figure. Here the figure is depicted in an orant stance, in slightly larger proportions than the others, and therefore, symbolically more significant[160] (fig. 123).

The unique scene of a mother surrounded by her five small children, painted directly on the closing bricks of a *loculus* on the second floor of the Catacomb of Priscilla, should also be considered within a heavenly setting, as suggested by the bucolic context. This does not imply, however, a complete abandonment of the level of reality to which the representation can be traced, portraying the dead woman as a mother during her earthly existence[161].

Other more or less popular themes of catacomb art can also be traced back to contemporary daily life in generic terms. First among these are the bucolic and hunting scenes that spread in various ways in painting, sculpture, and grave reliefs.

The bucolic subject matter lent itself naturally to the expression of the concepts of *quies, felicitas, and tranquillitas*. It enjoyed long literary success and was exploited iconographically in funerary sculpture during the third century, channelled within the figurative trend of plebeian art and marked by a spontaneous and immediate realism. In catacomb art, this subject matter was defined immediately in heavenly terms. Thus, a bucolic scene appears below the arch of an *arcosolium* in the Catacomb of Domitilla[162], or in a lunette of the *Coemeterium Maius*, in which two shepherds, one of whom is busy milking, serve to set the orant image of the deceased at the centre of the composition in the afterlife[163].

While describing pastoral life in detail, associating canonical instruments such as the pan-pipes and *mulctrae* to the images, surrounding them with more or less numerous flocks and having the figures move according to the vivacious gestures typical of shepherds, the scenes are elevated above daily events. In the same way, the much rarer hunting scenes embody the concept of *otium*, withdrawal to a peaceful sojourn in contact with nature, freed from the burden of daily, urban worries[164].

This theme of hunting, only generically tied to the real world, appears only twice in Roman catacomb painting. One of the two frescoes decorates the area between two *lo-*

culi in one of the niches of Via Anapo[165] (pl. III, p. 70). This monument, dated to the Constantinian period, displays a serried Apostolic College in the summit of the intrados, while on the sides appear canonical scenes of Jonah, Daniel, the three Babylonian youths, Abraham and an orant figure. Celestial images (genies, birds, flower pots, garlands, petals, buds) are represented on the back wall of the two inter-*loculi* above. Below, there is a hunting scene in which the hunter is depicted running, preceded by a dog that in turn chases a boar and a pair of deer that have already fallen into a net. The insertion of the hunting motif within this context pervaded by a completely salvific meaning around the commemoration of the deceased, uniquely stressing the concepts of *vis* and *fortitudo*, the insuppressible clash between brute strength and courageous intelligence, between destiny and the mystery of death[166].

It should also be added that this theme located "*en plein air*" could have been influenced by the idyllic/paradisial motifs scattered here and there in other inter-*loculi*. Finally, influence from contemporary funerary sculpture cannot be excluded. On sarcophagi, the hunting theme sometimes appears, especially on sarcophagi lids, whereas biblical and symbolic scenes occupy the side and front panels. It is also possible that the rectangular site of the inter-*loculus* recalled a theme typical of the front of sarcophagus lids, that very often were decorated with hunt scenes as also seen in the fragments reused in the Roman catacombs[167].

More complex is the question raised by the Hypogeum "dei cacciatori" on Via Appia[168]. The cemetery, that displays the characteristics of catacombs, has also preserved a number of inscriptions of undeniable Christian nature[169]. The hypogeum lies in the immediate vicinity of that of *Vibia*, so close in

122 Catacomb of Calepodio: detail of the decoration of the the tomb of Pope Callistus

demonstrates how, during the late Antique period, the theme had abandoned its courtly level that had distinguished its genesis. In contrast, meanings of a more self-representative character were adopted, that all centred

123 Catacomb of Priscilla: cubiculum of the velatio, the lunette on the back wall

108

fact that in the past a connection between the two cemeteries was suggested[170]. Two *arcosolia* of this underground area contain primarily hunting themes. In the first of these, a figure is portrayed in the lunette on the back wall with tools useful for the capture of birds; he is placed in a forest, populated by birds. The intrados is decorated with floral specimens that locate the scene in the afterlife[171]. In the back lunette of the second *arcosolium* are found putti harvesting, as they press the grapes. In the front of the arch unfolds a hunt of deer with nets, one of a hare with a dog that rips apart the animal and a wild boar hunt. Again, the portrait of the deceased appears above[172]. The hypogeum, on the basis of its decorative and stylistic traits documented by photographic records taken in the past, can be dated to the fourth century. It is no longer visible today and therefore, it is not possible to reconsider the questionable hypotheses concerning the syncretic nature of the monument. The theme probably derives from a more generic paradisial iconography, produced by the representation of the hunt, or possibly alluding to the leisurely attitudes and activities of the deceased.

Another theme that oscillates between the spiritual and realistic realms is that of the banquet, rather widespread in catacomb art. Appearing very early, still in the first half of the third century, in the famous controversial *convivium* of the Hypogeum of the *Aurelii*[173] (fig. 124), the image of the banquet enjoyed constant popularity in Roman catacombs and became one of the traditional features of Early Christian imagery.

Notwithstanding the numerous efforts of iconographers to understand the significance of these scenes[174], many questions of interpretation still need to be resolved, perhaps due to the semantic stratification that these images often assume. These representations evoke in the first instance ancient Hellenistic funerary banquets, of sacrificial, ludic and indeed funerary type. These meals were well established in the Italic, Etruscan, and Roman traditions. Various types of funerary banquets existed: the *silicerium*, held

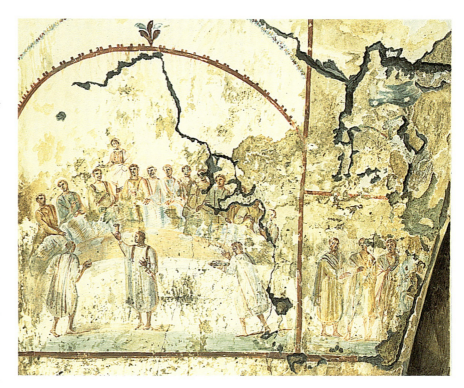

after the burial; the *novemdiale*, that, nine days after the burial, symbolised the return of the family to society; the better known ones organised during the *parentalia*, especially the banquet organised on 22 February on the occasion of the *caracognatio*. In this latter solemn *convivium* that took place near the burial site, only the relatives of the deceased participated; thus, they could remedy family tensions, taking advantage of the affectionate climate that was established amongst the guests.

The most recent critical readings would like to assign a strictly funerary meaning to specifically Christian banquet scenes, such as appear in Roman catacomb paintings and sarcophagus reliefs[175]. These interpretations connect the images with *agapes* and *refrigeria*, and thus, with the most concrete and daily practices tied to funerary ritual[176].

In fact, in these banquet scenes depicted in the catacombs, it is possible in recognise the majority of the iconographic models and symbolic meanings created in the preceding figurative tradition. Yet, the Christian ritual and symbolic significance prevails and distinguishes itself over the other meanings[177].

124 Hypogeum of the Aurelii on Viale Manzoni: banquet scene

125 Complex of S. Se-
bastiano: mausoleum of
Clodius Hermes, *decora-*
tion of the attic with
banquet scenes

tiano[179] (fig. 125); the familial component predominates in the fresco scenes of the cemetery of SS. Marcellino e Pietro, characterised by vivacious gestures and various atmospheric touches[180].

But, it would also be better to consider a range of meanings for these scenes, excessively stripped of any symbolic significance by modern critics. In fact, some scenes display clear references to a funerary meal organised for or by the family of the deceased, with realistic details that record actual ritual practices. The suspension of some images and the atmosphere around others, such as, for example in the famous *"fractio panis"* of the *Cappella Graeca* at Priscilla[181], seems to elevate them to a more symbolic level. However, in my opinion, links to the Eucharistic liturgy or Tertullian *refrigerium interim* are not convincing[182].

The symbolic atmosphere that can be perceived in certain banquet scenes painted in Roman catacombs derives more simply from the theme of the "celestial *convivium*". Associated with it are other representations that decorate tombs of clear or suspected religious syncretism. Examples include the famous *coena celestis* of the already mentioned Hypogeum of *Vibia*[183], in which an animated banquet takes place in the Elysian Fields, and the already cited banquet scene of the Hypogeum of the *Aurelii*[184].

Some banquet scenes are endowed with an otherworldly atmosphere that seems to cast them in an Eden-like idealised setting[185], without, however, renouncing those iconographic devices that connect the images to actual funerary practices. For example, one banquet scene in the Catacomb of SS. Marcellino e Pietro[186], set *"en plein air"*, is characterised by the presence of a funerary urn that indicates that the banquet takes place in a necropolis.

In this last case, symbol and reality meet and clash with each other. In other paintings, specific elements of equipment and composition, such as the utensils and tools used for the preparation of the banquet, do not always convey a realistic meaning. Rather, they

In Roman funerary banquets, one can detect two components, one connected with euergetism, the other with the family. The first, derived from the Greek and Hellenistic tradition, was related to the desire to secure the memory of the deceased within a civic and historic context, through solemnity and its public aspect. The familial one aimed at describing the relative within the group[178]. These two components seem to have continued in Early Christian imagery, sometimes in a very distinctive manner. The euergetic component seems to prevail in numerous representations, such as that painted in the Mausoleum of *Clodius Hermes* at S. Sebas-

110

should be considered the remnants of schemes of hedonistic hunting banquets that continued in the late Antique period, especially in the mosaics of *villae rusticae*[187], and sarcophagus lids[188]. This is clearly seen in the *arcosolium* of *Sabina*[189] (fig. 126) and that signed by Pomponius Laetus[190]. The amphorae, beverage heaters, plates of food as well as the extravagant gestures of the banqueters result in an anecdotal interpretation, sensitive to detail, typical of the Italic and Roman traditions.

The banquet theme, analysed in all its nuances, covers a very wide range of meanings. Very often, one semantic level intersects and interacts with another level of meaning giving way to original and significant shifts. This is the case of the banquets of the *Coemeterium Maius* where the subject of the meal, the bread and fish, assume such large proportions that symbolic and New Testament interpretations are suggested[191]. According to an old and forgotten idea of de Rossi, these scenes constitute a narrative allusion to the miracles of the multiplication of the loaves and the wedding at Cana[192].

Bearing this in mind, one should not, however, dismiss a more concrete reading of banquet images nor ignore the tie that these scenes had with the funerary practices of the *refrigeria*, also in light of the newest archaeological finds in different sites[193]. Yet, one cannot deny the symbolic character that these scenes can sometimes assume. For example, in the banquet painted in one of the Chapels of the Sacraments in S. Callisto, the representation is accompanied by a unique laying of hands (*impositio manum*) on a tripod that holds a loaf of bread and a fish[194] (fig. 127). A similar scene of "*impositio*" is found in the cemetery of SS. Marcellino e Pietro[195]. In the complex of S. Callisto, one also encounters extreme syntheses of banquet scenes. One is recognisable in the vault

126 Catacomb of SS. Pietro e Marcellino: arcosolium with banquet scene

111

of one of the Chapels of the Sacraments where only the tripod remains, with a fish and seven baskets of bread[196] (fig. 128). In a *cubiculum* of the Crypts of Lucina, a couple of large fish are associated with baskets of bread and glasses of red wine, alluding to the now famous scenes of "Eucharistic fish"[197] (fig. 129).

The unique painting found in the cemetery of SS. Marcellino e Pietro oscillates between reality and symbol. It represents a couple banqueting, next to a scene of the purchase or withdrawal from a *fullonica* of cloth used for the preparation of the banquet[198]. Rather than to the work of the dead woman, the fresco seems to allude to her talents, since she is presented in her role of looking after the household.

127 Catacomb of S. Callisto: Chapels of the Sacraments A3, scene of impositio manuum

128 Catacomb of S. Callisto: Chapels of the Sacraments A2, tripod and bread baskets

If, according to more advanced interpretations, the banquet scene came to express a heavenly *status*, overtaking above any other meaning that inspired its origins and success, the concept of *refrigerium* in a strict sense, nevertheless, continued to pervade many iconographic examples found in Roman catacombs. First among these is the incised gravestone of *Criste* in the Catacomb of Domitilla[199]. The deceased little girl is depicted in paradise with her arms outstretched and a dove with an olive branch. Her father, *Cristor*, who commemorated her with a *refrigerium*, is portrayed drinking and offering the last bite of his meal to a small dog, perhaps particularly dear to his small patroness (fig. 130). This example, so immediate and evocative, is echoed in others, such as the gravestone of *Eutropos*, on which the deceased is represented at work as a sculptor of sarcophagi in his workshop, as well as at the *refrigerium*[200].

Other, more simple incisions also seem to allude to the *refrigerium* in a generic way, by exclusively representing kitchen utensils and containers, as in a small inscription from the Catacomb of Commodilla[201]. An investigation into the actual meaning of these incised signs becomes problematic, since one must decide whether these images express a solely concrete concept or whether they extend to a symbolic level. Such is the case with the incisions that represent vases, small bottles, or other containers that perhaps alluded to funerary banquets in a very summary fashion.

The only realistic figurative representations found in Roman catacombs that remain as such, even when they come into contact with the Christian religious repertoire, are those that depict occupations and trades. Scenes of daily work display a natural origin in mid-Italic art, with images stamped by an immediate realism, with veristic and anecdotal touches that often lead to humorous interpretations and caricature. This refreshing and popular figurative trend was exploited in provincial art and continued throughout the late Antique period[202].

129 Catacomb of S. Callisto: "Crypts of Lucina", detail of the "Eucharistic fish"

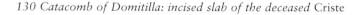

130 Catacomb of Domitilla: incised slab of the deceased Criste

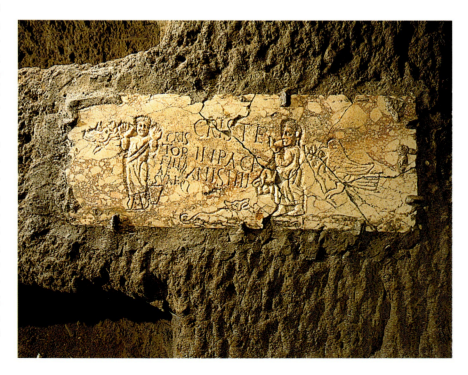

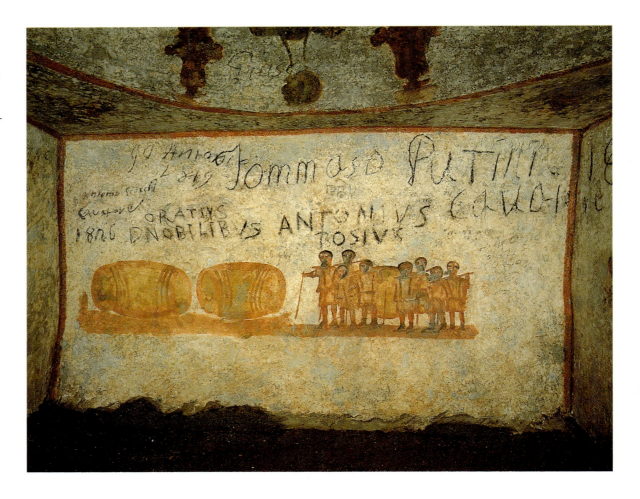

The monument that best introduces this theme is certainly the Hypogeum of Trebius Justus on Via Latina, datable to the first half of the fourth century[203]. The completely frescoed burial chamber, dedicated by his parents to the twenty-one year old *Trebius Iustus*, also affectionately called *Asellus*, presents a complex example of "aptitudinal" iconography. Thus, the various virtues of the young man are portrayed through his representation as a man of culture, a rich landowner and a supervisor of the construction of a country villa. The boy is omnipresent as the protagonist of these refreshing and immediate scenes of daily life.

In Roman catacombs, allusions to the professional activities of the deceased often appear, either inscribed in funerary epigraphs[204], or also in images, beginning with those professions associated to stone work. One interesting example is the epitaph of *Alexius* from the Catacomb of Domitilla that bears, beside the inscription, an orant image of the deceased and an axe with a chisel, to be interpreted as the tools of his occupation as *quadratarius*[205].

The entire humble world of workers, craftsmen and shopkeepers is documented by the simplest iconographic representations that the catacombs have preserved. A slab with a scene of sowing[206], one with the harvesting of grapes[207], another with generic farming activity[208], one with an allusion to the harvest[209], another that immortalises the gathering of firewood[210], all summarise agricultural life.

The lively world of commerce is referred to in many inscriptions and wall paintings. For example, a greengrocer is depicted in a fresco in the Catacomb of S. Callisto[211], bakers, in the prestigious *cubiculum* at Domitilla[212], barrel sellers in the fresco found in a

114

well-known *cubiculum* in Priscilla[213] (fig. 131). Wine merchants appear in the scene from an *arcosolium* of the Hypogeum of *Vibia*[214], blacksmiths, in a detailed marble incision found in Domitilla[215], shoemakers, on a number of epitaphs on which the tools of their trade are incised[216]. Barge transporters on the Tiber are documented by a frescoed *cubiculum* in the Catacomb of Ponziano[217], cargo workers, in the *Coemeterium Maius*[218], traders of pack mules, in the well-known incision of *Constantius* at

Domitilla[219]. Barbers and doctors[220] are attested to by an incision representing an eye doctor or a dentist in the Catacomb of Domitilla[221]; fish vendors appear on a slab from the Cemetery of SS. Marcellino e Pietro[222].

In this very complex and vivid social map[223], its diffusion and specificity distinguish the iconography of the *fossores*. While these representations betray a particularly realistic inspiration, when, that is, one considers the gifts and fancy goods associated with

132 Catacomb of S. Callisto: Chapels of the Sacraments A3, back wall

115

most realistic compositions of Roman catacomb painting. Here, the man is represented against the background, caught in the act of striking a tufa spur with his pick. Several rapidly executed yet precise details set the scene within a catacomb setting, such as a hook in the tufa wall from which a lit lamp hangs. The realism detected in all of these representations is also due to the clothing of the *fossor*, that is, the short tunic and characteristic headgear.

Less vivid is the painted figure of a *fossor* found at the highest point of a gallery in the Hypogeum of Via Dino Campagni[230], dated to the second half of the fourth century. The figure is depicted frontally, with a lamp and a bucket for dirt on his shoulder, between two floral garlands that hang from the sides, like gathered curtains, to project the image of the afterlife (fig. 134). This is the same device adopted, in the same years, by a painter in the "Catacomba Anonima" of Via Anapo who sets the *fossor Trofimus*, already mentioned[231], in a floral garden that can only be paradise.

Thus, as in the case of banquet scenes, an oscillation between reality and symbol can also be recognised for images of *fossores*. The former can be seen especially in incisions on funerary slabs. Examples include the famous one from Commodilla, with the *fossor* intent on burying a deceased already wrapped in his shroud[232], or the graphically more accurate depiction of the Catacomb of SS. Marco e Marcelliano, with the digger characterised by the *dolabra* and a large lamp[233]. The symbolic aspect, in contrast, is well documented in the earlier frescoes already discussed. But to completely understand the dynamic of fluctuation between reality and symbol involved, the representation of the *fossor* Diogenes found in Domitilla must be taken into consideration[234], sadly famous for its detachment and destruction in the eighteenth century. Here, the man no longer represents an anonymous image but a dead man, whose identity is known from a funerary inscription. His image stands at the centre of the lunette surrounded by the tools typically used for excavation, against the background of a cemetery network, in which galleries and *loculi* are schematically depicted. Everything seems to indicate a realistic representation, which can be traced back, however, to the trend of "self-representation" typical of late Antique art, framed by the nouveau riche.

The conspicuous and constant presence of images of *fossores* in Roman catacombs produces a type of osmosis until they either symbolise or are identified with the burial site. This suggests that their representation may also have been used as a type of sign of the inviolability or "novelty" of the tomb, as if to substitute the meaning that the symbol of the axe had in the Roman funerary tradition.

At the same time, the conspicuous recurrence of these images testifies to the increasing power of these *fossores* within both the context of funerary activity and within the social structure of the Early Christian communities[235]. This evolution, as is known, resulted in ever more consistent abuses and the progressive decadence of the group[236].

By describing the atmosphere and contexts of catacomb art, it has been possible to note how the repertoire, that originated and developed within these underground locations, found a special connection to the spiritual realm, if one excludes these more or less realistic images. Thus, it conforms perfectly with the salvific language especially of biblical inspiration that spread simultaneously in the East and West between the end of the second and the beginning of the third centuries[237].

These characteristics are very evident in the already mentioned Hypogeum of the *Aurelii* on Viale Manzoni. This tomb deserves additional attention to fully demonstrate the important role that it assumed as an antecedent of catacomb art.

This small hypogeum, composed of three painted chambers of which two are underground and one semi-underground, has aroused the interest of historians and iconographers alike since its discovery[238]. The debate focuses on whether the *Aurelii*, the commissioners of the tomb, were true Christians[239], heretics[240], Gnostics[241], or simply pagans[242].

118

135 Hypogeum of the Aurelii on Viale Manzoni: Homeric scene

In the course of this tormented interpretative journey, scholars have lost sight of the early and secure chronology of the monument, preceded by the construction of the Aurelian walls within which the tomb is located. Its special significance is as a meeting ground between different figurative trends, either derived from the well-established Classical tradition or driven by the expressive needs inspired by Oriental religions and mystery cults. Everything merges to produce and frame a unique form of private syncretism[243].

The back wall of the upper *cubiculum* displays, in a pleasant setting, Adam and Eve with the serpent (or Heracles in the garden of the Hesperides) and the scene of the creation of man (or the creative Demiurge). On the lateral walls, figures of philosophers are depicted against urban backdrops. On the lower level, one *cubiculum* contains a vault transversed by a close network of red and green lines with images of shepherds, peacocks, vegetal candelabra and small scenes from the standard repertoire. In the middle register are recognisable a shepherd who guards his flock, a scene of an entrance into a city, a legal scene, a banquet and a Homeric scene inspired by the return of Odysseus to Ithaca (fig. 135). Several life-size figures of philosopher type, wearing tunics and *pallia*, are represented around the socle. The connecting area and the other *cubiculum* present a more rarefied decoration, with figures carrying *pallia*, staffs and scrolls. One of these seems to point to a cross, although recently it has been proven that this element is none other than the ends of a garland[244].

In the context of the two fundamental themes, bucolic and philosophical that span the entire programme, it is not difficult to recognise the representations of the dead *Aurelii* dispersed throughout the hypogeum. Sometimes they are placed in majestic processions, sometimes within more ethereal and symbolic contexts, sometimes as part of a mysterious triad in the vault of the last *cubiculum*. The three *Aurelii*, recorded in a mosaic inscription set up as the pavement of the first underground room, were depicted in the afterlife in a frieze in the same room. One of them is represented in the guise of a shepherd, another is about to enter the afterlife as a dignified horseman, to sit at the centre of an urban forum, and lastly, a deceased woman participates in a celestial banquet. Such celestial *flashes*, not uncommon in contemporary funerary sculpture, result in other guises and additional symbolic metaphors for the deceased. This begins with the image of the orant figure that, while assuming the pose of the ancient personification of *pietas*, came to signify the beatified and happy condition of the deceased in the afterlife. The orant figure type spread from images of ordinary Christians to historical and devotional figures that infer a movement away from the concept of prayer, understood as a request for divine intervention, towards an interpretation closer to the Pauline concept of continuous prayer[245].

In catacomb art, the Good Shepherd also came to signify different concepts. The figure could be intended to simply represent the calm and beatified deceased in a pleasant environment, but the range of meanings could be richer and more complex. While the origin of this image is to be found in figures of Oriental sacrificial figures that continued in representations of Hermes carrying a staff, the more direct model of the Christological symbol assigns the concept of philanthropy to the image[246]. Considered within the general context of Early Christian art, the "Good Shepherd" image now appears to have been a concise symbol of the idyllic/bucolic theme that transmitted in particular good wishes for peace and tranquillity[247].

However, as soon as it came in contact with the Christian vocabulary, the figure of the Good Shepherd assumed new meanings, eluding and modifying its original significance while enriching itself, as could be imagined, with Christological parallels. This process gives the image the power to move into both sculpture and painting, to spread through all the iconographic categories and to become an indispensable term in Early Christian figurative language. It is clear that the parable of the lost sheep (Luke 15.6–7; Psalm 23) that attributes a baptismal, penitential and salvific meaning to the image played an important role in this process of enrichment.

In the vaults of Roman *cubicula*, the salvific meaning prevails over the various intertwined significances of the image. Thus, the Good Shepherd represents the Saviour or the agent of salvation for the deceased believer, personified by an orant figure. This can be verified in the ceiling of *cubiculum* Y in the area of Lucina at S. Callisto[248]. The vault displays a rich sampling of models that bore good wishes such as protomes of the Seasons, Erotes, birds in flight and garlands. On the sides, a pair of shepherds carrying sheep or rams alternates with a pair of orant figures set on top of vegetal pedestals to emphasise their symbolic meaning. Here, the conversion to Christianity has already occurred. This is indicated not so much by the image of Daniel in the lions' den that occupies a central position, but by the presence of Jonah depicted at rest on the right wall, and the famous "Eucharistic Fish" on the back wall.

In this extremely fluid context that demonstrates a true evolutionary process, it is easy to recognise the modifications of ancient Classical figures that result from contact with Christian imagery. Thus, in this context, the shepherd and the orant figure, that through to their placement and repetition immediately indicate a symbolic meaning, also express the insoluble link between "saviour and saved". At the same time, they participate in the joyous and happy ambience of the afterlife.

In these early paintings, a delicate selection is being carried out of those images that appear in similar circumstances in the so-called "paradisial" sarcophagi that include the well-known examples in La Gayole, Via Salaria, Via della Lungara, of Basel and S. Maria Antiqua[249]. Amongst this range of models, in addition to the shepherd and orant figure, the fisherman and the philosopher also appear. All of these figures together represent the beatified condition, a happy otherworldly *status*. In this quartet, the true counterpart of the shepherd is the fisherman, in so far as the combination of the bucolic and maritime idylls expresses the augural concept of "peace on land and sea". Very quickly, however, this successful combination loses the second of its components, the fisherman, who, as is well known, was substituted with the story of Jonah.

In Roman funerary painting, in fact, the image of the fisherman is abandoned almost immediately, if one excludes the figures depicted in the two Chapels of the Sacraments in S. Callisto[250] and in a niche in the gallery of the *Flavii* at Domitilla[251]. Nevertheless, one must not forget that, a century later and thus almost at the end of the fourth century, an *arcosolium* of the "Catacomba Anonima" of Via Ardeatina offers one of the more unique digests of these two idyllic images. Thus, a hybrid figure of a shepherd who tends a flock of sheep and fish is represented[252] (fig. 136).

The philosopher figure also undergoes a gradual shift in meaning. Evolving from the Hellenistic prototype of the wise man surrounded by muses, it comes to symbolise knowledge in a much more general sense, and later doctrine and catechesis[253]. In catacomb art, the philosopher appears as the embodiment of the deceased as *lector*, as on the entrance wall of a *cubiculum* of the Catacomb of SS. Marcellino e Pietro, dated to the Constantinian period[254]. Here, the wall surface is divided into four squares that constitute a small but well thought-out decorative programme. Clear allusions to a salvific environment in scenes of Adam and Eve and the Resurrection of Lazarus are flanked by images of a shepherd milking his flock and a philosopher.

The figures in the famous "anatomy lesson" in Via Dino Compagni[255] also refer to the image of the philosopher. They display many similarities as well with the groups of Apostles painted in the Catacombs of Domi-

136 *"Catacomba Anonima" of Via Ardeatina: fresco of the Good Shepherd flanked by sheep and fish*

137 Catacomb of
SS. Pietro e Marcellino:
detail of the cubiculum
of the Athletes

the result of a combination of diverse materials, many of which derive from the Greco-Roman tradition[259].

But within these traditional schemes, new iconographic models were inserted, sometimes in a traumatic fashion, such as when pagan hypogea were transformed into Christian catacombs. Typical of this phenomenon is the hypogeum in the Circus Maxentius in which the cycle of Jonah spreads out and superimposes an earlier neutral decoration[260]. At other times, this shift occurs in a less conspicuous way. Thus, scenes of a certainly Christian significance were painted in the remaining spaces of the gallery of the *Flavii* at Domitilla, as if one were to hang new paintings in a pinacotheca already very rich with funerary themes[261] (fig. 138).

Irrespective of the force or caution used, the insertion of Christian themes into "pagan" or "neutral" contexts provokes eclectic decorative programmes. This seems to be slightly reduced by a connecting thread, sometimes tenuous, at others more substantial, that attempts to amalgamate the heterogeneous themes in the earliest Roman *cubicula*.

138 Catacomb of Domitilla: Hypogeum of the
Flavii, scene of Daniel in
the lions' den

tilla, S. Ermete, Marco e Marcelliano, Marcellino e Pietro, Ponziano, S. Tecla, Via Anapo, Via Latina, and the *Coemeterium Maius*[256].

Thus, the orant, shepherd, fisherman and philosopher figures develop in significant yet diverse ways. At the same time, they also served to "disguise" the deceased, who also enjoyed being represented, irrespective of their true occupations, as charioteers and soldiers, as in two frescoes in the cemetery of the Giordani[257]. Alternatively they can appear in the guise of athletes as in the decorative programme of the *cubiculum* of the same name in the Catacomb of SS. Marcellino e Pietro, datable to the end of the third century[258] (fig. 137).

The repertoire of these early catacomb paintings of Rome can hardly be considered homogeneous if analysed in its entirety. Such programmes, in fact, are nothing other than

This connecting thread has strong salvific significance with clear paradisial aspects. The conception wishes to express the exceptional and positive beatitude enjoyed by the deceased in the afterlife. This conception of beatitude is enlarged to encompass every aspect, sign, and image. Thus, it creates a fundamental mood that unites all of the single elements of the decorative programme that would otherwise have incongruent and inorganic meanings.

The genesis of the iconographic signs, themes, and programmes rarely demonstrates a respect, at least rigorous, for pre-established laws and norms. Fundamental geometric schemes (symmetry, balance, mirror images, juxtaposition) are an exception; these, however, are always taken into account in every iconographic repertoire that revolves around the spiritual realm in a symbolic way. Irrespective of these rules, the vocabulary drafted by the artists of Roman catacombs, like all new artistic languages, suffers from clear phenomena of irrationality, paradoxes and contradictions. Indeed, it can be asserted that from the time of its inception, catacomb art constituted a true experimental laboratory for both the *artifices* and commissioners. There, themes and schemes were selected that sometimes proved to be inadequate or difficult. Thus, they could be abandoned after just one formulation, appearing and disappearing like meteors[262].

These experiments were carried out particularly with biblical subject matter that entailed works of invention or, at any rate, the introduction of new figurative schemes into the developing repertoire. The complete reverse is true of the process that selected a group of images that were considered suitable for the decoration of the catacombs from the huge repertoire of the Classical tradition. This selection, seemingly not very demanding in that it involved appropriation rather than invention, was however a very delicate process since it always or almost always involved deliberation on their original meaning, a process that was useless or less vexed for biblical themes. The decorators of the catacombs employed models taken from the Classical tradition in even the simplest schemes. It seems a given that Early Christian figurative production, and thus also catacomb art, did not represent itself as an autonomous initiative. Thus, many schemes adopted by the Early Christian *artifices* can be interpreted as reworkings, developments and elaborations of earlier iconographical signs and themes. These same signs and themes once depicted situations and images extracted from the rich imagery of Classical mythology.

This phenomenon of continuity is seen especially in Old Testament themes. Typical and already well known are the parallels between the sleeping Endymion and Jonah resting under the pergola[263], Noah in the Ark and Deucalion and Pyrrha[264], Adam and Eve and Jason and Medea[265] and Moses who loosens his shoe strap and Hermes who ties his sandal[266].

Turning to a comprehensive reading of the iconography of Roman catacombs, it must be stressed that every unambiguous consideration is rendered difficult by these inverse operations of addition and subtraction that produce mixed and non-classifiable results that can be applied only when the figures emerging from a preliminary selection are placed in pre-meditated symmetries.

True Christian art, grafted onto this extremely eclectic picture still informed by ancient iconographic ideas, emerges in the Roman catacombs between the second and third centuries. This debut was expressed in two distinctive iconographic forms. At times, Christian art aligned itself with contemporary iconographic tendencies, namely, with biblical events reduced to extremely abbreviated vignettes that rejected the narrative intent that characterised Roman art of the preceding centuries. At other times, it invented an even more cryptic language composed entirely of symbols, sometimes difficult to interpret.

Both iconographic approaches coexisted even within the same compositions and were expressed simultaneously in the same period. Thus, in the earliest Roman catacomb paintings, biblical scenes as well as symbolic figures can be found, as can be verified in the early examples in the Chapels of the Sacraments and Crypts of Lucina in the complex of S. Callisto.

To understand these coexisting phenomena, one can refer to the *cubiculum* of the *coronatio* in the cemetery of Pretestato, now dated to the first half of the third century[267]. The *cubiculum* takes the form of a vast whitewashed room, completely covered by a system of red and green linear decoration. These red and green lines outline fields within which are set motifs from the cosmic and seasonal repertoire (deer, peacocks, ducks, flowers) that, in the ceiling, are arranged around the central image of a shepherd. On the walls, New Testament scenes are inserted into this neutral context, or at any rate, it is not properly symptomatic of Christian iconography. Reduced to concise images, generally with no more than two or three figures, they depict the Samaritan woman at the well, the Resurrection of Lazarus, the healing of the haemorrhage, the famous crowning with thorns (fig. 139).

This last scene represents an extremely unusual iconographic scheme for such an early period. Scenes of the passion were usually introduced into the Early Christian figurative repertoire after the Constantinian peace, particularly in funerary sculpture. The appearance of this scene in the Catacomb of Pretestato should, therefore, be considered as an iconographic "meteor", an early example attributable to the needs of a strong-willed commissioner. Perhaps, he was close to the ecclesiastical *entourage*, or at any rate, extremely well educated in biblical imagery, so as to introduce new scenes or scenes excluded from the contemporary repertoire.

While at Pretestato one is still dealing with narrative art, even though in the abbreviated version typical of "catacomb art", in the central *arenaria* of Priscilla the figurative language becomes more symbolic and complex, although it is entirely prompted by a composition of extreme simplicity and immediacy. Based on the latest restorations, the niche of the Madonna with the prophet at Priscilla dates to the third or fourth decades of the third century[268]. It provides evidence for a decorative workshop that began in the early third century and was operative into the next century. In the Madonna painting, the Old and New Testament come into intimate contact to stress the cohesion between the two Testament traditions. They are set in front of the image of the Madonna and Child and a prophet of uncertain identity, perhaps Balaam, or Isaias or a generic personification of prophecy. Nevertheless, the symbolic language is still presented in a discursive and easily legible fashion (fig. 140).

The language becomes concise and more difficult to decipher, however, at S. Callisto. This is particularly true of the scene of the "Eucharistic Fish" in the Crypts of Lucina as well as in the scenes with an isolated tripod and the *impositio manuum* in the Chapels of the Sacraments. The chronological development of these much-discussed scenes extends from the end of the second century to the middle of the third. In all these scenes, one sees a symbolic language, predominantly aniconic and based on symbols, that was especially dear to the biblical religious tradition and that was used or perhaps introduced by Jewish art. The process of symbolisation reaches its highest point until it becomes encoded. The fish of

139 Catacomb of Pretestato: cubiculum of the coronatio, detail of the scene depicting Christ being crowned with thorns

Lucina, the tripod and the *impositio* of the sacraments, as has already been stressed, are condensed forms of the *convivia* represented contextually in the same monuments, where they allude both to funerary ritual and to a more strictly heavenly environment.

But the language becomes truly symbolic in several early incisions on funerary slabs from the catacombs in which it still seems difficult to judge the "Christianity" of the iconographic material. Several slabs used to close off the *loculi* in the area of the *piazzola* at S. Sebastiano record the initial phase of Christian epigraphy. This phase is characterised by formulae perfectly aligned to contemporary pagan forms but also by signs, namely, the anchor and the fish, that, moving away from a neutral context, take on Christian meanings[269]. Thus, the tomb of young *Atimetus,* who died at the age of 8, is decorated with an anchor and a fish[270]. The inscription of *Ancotia Auxesis*, which his parents *Ephaphroditus* and *Ancotia Irene* dedicated for his burial, is also enriched symbolically in the same manner[271].

One might query the profound significance of these simple signs that, at first glance, seem to refer to the vast marine imagery that, together with that pastoral, constituted one of the most frequent subjects of iconography of the late Antique period. In this sense, these signs could be considered abbreviations or "cut-outs" of broader figurative contexts and not proper symbols. But it is also true that at the same time that these signs were selected to represent specific contexts, they were judged as highly salient images. Moreover, the multiple aspects that these figures could adopt was stressed, complying with the tendency towards pluri-valent language typical of Early Christian Art.

In a brief passage of his *Octavius*, Minucius Felix seems to refer to this symbolic language when, enumerating the unmentionable behaviours of Christians, he records that they communicated and recognised one another through "signs"[272].

In reality, the phrase of Minucius is open to various interpretations, and in substance, wishes only to stress a mysterious and in-

comprehensible behaviour. However, it is not impossible that beyond these "signs" of an alphabet for believers are to be recognised also the symbols used by Christians in their initial, early iconographic schemes.

This suggestion finds surprising support in a famous passage of the *Paedagogus* of Clement of Alexandria in which anchors, fish, doves and ships are suggested as symbols for Christian seal rings[273].

The figurative repertoire that appears on the earliest inscriptions of Roman catacombs seems to reflect closely these two patristic passages. Thus, on the slab of *Faustinianus*, a sheep, dove on a branch, and an anchor converge[274], or on the slab of *Urbica*, the

140 Catacomb of Priscilla: fresco of the Nativity with the Prophet

125

text, enclosed in a circular mirror, is flanked by a fish and a dove[275]. Finally, on the slab of *Valeria* at Priscilla, anchors and palm trees emphasise the text painted in red on the closing bricks of the *loculus*[276].

Although these symbols clearly display their pagan ancestry based on magic and ritual, they began to systematically appear in catacombs, triggering a mechanism that must have altered the significance of many of them towards a Christological and soteriologic significance[277].

While Christian iconographic imagery underwent these drastic reductions and the original *artifices* learned the language of the symbols, some more discursive figurative schemes also continued to appear. One example is the *cubiculum* of the *velatio* located at the edge of the *arenaria* of Priscilla, dated to the second half of the third century[278]. Here, as one could have already anticipated, a complex, securely articulated and mature story is found. Thus, the specifically cosmic meaning, represented by Christ the Shepherd surrounded by diverse animals in the vault, and probably the soteriologic one, represented by the stories of Jonah, Abraham and the youths in the furnace, are associated with a lively trilogy in the lunette on the back wall[279]. In this lunette, the realistic tradition of Roman art, completely engaged in translating quickly and simply a humble and ordinary *cursus vitae,* is merged with a new imagery that through signs and metaphors provides glimpses of another life and a new world.

An advance in terms of chronology and the organisation of the decorative programme can be seen in the *Cappella Graeca* of the same cemetery[280]. In this room, as mentioned earlier, meanings gravitate towards each other, interact or move in a parallel fashion. Everything seems to converge in the nucleus of the so-called Eucharistic banquet. In reality, as has been seen, it represents a suspended banquet scene, presumably only of a funerary nature, on a Pompeian red background. From this central hub uncoil the themes of resurrection (Lazarus, and the phoenix), salvation (Daniel, Abraham, the

three Babylonian youths, Susanna), baptism (Noah, the paralytic, Moses striking the rock), as well as iconography that is more properly and solemnly Christological (the adoration of the Magi). All these themes are spread out in a not very homogeneous way within a cosmic regenerative context that, as mentioned, unfolds especially in the vaults of the two chambers into which the *cubiculum* is divided (fig. 141).

With these schemes in formation and these iconographic medleys still barely amalgamated, one approaches the fourth century, when the paintings of the Roman catacombs discover a more considered, reasonable, geometric and less improvisational order. The natural order of the cycle is rediscovered as well as the preference for biblical scenes recounted in a logical sequence or with an alternating rhythm, such as in the *cubiculum* of the two banquets in the Catacomb of SS. Marcellino e Pietro, dated to the Constantinian period[281]. Here, the figure of Christ the Shepherd is placed at the centre of the vault; eight scenes rotate around his image as if in a merry-go-round. Derived from a biblical repertoire, these scenes alternate in perfect rhythm between Old and New Testament images: the miracle of the rock, the healing of the paralytic, Daniel in the lions' den, the multiplication of the loaves, Noah in the Ark, Job, a Baptism scene, the Resurrection of Lazarus.

At the same time and according to the same schemes, vast parades of biblical scenes unfold on the front and side panels of sarcophagus lids, in continuous friezes, also organised in two registers. Typical, it seems to me, is the famous sarcophagus of Lot found in the complex of S. Sebastiano (fig. 142)[282]. While the un-inscribed lid holds small scenes inspired by the return from the hunt, portraits of a couple within a shell are set in the centre of the front panel, divided into two registers. The biblical scenes unwind without a sense of continuity: the resurrection of Lazarus, the denial of Peter, Moses receiving the Ten Commandments, the sacrifice of Isaac, Adam and Eve receiving the symbols of work, Lot leaving Sodom, the expulsion from paradise, the massacre of the innocents.

141 Catacomb of Priscilla: Cappella Graeca

Roman catacombs and the buildings above ground have preserved a considerable number of these sarcophagi with continuous friezes. Although they appear at the beginning of the fourth century, they achieve their highest expressive form in the course of the Constantinian period. Among the most significant examples, one should record the famous one of Balaam at S. Sebastiano[283], that of a child at S. Callisto[284], as well as several from the Catacombs of Pretestato[285], Marco e Marcelliano[286], and Novaziano[287].

The cyclical and narrative tendency is evident in the ceiling of the so-called *cubiculum* of the Exodus in the Giordani cemetery on Via Salaria Nova, dated to the Theodosian period[288]. Here, the centre and foundation of the iconographic scheme, namely, Christ and the

Bible, are associated in the central tondo that holds the former seated on a *subsellium* holding a *codex* in his hands following the typical iconography of the teacher. Anonymous orant figures rotate around him, as well as four episodes from Exodus, specifically, Moses receiving the Ten Commandments, Balaam who admires the encampments of Israel, a Hebrew who gathers manna in the desert, and the capture of the quails.

The narrative scheme, so popular for the decoration of cult buildings and certainly connected to the decoration of illuminated bibles, finds its greatest expression in the Hypogeum of Via Dino Compagni[289]. Between the middle of the fourth and the beginning of the fifth centuries, the tomb received pictorial decoration of an extraordinary eclectic

127

nature on the walls of the complex rooms, articulated by a truly audacious negative architecture. Here a cyclical tendency specifically inspired by Old Testament sources prevails, but one also finds *revivals* of pagan schemes due, among other things, to the religious policy of Julian the Apostate, memory of the Hellenistic figurative tradition and newly invented theophanic scenes. The complexity of the decorative programme of Via Dino Compagni betrays the strength of the intentions of a private commissioner of high social class and conspicuous economic means.

This cyclical approach, also enriched by stories of the passion, continues with great popularity also in sculptural production from the Constantinian period to the end of the fourth century[290]. Almost all the tectonic typologies that develop during this period are found in Roman catacombs. Panel and columnar sarcophagi as well as those with trees or city gates, the passage of the Red Sea to those with stars and crown, from the so-called Bethesda ones to those of the *anastasis* are all represented.

These theophanic themes seem to emanate precisely from the sphere of the pro-

128

duction of Roman sarcophagi, as for example, that of the *traditio legis* that seems to first appear on a sarcophagus from S. Sebastiano[291]. Among the sarcophagi discovered in Roman cemeteries, in fact, one finds examples with scenes of *maiestatis Domini*, such as the one from S. Sebastiano[292] and one from Domitilla[293]. The *anastasis* appears on several examples from S. Sebastiano[294]; an isolated and central cross is depicted, again in an example from S. Sebastiano[295].

This last complex has preserved the greatest number of sarcophagi, perhaps due to the great proliferation of mausolea annexed to the *basilica apostolorum* that held these marble tombs. Among the most interesting examples is the so-called Albani sarcophagus[296], dated to the first half of the fourth century. The front panel is articulated by strigillated and figurative panels with scenes of the *maiestas Domini*, the symbols of work, the resurrection of Lazarus, the miracle of the blind man, the Petrine trilogy and the miracle of the paralytic.

The so-called Sarcophagus of the Two Sisters, again conserved in the museum of S. Sebastiano, dates to the end of the fourth century[297]. The front panel is articulated by figurative and strigillated panels, with two figures of saints who, from their extreme positions, indicate the central representation of two women set in a *clipeus*. Once interpreted as two sisters, they most probably refer to the personifications of *ecclesia ex gentibus* and *ecclesia ex circumcisione*. Thus, the two entities of the Early Church are represented as women in an orant stance; behind them stands a cross as the Christological symbol of cohesion between the two parts.

In Roman catacombs, many theophanic scenes were introduced during the second half of the fourth century. After having undergone their first figurative use in funerary sculpture, they entered pictorial decoration. This symbolic atmosphere was created by the first representations of paradise with the martyrs and deceased as protagonists, such as in the famous fresco of an *arcosolium* located near the Basilica of SS. Nereo ed Achilleo at Domitilla[298]. Dated to the second

half of the fourth century, the martyr Petronilla, who already enjoyed fame and a cult at Rome, introduces the deceased aristocrat *Veneranda* into the garden of paradise with gestures of great intimacy (fig. 143).

Between the martyrs and the deceased a kind of religious friendship was established, an intimate relationship *inter pares* that characterised the saints as protectors, patrons and intercessors. To be close to them and be represented in their company meant shattering the limit between heaven and earth, a concept expressed well in the Roman catacombs by the creation of *retro sanctos* areas[299].

The relationship of patronage between martyrs and the defunct is well illustrated at the end of the fourth century by the *Cubiculum Leonis*. Precisely at the entrance and especially on the sides of the painted *tabula inscriptionis*, where one would expect to find the representations of apostles, one finds instead the figures of the eponymous martyrs Felix and Adauctus. These martyrs, venerated in the Catacomb of Commodilla where the *cubiculum* is located, elevate crowns as symbols of their martyrdom and triumph[300].

A document of great figurative impact expresses the rapport between saints and the deceased in an important manner. In the aristocratic *cubiculum* in the cemetery of SS. Marcellino e Pietro on Via Labicana, the four most venerated martyrs are arrayed at the base of a pyramid with Christ at the summit between the princes of the apostles[301]. Tiburtius, Gorgonius, Peter and Marcellinus indicate with eloquent gestures of acclamation the celestial vortex composed by the triad of Christ, Peter and Paul (fig. 144).

Dated to the beginning of the fifth century, this seems to be the last testimonial to devotion to the saints by affluent Roman classes. But perhaps along these lines one can situate a painting in the small Basilica of Commodilla dated more than a century later. The picture shows the eponymous martyrs who present the widow *Turtura* in front of the Virgin, mother and queen. But, by now these are spaces designated for pilgrimages and this is one of the last burials in the catacombs[302] (fig. 145).

143 Catacomb of Domitilla: arcosolium of Veneranda and Petronilla

144 Catacomb of SS. Pietro e Marcellino: fresco of Christ with SS. Peter and Paul and the Saints of the catacomb

When Roman catacombs assumed the role of pilgrimage sites, a new decorative phase commenced that was characterised by the appearance of images of the venerated martyrs[303] along the *itinera ad sanctos*. One early example is the grandiose group of SS. Sebastian, Policamus, and Quirinus in the skylight of S. Cecilia at S. Callisto, dated to the beginning of the fourth century[304].

These last manifestations assume the arrangement and complexity of the apsidal programmes of buildings above ground. Examples include the fresco of Christ between the martyrs at Generosa, the *traditio clavium* at Commodilla, the apses of S. Felicita and S. Ermete, the procession of saints at S. Valentino, the panels of Lucina, Ponziano, and the Crypt of S. Cecilia and the decoration of the tomb of S. Callistus at Calepodio[305].

4. THE HISTORY OF SCHOLARSHIP

Catacomb art immediately attracted the attention of the first discoverers of the Christian cemeteries in Rome. The explorers of the sixteenth century, walking through the meanders of the catacombs with difficulty by torch light, stopped in front of the frescoes, sarcophagi, and mosaics, so simple in form but so profound in meaning[306].

The great Church historian Cesare Baronio, describing the first catacomb to come to light in May 1578, the "Catacomb Anonima" of Via Anapo, expressed his great admiration of the newly discovered *subterranea civitas* and rejoiced in the fact that these were *ampliora spatia sanctorum imaginibus ornata*[307].

Baronio, along with other scholars of that period, such as De Winghe, Ciacconio

130

145 *Catacomb of Commodilla: fresco of Turtura, detail of the face of the Madonna*

as a result of the urgency and haste of painters little disposed to remaining for a long time in these dark and narrow settings. Alternatively, it was considered the mechanical and obsessive repetition of themes and schemes, verified by the dearth of originality[308]. Sometimes, the catechetical role has been stressed, or it has been disavowed in that the decorations were very often "imprisoned" within the *cubicula*[309].

All these evaluations do not fully reflect the impact of an art that, even in the soft light of the lamps, depicts a salvific imagery that is amongst the richest and most meaningful drafted by the ancient religious tradition. It was an art that, although it expressed itself in the shadows, was able to create a positive and joyous atmosphere that immediately annulled the dark umbra of the burial chambers.

Up until the 1970's, Catacomb art, like Early Christian art more generally, was considered a practically autonomous and original phenomenon with strong connotations and therefore decisively separate from any other figurative expression, even those intimately close to it in time and place.

To this day, to speak only of "Christian art" and "catacomb art" seems to indicate a figurative island immersed in a non-existent sea insensitive to these strong, expressive, rich, complex images, diversified in expressions particularly original.

For a long time, in the interpretation of catacomb art, as in the case of all Christian art, exegesis and theological speculation have been used as analytical tools rather than those proper to the history of art. In addition, scholars of Christian antiquities looked on these early artistic expressions as an extraordinary *test* of verification of their Counter-Reformation theories. Since this time, Early Christian archaeology has been the subject of investigation, even though not yet of scientific research.

At the beginning of our century, this situation led to the creation of a "science of Christian art" and thus a "study of catacomb art" impregnated with powerful apologetic aims, clear confessional character, to a con-

and the great Antonio Bosio, made every effort to record these evocative paintings in watercolour so they could be appreciated and studied better.

From the very beginning of Christian archaeology, the art of the catacombs struck experts who, however, attributed a dismal functional role in the complex Reformation debate to these precious iconographic documents.

Art historians and iconographers of every age have always disregarded catacomb art, in that it has been considered a sort of artisan production. At times, the spiritual component has been emphatically stressed by separating it in an anti-historical fashion from the art-historical context of the period; at others, it has been attempted to underplay this aspect in comparison with the preceding pagan tradition. At still other times, the condensed and eclectic stylistic character of catacomb art has been stressed, interpreting it siderable extent defined by speculation, preconceived hermeneutic methods and heavily dogmatic interpretations. All these methodologies merged in the thought, scientific activity, and iconographic approach of Joseph Wilpert. Fifty years after his death, all the power and intelligence of his review of Early Christian iconographic models can be recognised, but also his serious responsibility for having plotted profound trenches between the diverse Christian and non-Christian artistic traditions[310].

Wilpert contributed to the design of a specific physiognomy of Early Christian art, privileging in particular catacomb art and especially funerary painting. He specifically focused on Rome, dividing the material into three large typologies, namely, paintings, sarcophagi and mosaics. He assigned only a secondary role to all other art forms. All these steps facilitated his desire to gather iconographic material and document it following to the most modern criteria, using water-coloured photos to record the paintings and graphic reconstructions for sarcophagi. However, they also erected insurmountable barriers between the different artistic categories.

Nevertheless, the *corpora* of Roman catacomb paintings[311] and sarcophagi[312] compiled by Wilpert still constitute an attractive point of reference for scholars of Early Christian iconography. Still, they await more updated repertoires drafted according to criteria more aligned with modern criticism of the figurative arts of the late Antique period.

Only in the last thirty years has Early Christian art been studied from a less specialised point of view and contextualised within the framework of art production of the period. Scholars no longer consider only its specific, defined characteristics, but rather all the phenomena of continuity that stimulated Christian imagery to evolve naturally from late Antique art.

While an old prejudice still considers catacomb art as a separate field[313], scholars have begun to set the Early Christian figurative tradition in context[314], in the sense that,

art-historically, it has come to be treated in tandem with the pagan tradition.

In these same years, the first observations were pinpointed by Bianchi Bandinelli[315], who detected in late Antique production, and especially in the pictorial decoration of catacombs, a precise phenomenon of continuity with Hellenistic imagery. Alongside these presentations of its general and specifically figurative character must be set the work of Ernst Kitzinger. Using an art-historical approach, Kitzinger invented the term "perennial Hellenism" to intend a periodic and continuous return throughout the centuries of the late Antique period to the imagery developed by Graeco-Roman art[316].

At the same time, Christian iconographers were defining their critical positions. Distancing themselves from the typologies established by Wilpert's symbolic view, they immersed themselves in a continuist position that saw a gradual evolution of scenes and figurative models in the development of Christian imagery[317]. The most consistent contribution was made by Theodor Klauser[318], but later Dassmann[319], Engemann[320], Brandenburg[321] and Deichmann[322] made important contributions.

Based on these most recent studies, Early Christian art seems to have freed itself from unambiguous interpretations that united the various figurative models using a connecting thread that related them all to a single fundamental reference.

In the past, these ideas were ready-made to be mechanically applied to the figurative arts. Sometimes, they were recognised as expressions of the soteriologic and sacramental power detected by Wilpert[323], and enriched with slightly different nuances by Sauer[324], and Casel[325]. Sometimes, and particularly recently, the figurative expression of hope in immortality and the resurrection has been recognised[326].

While, during the last thirty years, all the theories of the past have been questioned due to the unilateral views they proposed, "catacomb art" has been subjected to further negligence. For example, about twenty years ago, in a broad article that attempted to analyse Roman painting of the fourth century[327], catacomb painting was eliminated from the comprehensive picture. Its exclusion was attributed to the excessive chronological fluctuations of the different regions of catacombs.

This serious omission seemed to find further backing in an article that denounced the state of things at the time[328]. It declared that modern criticism had entered a blind tunnel regarding progress in understanding the chronology of Roman catacombs.

The debate in these last thirty years seems to have concentrated especially on the vast pictorial production of SS. Marcellino e Pietro on Via Labicana. Since the initial arguments that took the form of a confrontation between Kollwitz[329] and De Bruyne[330], the debate in these last years seems to be focused on a wider and methodologically more involved area. Thus, the debate now entails not only and not so much the chronological definition of the paintings, but it has expanded to consider the absolute dating of catacombs[331].

The debate seems to be circular, since on the one hand it considers the pictorial patrimony of the catacombs on Via Labicana in isolation according to an art-historical approach that attributes rather late dating to the paintings. On the other hand, the paintings are placed rather unnaturally in their monumental context in which they serve as nothing more than verifications, rather than as effective contributing elements, for the definition of the history of the different regions of the cemeteries[332].

In both cases, the pictorial decoration of the cemetery of SS. Marcellino e Pietro is used for different aims. On the one hand, its expressive significance is diminished in favour of solely chronological deductions. On the other, by considering the frescoes in an isolated fashion as if in a picture gallery, its intimate connection with its surrounding context is ignored.

The iconographic spectrum of the pictorial production of the cemetery displays rather the typical development of catacomb decorations, with a series of phases already provided for in both the design and creation of the tombs and later in their decorative programme. This phenomenon of interruptions, second thoughts and variations in the course of the work is also seen in the hypogeum of Via Labicana.

For this reason in particular, one should scale down or consider suspect the presumed "fashion" that interprets the spread of white cubicula as a tired habit or as a sign of the irreversible process of impoverishment of the decorative programmes. Very often the only whitewashed cubicula present evidence of a building site, with the area completed to the point of placing a layer of plaster on the walls of the cubicula. In this state, they awaited the acquisition of the various chambers and the definitive decoration, left to the choice of the commissioners.

All this implies a dichotomy between the actual digging of the catacomb area and the decoration of the individual tombs. It is enough to cite the example of the famous hexagonal room in the Hypogeum of Via Dino Compagni, where one cubiculum that is only dug out and another that is only whitewashed coexist with frescoes of great iconographic significance such as the so-called "anatomy lesson"[333]. Alternatively, in the so-called area of "Novella" in the complex of Priscilla, the arcosolium of the shepherd with roosters represents the only frescoed monument in a series of other white arcosolia, prepared for decoration but never finished[334].

In addition, one cannot forget several niches of the "Catacomba Anonima" of Via Anapo that involved the decision to decorate the individual oblong arcosolia with paintings only after having systematised several tombs on the back wall[335]. These examples do not represent rare exceptions, but rather widespread and interesting signs of a dynamic that very often did not involve a harmonious rhythm between the progression of the digging, the creation of tombs, and their actual decoration. Likewise, it should be remembered that many nuclei of Roman catacombs developed within pre-existing underground cemeteries[336], where fossores and painters could move freely in different points of the area without following a set order[337].

With this in mind, one should exercise caution in considering catacomb paintings as reliable evidence for a chronological definition of a catacomb area, especially since these iconographic documents are also themselves subject to internal difficulties of chronological evaluation. Catacomb paintings, developing over a time span of approximately two centuries and often repeating themes and schemes according to slightly differentiated structures, do not always offer valid reference points for a reliable and absolute dating[338].

This does not mean that the role of painted decorations should be diminished within the comprehensive analysis of an area or a cemetery, but rather that these frescoes should be considered within the historical development of the monument. It is for this reason that scholars of Roman catacomb painting have taken some time out to reflect on their research and to abandon both the specifically iconological disputes as well as the purely chronological debates. Today more attention is being focused on the documentary[339] and technical[340] evidence and to research into the most profound roots of the figurative phenomenon, resuming the study of the execution of the catacomb frescoes. This approach also suggests the urgency and the manner of applying immediate conservation measures, drafting, as has been mentioned, a precise and detailed census of the paintings to obtain a broad and clear panorama that can serve as a reliable foundation for all future in-depth and specialised studies.

These observations betray the weakness of chronological analyses of catacomb paintings as compared to those applied for the study of sarcophagi. Sarcophagi seem to display a more reliable periodicity[341], despite the fact that there is a less intimate relationship between them and the monuments in which they are placed, due to their mobility and the long lapses of time that can separate their production from their use.

Both frescoes and sarcophagi, the most important decorative elements of Roman catacombs, still await more profound and combined study to prepare a real history of art of the catacombs. After the "separate" treatments of Wilpert[342] and those more interested in pictorial decorations of De Bruyne[343], the observations of Testini appear rather recapitulatory and spoiled by their collection in a manual[344]. Some of the most recent monographic studies[345], manuals[346] and even general[347] and uncritical[348] texts also provoke the same feeling.

The history of the art of the catacombs still needs to be written. Perhaps one could start from the faces, the physiognomies that appear like visions out of the shadows of the galleries. Faces, for the most part anonymous, repeated according to simplified schemes and more often engaged in rendering a simple figurative "unit" rather than a specific iconographic "personality". But scanning the rich repertoire of painted and sculpted faces found in the catacombs, one encounters gazes of great psychological impact, beginning with the famous philosopher, once identified as Paul, in the decorative programme of the Hypogeum of the *Aurelii* in Viale Manzoni[349] (fig. 146). Here, all those elements that characterise portraits of the late Antique period in their earlier renditions converge, but they are already intent on relaxing all the rules and peculiarities that had made Roman portraiture famous. Every reference to the physiognomic characteristics of the individual seems to be forgotten. Rather, the stress is on expressions that are tense and self-possessed at the same time, resigned and yet agitated, in an intensive and simultaneous sense of seeking a distant and indefinite yet secure point in which to attain a definitive internal peace.

The faces of the *Aurelii*, like those of many sarcophagi of the late Severan and early Gallienic periods, present an inspired almost visionary look. They fall into that figurative conception that must have expressed "the anguish of living in these tragic times" through ephemeral and vacuous psychological expressions and a "painful stupor"[350].

146 *Hypogeum of the Aurelii on Viale Manzoni: head of a philosopher*

the art of the catacombs[351]. Passing through the Roman catacombs, one finds dozens of inspired faces, all pertinent to the late Severan or early Gallienic period. Examples include the fragment of a paradisial sarcophagus in Priscilla with a reading *matrona*[352], a female portrait on a fragmentary lid from S. Callistus[353], the melancholic portrait of *Bassa* recalled together with her husband on a gilded glass still *in situ* in the cemetery of Panfilo[354], the figure of a young girl on the front panel of a sarcophagus also from Priscilla[355].

From the beginning of the fourth century until the Constantinian period, the faces found in catacombs, like all Roman portraits, are affected by the expressionist stimulus that arrived at the capital together with Oriental ideas and religions. At the same time, portraiture was influenced by the plebeian figurative tradition, namely, the reemergence of the autochthonous figurative concepts properly defined as "sub-antique"[356].

This strong figurative tendency produced portrait masks with an extremely strong impact, almost violent and shameless in presenting staring, over-sized eyes framed by wrinkles, sometimes as deep as scars, that run across the foreheads. Many faces depicted in the catacombs, dating to the tumultuous period extending from the Tetrarchy to the Constantinian period, express this important shift in the history of late Antique portraiture. The best examples are the faces of the orant figures in the Giordani cemetery that, according to the Roman dialect of the workers of the beginning of this century, were referred to as the *pignone* (fig. 147). These two faces[357] present grotesque physiognomies, at most tragic masks, in which the entire expressive focus is assumed by the pathetic gaze, greatly exaggerated and heavily engaged in a dramatic and painful purpose.

These tragic faces often recur on Roman sarcophagi. Perhaps the best examples are the polychrome slabs in the Museo Nazionale Romano[358] that, while not presenting real portraits, display a rather close sequence of extremely characterised faces.

Many faces of the catacombs, and especially the oldest portraits, present this paradoxical coexistence of agitation, depression and dissatisfaction, but also of a strange calm, total confidence and freedom attained through knowledge and doctrine.

The expression of tense and grave spirituality of the "philosopher" of Viale Manzoni is also the product of a rapid "impressionistic" technique. Between 250 and 260, this relationship between expression and technique is seen again in the faces of the back lunette of the *cubiculum* of the *velatio* in Priscilla. These represent some of the most successful pneumatic portraits left to us by

This is true of both the portrait of Christ, always hieratic and inspired by the typology of the philosopher, as well the figures of the miraculously healed, who have rather anonymous, repetitive but strongly expressive faces.

As one gets closer to the Constantinian period, it becomes easier to detect a "bi-polarity" in catacomb art. This is composed, on the one hand, of the expressionism in fashion from the beginning of the century, and on the other hand, of a well-considered and clear Classical *revival* that reaches its culmination and most defined expression in the mid-fourth century.

The first tendency is again documented by the physiognomies and painted portraits. One example is the Madonna in the *Coeme-terium Maius*[359] (fig. 148) that, through its absolute frontality, but especially through its exaggerated over-sized eyes, very closely recalls the many effigies of Constantinian ladies. Similarly, several powerful portraits found the circular *cubiculum* of Via Dino Compagni[360], such as Balaam, the angel, Christ, the Samaritan woman (fig. 149), Samson (fig. 150) and several Philistines, evoke anew the many stereotypes and *chiaroscuro* contrasts of official reliefs of later Constantinian sculpture.

The other figurative trend is best represented by the "beautiful style" of famous sarcophagi such as those of Junius Bassus[361] and of the Two Brothers[362] or the so-called "dogmatic" sarcophagi[363]. It is also reflected in the Roman catacombs by several famous portraits such as the soft and classic one of the girl in Via Dino Compagni[364], or the more faded yet stately one of a young man in Domitilla silhouetted against the neutral background[365]. But these Classical faces that are smoothed out, organic and coherent from a formal point of view, are better appreciated in sculpture. The best examples are a splendid continuous frieze from the cemetery of Pretestato[366], a sarcophagus from the cemetery of Novaziano[367], in a well-balanced front panel from the Catacomb of S. Sebastiano[368], but especially in a recently discovered small fragment in the eastern *tricora* of

S. Callisto with two Classical faces, that of Christ and S. Paul, perhaps involved in a scene of *maiestas Domini*[369] (fig. 151).

Also during the period that extends from the second half of the fourth century to the beginning of the fifth, corresponding to the last figurative phase of Roman catacombs,

147 Catacomb of Gior-dani: fresco with the portrait of a deceased woman

137

148 *Coemeterium Maius: fresco with the "Madonna" and child*

one finds many portraits and physiognomies of the period. For example, the typical face of Petronilla in the *arcosolium* of Veneranda at Domitilla[370] presents the characteristics, the immobile expression and the typical hairstyle of portraits dated 360–370. Similar are the two more anonymous faces, already informed by the stereometric canons of personifications, depicted in the sarcophagus of the "Two Sisters" from S. Sebastiano[371], already datable to the end of the century.

Even the faces of Christ and the princes of the apostles acquire during these years special peculiarities that proclaim the graphic and fixed tone of Byzantine portraiture, as exemplified by the bust of Christ in the centre of the ceiling of the *Cubiculum Leonis* at Commodilla[372] (pl. I, p. 8). Such faces, bloodless in their layout and vibrant in the violent juxtaposition of the earthly hues,

predominantly browns and reds, can also be found in the images of S. Paul in the Hypogeum of Via Dino Compagni[373] and in the *cubiculum* of the *fossor* Diogenes at Domitilla[374]. Alternatively, in the face of Eve in the *cubiculum* of the Exodus at Giordani, the eyes are circled with dark lines, as if she is wearing glasses[375].

Abandoning for the moment the evolution of portraiture, and following the path marked out by the history of iconographic and figurative contexts, it is possible to reconstruct a formal development. Although critics have still not formulated this development, it is nonetheless extremely interesting for an understanding of the genesis and evolution of an artistic language that pervaded catacomb art.

Discussion could begin with an analysis of several painted scenes still sensitive to a

138

setting "*en plein air*" and a bird's eye point of view derived from the Roman figurative tradition. The generic scenes record in turn the Hellenistic tradition. This figurative typology finds particular expression in several pictures in the Hypogeum of the *Aurelii*[376], the pastoral scenes in the attic of the Mausoleum of *Clodius Hermes* at S. Sebastiano[377] and the so-called "Shepherd" sarcophagi that survive in both intact examples and numerous fragments[378].

From these open settings, an iconographic reality that was more ephemeral and more organised geometrically began to be created, as for example, in the paradisial scene in the painted *loculus* on the second floor at Priscilla[379]. Still within the third century, one finds reductions or, better yet, "cutouts" from typical and powerful scenes that, set in the foreground, reveal their emblematic role. Examples include the Madonna and prophet at Priscilla[380], the scenes of the Sacraments[381] and of Lucina at S. Callisto[382], the shepherd who divides the flock from the wild animals[383] and the New Testament vignettes in the *cubiculum* of the *coronatio* of Pretestato[384], the oldest frescoes of the cemetery of SS. Marcellino e Pietro[385] and the decoration of the *cubiculum* of Nunziatella[386].

The simplification of figurative scenes also implies an impoverishment of the iconographic models, reduced to a few essential elements, that coincided as well with the "interpretative codes" to decipher the various scenes. Another measure for the de-codification of images immediately adopted by the decorators of the catacombs was that of attributing perfectly functional proportions to the diverse figures. Thus, the Christ figure, in comparison with the people healed, is always of greater proportions, even more emphasised by his solemn gesture of *impositio manum* or by the use of the miraculous *virga*. In the scenes of the baptism of Christ, for example, the roles are inverted. Larger proportions are given to the figure of John the Baptist to indicate the action, hierarchy of the figures and dynamic of the scene.

A characteristic typical of all late Antique art, but specifically of its figurative re-

ligious tradition, became constitutionalised in the art of the catacombs. This is the projection into the foreground of every image not only in the frescoes and reliefs but also in incisions with biblical themes preserved in the Early Christian cemeteries of Rome. By this procedure, the symbolic atmosphere and didactic finality are further stressed to the point of transforming these biblical proverbial extracts into formidable religious manifestos.

All these characteristics distinguish the art of the catacombs of the third and fourth century, and denote a progressive evolution and definition. In the Constantinian period, the walls, vaults, *arcosolia* of the *cubicula*

149 Hypogeum of Via Dino Compagni: cubiculum of Samson, detail of the face of the Samaritan Woman

139

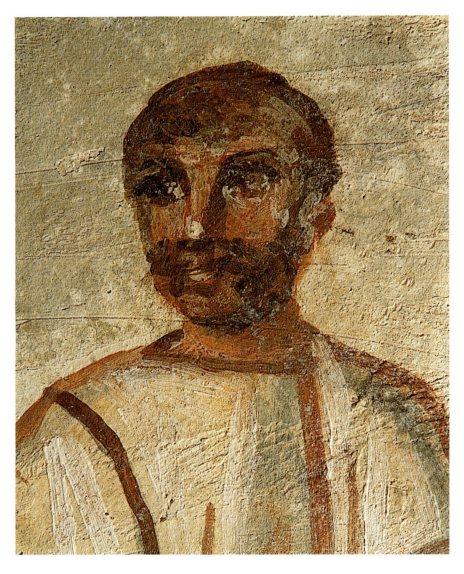

150 Hypogeum of Via Dino Compagni: cubiculum of Samson, detail of the face of Samson

iconographic organisation of the sarcophagi of the first half of the fourth century. Examples include the *loculus* of *Grata* in the cemetery of the Giordani[387] and the *loculus* of *Ianuarius* at Domitilla[388]. In the catacomb of the Giordani, one might also consider the *loculus* with a series of biblical scenes. These include the miracle from the rock, the multiplication of the loaves, the adoration of the Magi, Noah in the Ark, the resurrection of Lazarus, Daniel in the lions' den, Tobias and the archangel, the healing of the paralytic, the personification of the Tigris[389].

Catacomb painting, during a long period that extended from the Tetrarchy to the Theodosian periods, presented schemes that were extremely similar and altered only the stylistic language, that underwent two "renaissances" of "Classicism" in the middle and end of the fourth century. In contrast, sarcophagi mark the passage of time better, both through the adoption of diversified tectonic types and by the assumption of figurative stylistic features in continuous modification.

In this slow but easily judged evolution, one sees a progressive reduction in the anatomical volumes of the figures, that goes so far as to imbue the images with a sinuous and insubstantial effect, with *silhouettes* more drafted than rendered in relief. Sculpture is no longer concerned with the production of high relief but is inclined towards the rendition of optical effects with more or less profound lines that, capturing shadow, produce a negative relief.

This feature reaches its culmination in the Theodosian age, when the drapery of the figures assumes a geometric configuration of sinuous lines. At the same time, the images are elongated until they touch the edges of the sarcophagi. Examples include the sarcophagus with stars and crowns from S. Sebastiano[390] and the sarcophagus of Bethesda from Pretestato[391].

These examples as well as the latest pictorial expressions, such as the earlier rooms of Via Dino Compagni[392], the *cubiculum* of the Exodus of the Giordani[393], the *Cubiculum Leonis* at Commodilla[394], the *cubiculum* of the eponymous saints at the Catacomb of

but also the inter-*loculi* of galleries and the closures of the tombs, whether incised, painted or decorated in relief, the front panels and lids of sarcophagi all become undifferentiated versatile supports for decoration. This embellishment took the form of parades, pinacothecae, sequences, friezes and series of biblical scenes, extremely reduced in terms of their figurative development, barely open to judgement on a hermeneutic level were it not for the obsessive interaction of the schemes.

The spaces between the *loculi* receive "continuous frieze" decorations that demonstrate a confident inter-relationship with the

140

Archeologia Sacra, cf. most recently, Bordignon 1991–1992.
341 Stutzinger 1990.
342 Wilpert 1903; Wilpert 1929–1936.
343 De Bruyne 1959.
344 Testini 1966.
345 Tronzo 1986.
346 Deichmann 1993.
347 Grabar 1968.
348 Dorigo 1966.
349 Nr, p. 46, n. 2.
350 Bianchi Bandinelli 1984, p. 87.
351 Nr, pp. 23–24, n. 7.
352 Salvetti 1993.
353 Bisconti 1989a.
354 Pillinger 1984, p. 84.
355 Ramieri 1993.
356 Kitzinger 1989.
357 Nr, p. 16, n. 11.
358 R, n. 773.

359 Nr, p. 36, n. 22.
360 Ibid., pp. 78–79, n. 6.
361 R, n. 680.
362 Ibid., n. 45.
363 Ibid., n. 43.
364 Nr, p. 83, n. 13.
365 Ibid., p. 130, n. 67.
366 R, n. 55.
367 Ibid., n. 663.
368 Ibid., n. 183.
369 Bisconti 1993a.
370 Nr, p. 123, n. 15.
371 R, n. 240.
372 Nr, pp. 142–143, n. 5.
373 Ibid., pp. 79–81, n. 9.
374 Ibid., p. 123, n. 19.
375 Ibid., pp. 14–15, n. 7.
376 Ibid., pp. 45–48.
377 Ibid., p. 88, n. 7.
378 Bosio 1993.
379 Bisconti 1990.

380 Bisconti 1996b.
381 Nr, pp. 106–107, nn. 21–25.
382 Ibid., p. 103, nn. 1–2.
383 Ibid., p. 92, n. 7.
384 Bisconti 1997a.
385 Nr, pp. 50–51, nn. 9–14.
386 Ibid., p. 139, n. 4.
387 Ibid., p. 14, n. 5.
388 Ibid., p. 124, n. 26.
389 Ibid., p. 14, n. 6.
390 R, n. 175.
391 Ibid., n. 556.
392 Nr, pp. 81–85, nn. 10–13.
393 Ibid., pp. 14–15, n. 7.
394 Ibid., pp. 142–143, n. 5.
395 Ibid., p. 50, n. 3.
396 Bisconti 1995c.
397 Farioli 1963; Osborne 1985; Bisconti 1995.

VENERI
OSNSPIR
IIVSIVSINTE
RSANTOS

III. INSCRIPTIONS IN ROMAN CATACOMBS

Danilo Mazzoleni

1. Christian Inscriptions in the Catacombs

"Christian epigraphy of the late Antique period seems conservative, in that it continues secular schemes and formulae, and, at the same time, innovative, since it reflects new sentiments and situations. Thus, by expanding the use and meaning of some vocabulary and expressions, and creating new words and declarations of faith that were unknown in pagan funerary epigraphy, it took on a true wealth of signs and images"[1].

This observation is fundamentally correct. One could also add that hardly anything would be known about the genesis and evolution of Christian epigraphy were it not for the more than 40,000 inscriptions that survive from the Roman catacombs. The inscriptions are mostly datable to a chronological span between the beginning of the third century, in the oldest galleries of the cemeteries, to the fifth century, when underground burial was progressively abandoned[2].

These inscriptions constitute an enormous, heterogeneous group of material, from which it is possible to draw a number of important observations. For example, discrediting a commonly held belief, it has been noted[3] that, in comparison to the enormous mass of surviving funerary inscriptions, the religious inscriptions constitute only a small minority. Most of them date to the post-Constantinian period.

It is certainly true that the study of the numerous elements contained in so many thousands of Roman epitaphs has only just begun and the future is very promising. No doubt, the completion just a few years ago of the monumental collection of the *Inscriptiones Christianae Urbis Romae septimo saeculo antiquiores* (known by the acronym ICUR) will have an enormous impact on future research in this field. The collection, begun in 1922 by Angelo Silvagni, was later continued by Father Antonio Ferrua and the author, under the auspices of the Società Romana di Storia Patria and the Pontificio Istituto di Archeologia Cristiana.

Pl. III Catacomb of S. Callisto: Crypts of Lucina: gravestone of Veneriosa (ICUR IV, 9451)

152 Catacomb of Panfilo: gilded glass with a portrait of a bearded man, set into the closing mortar of a loculus in a gallery of the second floor

153 Catacomb of the Giordani: small ivory doll set in the closing plaster of a loculus of a child in a passageway

While much remains to be done, it should be remembered that Christian epigraphy is a relatively young science. Giovanni Battista de Rossi (1822–1894), the man who has been rightly called "the father" of Christian archaeology, defined its methodological foundations in its essential form. Only a few scholars, first of all, the already mentioned Angelo Silvagni, and Father Antonio Ferrua, followed in his footsteps. The latter, who can rightly be considered the greatest scholar of this century, was the author of an extremely vast series of

monographs and articles that resulted in extremely important developments in this discipline[4].

Examining the various anthologies that gather these inscriptions in critical editions, it is noteworthy that there are a great many from which emerge features useful for an understanding of interesting and sometimes unpublished aspects of these ancient communities. These include issues such as the spoken language of people in the late Antique period, their religious feelings, affections and ideas concerning the mystery of death. At the same time, many details of life in the Early Christian communities can also be reconstructed, such as their social structure, the presence of foreigners and immigrants[5], their level of education as well as many small everyday events that history generally does not record.

Thus, it is possible to discredit or at least place in perspective several beliefs, such as that, for example, concerning the not at all sporadic presence of members of the higher social classes and military personnel of every rank and division in the Christian communities. Thus, those who speak of Christianity as derived essentially from a plebeian or petite-bourgeois background, barely represented among soldiers, can be refuted by the factual evidence.

Likewise, walking through the long galleries of many catacombs, one easily becomes aware of another phenomenon worthy of attention, that is, the high incidence of illiteracy among the faithful. In fact, it is noteworthy that a majority of the tombs still intact do not have any inscription, whereas a certain number of the tombs have only small objects of every type fixed into the closing mortar. These objects include necklaces, shells, bronze coins, bases of glasses or cups with finely worked images in gold leaf (fig. 152), bone or ivory dolls (fig. 153), small bells, small terracottas and glass vials. These were all signs that could have had an ornamental value, but they could also have helped to identify the *loculus* in which a dear one was buried amongst so many others that were apparently equal[6].

Evidently, there were also Christians who could not afford the extra cost of an inscription placed on the tomb. However, it is also true that, if one really desired a written dedication, a short and economical graffito incised with a hard point on the still fresh mortar that sealed the closing slabs of the tomb would have been sufficient (fig. 154). Therefore, the absence of an inscription was more likely connected with the illiteracy of the commissioners, rather than a choice dictated by a lack of economic means.

2. THE ORIGINS OF CHRISTIAN EPIGRAPHY. THE EVOLUTION OF FORMULAE

The first appearance of conspicuous groups of inscriptions of a certainly Christian nature is dated to the beginning of the third century; however, they do not occur everywhere simultaneously. In general, an extreme simplicity prevails at first, the so-called "archaic laconism" (fig. 155), whereby the lone name of the deceased is accompanied at most by a symbol, such as an anchor, fish (a symbolic image of Christ), or dove (fig. 156)[7].

It is clear that the new language was developing slowly. Soon other elements were added, such as, for example, reference to the dedicators who commissioned the gravestones for their deceased relative (fig. 157), and wishes for a life in Christ, peace and participation in the celestial "*refrigerium*", in other words, for an eternal life in paradise.

The date of deposition in the grave, which usually coincided with the actual date of death is often present; this date had earlier been omitted because it was considered inauspicious or a bad omen. In Christian epigraphy, the date of burial became important, since for the faithful the day of death also represented the date of passage to a new life. It also marked the anniversary date on which relatives annually celebrated rituals in honour of their dear ones and often ate a small symbolic meal in the ideal presence of the deceased.

While the community as a rule provided for the poorest members, the faithful normally bought their tombs while they were still alive (as is often recorded in the inscrip-

tions) from the *fossores*, that is, those who actually excavated the galleries of the catacombs. To demonstrate that the purchase had been carried out regularly, the commissioners sometimes indicated on the gravestones the name of the person from whom they had bought the grave; sometimes even the sum that had been paid is included. Thus, an inscription of uncertain origin records that a certain *Serbulus* bought a tomb for two persons from the *fossor* Leontius[8].

154 Catacomb of Priscilla: funerary graffito

Pagan and Christian inscriptions

In general, the quality of writing on Christian gravestones was decidedly inferior to that

155 Catacomb of Priscilla: inscription of the small boy Aemerus found in situ on the first floor (ICUR IX, 24903)

156 Catacomb of S. Sebastiano: *fragment of a gravestone with a Christogram, fish and anchor (ICUR V, 13269 b)*

157 Catacomb of S. Sebastiano: *Greek inscription dedicated by* Marcus Ulpius Calocerus *to his pious mother Sempronia Agathous, in her memory. Beneath the gravestone, a fish (derived from Christological symbolism) darts through the waves. Traces of the original colours survive (ICUR V, 12905)*

of pagan ones, perhaps as a result of a variety of motives. These included amongst others, more limited financial means, the employment of less specialised workers (or those who did a bit of everything, such as the *fossores*)[9] and the diverse needs of the commissioners. The latter were perhaps more interested in the content rather than the exterior appearance of the inscriptions[10].

In Christian cemeteries, it was not rare for heterogeneous materials to be used; examples include plundered tiles or fragments of marble slabs, reused without even smoothing out the edges. The characters were incised hastily without any preparation to arrange them symmetrically. Irregular writing was adopted, mostly in upper case, which is defined technically as *capitalis attuaria rustica*; this script is characterised by elongated and slightly inclined lettering. Sometimes, other types of graphic script, such as unarticulated cursive script or rounded uncial script accompanied this form.

Although it is undeniable that the general quality of Christian gravestones was relatively low, texts incised with a certain elegance and regularity (apart from the significant exceptions of the epigrams of Pope Damasus) do exist, even if they are rarely comparable with the impressive Classical examples.

Despite the many differences between pagan and Christian inscriptions, there are also numerous similarities[11]. In contrast to the addition of many significant novelties in the formulae, especially in terms of content (fig. 158), various expressions, attributes and symbols persisted out of habit, although they perhaps increasingly lost their original significance.

For example, the appearance of an initial dedication to the *Di Manes*[12], the underworld divinities invoked by pagans to protect the tombs, in several hundreds of Christian inscriptions, might cause amazement. Also surprising might be the fact that the tomb sometimes continues to be defined as the *dimora aeterna*[13], since it is well known that the faithful considered the grave only a temporary resting-place for the body awaiting the Resurrection. In the first case, the custom of the dedication to the *Manes* probably persisted since, in some sense, by convention it allowed the tomb to be placed under the protection of Roman law as a "sacred place"[14]. The Christians then, just like the pagans, were afraid that their tomb could, after their death, be devastated or alienated, particularly when the burial area was in the open and therefore difficult to protect.

Other similarities occur in the use of rather generic expressions addressed to the deceased to celebrate their virtues, such as "worthy", "very dear", and "very sweet"[15]. Similarly, the same terms related to the pain and grief of those left behind, such as "suffering", "in everlasting mourning" appear in both pagan and Christian inscriptions. Citations from poets, especially Virgil, were also drawn from the Classical repertoire. It is precisely in Christian funerary poems, generally not of great artistic value, that schemes and images from the pagan repertoire are repeated. These were particularly diffuse during the Constantinian period[16].

Christian epigraphy of the Severan period

The Severan period, and more specifically the very first decades of the third century, marks the beginning of Christian epigraphy in Roman catacombs[17] It is only at the beginning of the third century that, in the oldest nuclei of the cemeteries, the first written documents that can be defined as Christian begin to appear. A very few (non-Roman) examples, dated with certainty to the closing decades of the second century, are the exceptions to this rule. These include the famous inscription of Bishop Aberkios of Hierapolis, dated between 161 and 180[18], and probably the equally renowned dedication of Pectorius of *Augustodunum*[19].

The two texts cited above already demonstrate a very developed and complex

formula, with a marked symbolic language not always susceptible to an immediate and unambiguous interpretation. In contrast, in other Roman funerary examples, the dedications are generally very different and are characterised by a great conciseness. Often, they contain only the names of the deceased and sometimes, some wish for peace addressed to them. In this same period, the first symbols begin to appear, either alone or beside the text. Anchors and fish are particularly common, to accentuate the Christological and soteriological significance of the inscriptions[20].

Other funerary inscriptions, in contrast, reveal close ties with pagan epigraphy, distinguishing themselves from these sometimes only by slight (and not always certain) indications. Not infrequently, the formula is still neutral (the same characteristic is also noted in texts of the later period); only the provenance of the inscription testifies in favour of its Christianity.

Recently, there has been an attempt to elucidate the peculiarities of the early period of Roman epigraphy. In particular, the focus has been on the "problems of the chronology, nature and true character of the oldest

158 Catacomb of the Giordani: fresco in the lunette of an arcosolium that depicts a scribe holding an open book with the inscription "the resting place of Silvestra" (ICUR IX, 24489)

epigraphic texts securely attributable to Christian commissioners"[21], that span down to the second half of the third century.

The Catacomb of Priscilla represents a monumental complex of considerable importance for the reconstruction of the delicate phase of the genesis of Christian epigraphy. The *arenaria* of this catacomb, in particular, was intensely used by the local community from the end of the second and the beginning of the third centuries onwards.

In this area, de Rossi discovered circa 300 Latin and Greek inscriptions, often still fixed to the *loculi*[22]. Significant results emerged from his detailed study which indicated that more than 80 percent of the inscriptions discovered in that region were neutral; in other words they lacked any element which could be considered specifically Christian. Most of these had in fact only the name of the deceased, whereas a much smaller percentage also included the name of one or more dedicator[23].

In contrast, a little more than 50 inscriptions contained unquestionably Christian wishes or acclamations of peace, perhaps intended as symbolic greetings addressed by the survivors to their deceased loved ones. Among the many cases of this type, it should suffice to mention the dedications of *Caelestina*[24], *Felicitas* or *Pomponius* painted in red lead in "priscillian" letters[25]. Another very well known example is the epitaph of *Vericundus*[26] in which the central abbreviation (an M underlined and cut by a horizontal dash) should be interpreted as *m(emoria)*, and not as a reference to a presumed martyr or as a Marian *ante litteram* invocation.

In other similar examples, also discovered in the Catacomb of Priscilla[27], one finds once again the anchor along with the fish as one of the first symbols to appear beside the text. The former was also among the first to be abandoned, from the fourth century. Thus, at first, images with an obvious Christological (connected to the famous Greek acrostic ΙΧΘΥΣ, symbolising "Jesus Christ, the Son of God, the Saviour") and soteriological significance[28] were introduced into the Christian repertoire.

An anchor, together with decorative motifs in the form of arrows and palmettes, appears in the famous inscription of *Filumena*[29]. During the last century, she was considered a martyr, but without the slightest archaeological or epigraphic evidence; a completely apocryphal hagiographic tradition was then created around her. Disregarding these widely known facts, it should be noted that the tiles of the *loculus* were probably inverted through the error or ignorance of a *fossor*.

According to the conclusions reached by de Rossi, the extreme simplicity of the Early Christian texts, despite a certain number of exceptions, continued for approximately half a century. Around 250, the formulae began to be gradually embellished with other elements, supplanting the extreme conciseness that characterised the original period.

An investigation conducted in 1975 confirmed the sporadic presence of written documents datable to the Severan period in all regions of the *orbis christianus antiquus*[30]. Nevertheless, in Rome, several catacombs have been identified in which at least a group of inscriptions could date with good probability to the first half of the third century.

In addition to the already mentioned examples from the Catacomb of Priscilla, de Rossi included in this period texts derived from the Crypts of Lucina and "Area I" of the Catacomb of S. Callisto. For example, on January 3, 236, the first pope, Anterus[31] was buried in the Crypt of the Popes in S. Callisto. In addition, nuclei of inscriptions of the first decades of the third century have been identified in the area of the *Flavii Aurelii* in the Catacomb of Domitilla[32], in the Catacomb of Calepodio, where the martyr pope Callistus was buried in 222[33], in the *Coemeterium Maius* on Via Nomentana[34] and at S. Ermete. In the latter, as shall be seen shortly, an inscription dated to 234 was found[35]. Presumably, other examples of the same period can also be identified in the Catacombs of Panfilo, Marco e Marcelliano, and Novaziano[36]. Nevertheless, it is often not at all simple to recognise them on the basis of convincing evidence; too often, there is only palaeographic evidence, in itself extremely ephemeral and inconsistent.

The Greek inscription of Κάρικος from the Catacomb of Panfilo, on a beautiful marble slab with a very careful script, is now in the Musei Capitolini[37]. Certainly, it is undeniable that the text is early. Nevertheless, it cannot reasonably be dated to the second half of the second century, as it has been suggested, essentially on the basis of the script. In fact, the earliest use of this cemetery on Via Salaria Vetus does not seem earlier than the third century and the existence of earlier hypogea has not been proven.

Nevertheless, the concluding phrase of this inscription is noteworthy, in which it expresses the wish that the soul of the deceased be remembered, equivalent to a request for prayer in his support.

Another important reality of Christian inscriptions of the first decades of the third century is the extreme rarity of dated inscriptions. This is, however, completely comprehensible, considering what has already been observed regarding the conciseness of the formulae, which normally did not include the date of death. The Roman funerary inscriptions of this period with a precise chronological reference, that is, with a secure consular date, are in fact extremely few.

The earliest inscription of this type, dated to 217, was found on a sarcophagus from the area of Torre Nova on the present day Via Casilina (the ancient Labicana), which was later brought to the Villa Borghese[38]. Here, *Marcus Aurelius Prosenes* is remembered. He was the freedman of two Augusti (that is, Marcus Aurelius and Commodus), major-domo to the emperor, the court economist, administrator of imperial goods, organiser of gladiatorial games, responsible for the wine supply, and entrusted by Commodus with court administration. The *liberti* of this freedman were the dedicators and commissioners of this sarcophagus, decorated with erotes, cornucopia, garlands and with the recumbent figure of the deceased, now headless, on the lid.

On the basis of such elements, this funerary monument exhibits nothing specifically Christian. But another inscription was added in a later period in the upper margin of the right side by the freedman *Ampelius* upon his return from a military expedition against the Parthians. It specifies that *Prosenes* was "welcomed before God" (*receptus ad deum*) on March 3, 217, during the consulship of Presens and Extricatus[39].

This expression quite logically tips the balance in favour of the Christianity of the text, which has, however, been questioned by several scholars. Nevertheless, while it refers to 217, it was most likely incised at least several years later.

In contrast, a gravestone from the Catacomb of S. Ermete[40] dates to 234. The inscription refers to a young girl, aged 10 years and eight days, *Cornelia Paula*, who died on 23 July, 234, when Massimus and Urbanus were consuls. In this case, there is no doubt concerning the nature of the text, in which one reads the verb (*decessit*), indicating death, followed by the date of the *dies natalis* of the small dead girl, that is, the date on which she ended her earthly life to begin that otherworldly.

The authenticity of an epitaph dated to 235[41], and found in the Catacomb of Commodilla, remains very controversial. On the other hand, the incised lid of a sarcophagus of uncertain origin in the Museo Pio Cristiano is datable to 238. It contains a dedication in Greek to another child Ἡράκλιτος who lived almost eight years; he died in the year that Pius and Pontian were consuls[42].

Other inscriptions, although lacking a consular date, may contain elements that nevertheless provide a secure date within this same period. This is the case of an epitaph of the slave Marcus, also from the Catacomb of S. Ermete, but more likely from the region above ground, now in the Museo Nazionale Romano[43].

Here too, the first part of the dedication does not have any clear signs of Christianity, but the last lines identify it without doubt as such. It was set up by Alexander, the slave of two Augusti, that is, with all probability,

Septimius Severus and Caracalla, colleagues in the Empire between 198 and 211. This reference makes it possible to date the gravestone with good probability.

The dead Marcus, who lived 18 years old, 9 months and five days, was one of the slaves assigned to the imperial wardrobe. He was known as *Caputafricesi*, namely, resident on the street of the *Caelimontium* where the *paedagogium puerorum*, a school for the training of the slaves of the imperial household, had its headquarters.

The last part of the inscription contains a deprecatory formula, with which the "good brothers", that is, the brothers in the faith, "in the name of the one God", are implored not to disturb the gravestone (and thereby by extension, to the burial monument) after the death of the dedicator.

It is certainly not rare to find this type of expression as well as warnings or threats of fines against tomb violators in Christian epigraphy. The phenomenon was widespread; pagans, Jews and Christians alike shared the same fear that their tomb might be damaged in the vain search for precious objects or to insert other bodies illicitly after their death[44].

Another famous inscription, that of *Licinia Amias*, found in the Vatican necropolis and now in the Museo Nazionale Romano, also dates to the beginning of the third century[45]. After the dedication, still of a pagan type, to the *Di Manes*, it begins with a Greek invocation to Christ, "the fish of the living", rendered in the form of the acrostic ΙΧΘΥΣ and followed by the image of an anchor and two fish facing each other. The term "living" was used from the second century onwards to allude to the faithful, revitalised by the sacrament of Baptism.

The lemniscate crown, inserted between the letters of the initials, D[is] M[anibus], reflects a convention of profane funerary monuments on which it was a figurative element. This symbol later assumed another meanings that alluded to the crown of martyrdom or the eternal prize which the faithful sought[46]. The rest of the surviving text is the same as other contemporary neutral inscriptions, with the generic *benemerenti* or "worthy", followed by the age of the deceased, now entirely lost.

A stele in black marble, originally from the Catacomb of S. Ermete and now in the Museo Nazionale Romano, is also dated to the first decades of the third century[47]. The text records that "here lies Protus in the Holy Spirit of God" and that his sister *Firmilla* dedicated it in memory of her brother. A sort of fusion of formulae is also found here, uniting the common pagan expression "here lies", with the eschatological formula of rest "in the Holy Spirit of God", rarely found elsewhere.

Another controversial inscription is that of *Iulia Calliste,* of unknown provenance, now in the Museo Pio Cristiano. It is dated either to the beginning of the third century or, according to some scholars, to the end of the second century. The stele has lateral acroteria. This type of funerary monument, with the exception of the early examples already noted, was very rare in the Christian communities of the West. In contrast, the form was extremely widespread in the East.

The text, introduced by the dedication to the *Di Manes*, was dedicated by her husband and children to their wife and mother respectively, *Iulia Calliste*[48]. The formula is neutral, but in the last line appears a P, a ligature between I and H and a Christogram, that has been interpreted as *p(ax) Ie(su) Chr(isti)*, and more recently as *p(uella) Ie(su) Ch(risti)*. The main difficulty is the presence of a monogram of Constantinian type, used as an abbreviation and not as a symbol, in an epigraph of the end of the second or beginning of the third century. This element, with the exception of several examples equally controversial in terms of interpretation and chronology, does not usually appear before the second decade of the fourth century. Some scholars have suggested that it is a later addition, noting the diversity of the model and the low incision of the letters, as well as the imperfect symmetry of the last line, in contrast to the other, more carefully rendered lines.

Others, however, have sustained the contemporaneity of the entire inscribed text, based on diametrically opposed observations. Apart from any other consideration, this example proves how interpretation of epigraphic details can be extremely subjective and variable. In the absence of indisputable elements, the wisest solution seems to be to defer judgement. Yet, the hypothesis of a text with a Christogram from the beginning of the third, if not even the end of the second century, is certainly attractive. At any rate, the only type of monogram of Christ commonly attested in the pre-Constantinian period remains that formed by the interweaving of the letters iota and chi. This form already appears in securely datable examples from Phrygia, from the mid-third century onwards[49].

Thus, the first decades of the third century represents a period of great importance for Christian epigraphy, but about which it is only possible to present very fragmentary and erratic data. Nevertheless, in inscriptions of this period, one can identify an important link in an imaginary chain of continuity and breaks, of conservatism and novelties that mark the progressive decline of Classical epigraphy and the always greater growth and diversification of Christian epigraphy. Christian epigraphy, although using the same languages (Latin and Greek) and sharing many common traits, was able to profoundly differentiate itself from Classical epigraphy not only by its content, but also through distinctive formal aspects.

3. CHRISTIAN NAMES

Study of the thousands of names recorded in the funerary inscriptions of the Roman catacombs reveals many significant features. For example, they divulge the most popular names of the Christians, both those introduced by them and tied to a particular meaning as well as those that they continued to adopt even if they were apparently less appropriate for the faithful. In addition, it can also be considered whether the cult of the martyrs buried in the cemetery could have had some influence on the diffusion of specific names[50].

First of all, it is easy to verify that in the majority of cases, only one name appears. This follows a practice already widespread in the late period. Beginning in the third century, in fact, precisely as the first Christian texts were diffused, several features of Roman nomenclature, such as the personal and

159 Catacomb of Priscilla: inscription, painted on two tiles, of L. Septimus Zoticianus (ICUR IX, 25575)

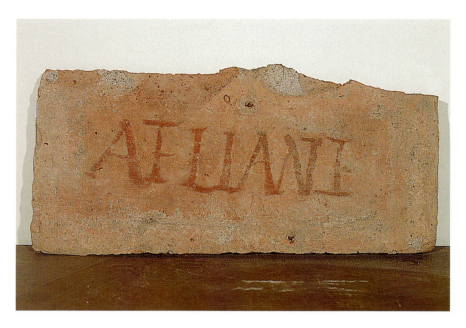

Although this was the general rule, conservative families, especially those of high social rank or in provincial cities, who were more closely tied to tradition, sometimes continued to adopt two or three names in the fourth and fifth centuries. And yet usually, when examples of this type are found, their form could constitute a valid reason to postulate an early date for the inscription, perhaps still within the pre-Constantinian period (fig. 159). In some cases, one might even interpret the continued use of "three names", which for centuries had distinguished Roman citizens, as a kind of pretentiousness or snobbism (to use a modern term). For example, in the Catacomb of SS. Marcellino e Pietro, a man, certainly of non-aristocratic lineage, vivaciously depicted with his merchandise in an incision on his gravestone, is called *Iulius Marius Silvanus*[51].

160 Catacomb of Priscilla: inscription, painted on a tile, of Aeliana (ICUR IX, 24896)

161 Catacomb of Priscilla: Greek inscription, painted on a tile, of Irene (ICUR IX, 26020b)

family name, fell progressively into disuse. This might have occurred because they had lost their distinct original function. Alternatively, they were abandoned because the main motive for specifying them in written texts gradually diminished with the evolution of society and the issuance of laws that extended citizenship to all residents within the confines of the empire (the *constitutio Antoniniana* of 211 A.D).

"Profane" and "Christian" names

From a close analysis of the mass of onomastic information recorded on Roman epitaphs, an initial point emerges which tends to discredit a rather widespread common belief. This is the fact that the Christians often continued to bear profane names, even of mythological origin that theoretically would seem to contradict their faith.

It is not difficult, therefore, to find in the catacombs gravestones on which the faithful are called Hermes, Hercules, Aphrodite, Apollo, Eros, Saturninus, Martial, Asclepiodotus, Athenodorus ("gift of Athena"), Achilles, Posidonius, Pentesilea (the Amazon queen), Isidorus ("gift of Isis", the Egyptian goddess), Aelius and other similar names (fig. 160)[52]. Among the many examples of this usage, it should suffice to mention that the older brother of S. Ambrose was called Satyrus! Evidently it was habit and fashion, more than etymology, that influenced similar choices. Other clergy members did not escape this usage, such as the priest Mercurius, later elected pope as John II in 533, namely, in the sixth century, when paganism had already been in decline for some time.

Although a considerable number of names reveal common usage, many can be traced back to a Greek or at any rate, Eastern origin[53]. In contrast, epithets of biblical origin (Maria, Susanna, John, Peter, Joseph, Judas)[54] did not occur with great frequency. Nor were names that could be defined as specifically Christian, connected with concepts of salvation, religious piety, resurrection and hope, very numerous.

Among the most common, however, one can cite *Agape* (which in Greek means "love"), *Irene* (peace) (fig. 161), *Anastasius* (alluding to the Resurrection), *Refrigerius* (that recalls the rite of the same name), *Martyrius, Benedictus, Spes, Renatus* ("born to new life"), *Quadragesima* (Lent), Πεν–τεκοστή (Pentecost), *Redemptus, Quodvultdeus* ("what God wills") (fig. 162), *Deogratias* ("thanks be to God"), *Adeodatus, Theodorus* ("gift of God"). The use of several of these epitaphs, of African origin, was probably fostered by the presence of immigrants from the other shore of the Mediterranean.

In addition, epigraphic documentation allows us to verify that, all things considered, the faithful named after the martyrs buried in the same cemeteries were not always numerous. The Catacomb of Cyriaca, the centre of the cult of the highly venerated deacon Laurentius, is an exception. Here gravestones have recorded some 3,000 Laurentius and about 15 Laurentia[55].

162 Catacomb of Priscilla: inscription with inset porphyry letters at the entrance to the double cubiculum of the martyr. Two freedmen dedicated the epitaph to their former owners, Teophilus *and* Pontiana; *one was named* Vitalius, *the other* Quodvuldeus *(!) meaning "as God wills" (a name of African origin) (ICUR X, 26460)*

157

Browsing through the onomastic indices of the collections of the Christian inscriptions of Rome, one encounters dozens of strange, curious, and often unique names[56]. Just as with pagan names, their origin can be traced back to different sources. One group is derived from good wishes (*Felix, Fortunatus, Fructuosus, Beneratus*), another from physical attributes (*Nigrinus, Albucius* ("rather white), *Rhodacilla* ("of red colour"). Other names evolved from the months of the year (*Ianuarius, Aprilis, December...*), from toponyms (*Afer, Syrus...*), or else from various animals, such as the bear, lion, ant, mouse, leopard, deer, swallow, dove and even the tench[57]. Still others are taken from affectionate epithets that evidently were created within the family, such as Cara or "Little One"[58]. The range of names is so heterogeneous that it is difficult to cite all the etymologies.

One last observation concerns the names of "barbarian" origin, namely, names that are neither Latin nor Greek, but, for example, Thracian, Vandal, Gothic or Longobardic. Taking into account that the chronological span of the majority of funerary dedications found in the catacombs spans the third to the fifth centuries (examples of later epigraphs are relatively limited), one can understand why such names were rather sporadic. For the most part, they appear in graffiti left by the pilgrims, who continued to visit the sanctuaries of martyrs through to the Carolingian period. Among the rare examples attested in epitaphs, one might note, from the cemetery of S. Valentino, *Herila*, a high Gothic official (*comes*), probably a converted Aryan, who could die "in peace with the Catholic faith"[59]. Alternatively, the Thracian *Valerius Dalat(ralis)* buried in the Catacomb of S. Felicita, is worthy of notice[60].

Humiliating names or nicknames

In Christian nomenclature, the so-called "humiliating names" or "shameful names" form a distinctive group. These names, when not defamatory, were sometimes used by some faithful as a life-long act of modesty, precisely because of their unpleasant significance[61]. Some refer to animals which generally had a negative connotation, such as the donkey (*Asellus*[62], *Asellica*[63], *Onager*[64]); others recorded vices or negative qualities, such as *Lascivus* (Lascivious), *Importunus* (Annoying)[65], *Fastidiosus* (Fastidious), *Calumniosus* (Liar), *Luxuriosus* (Lustful), *Iniuriosus* (Insulting), *Pannosus* (Tramp), or *Superbus* (Arrogant). For the last, an inscription from the Catacomb of Pretestato dated to 405 reads: "Here rests Superbus, called so only in name, whom the beatified saints recognised as meek and innocent; into this tomb his wretched father would have wished to precede him..."[66].

Other adjectives, of a shameful nature in themselves, may have been connected in certain cases with the social status of some of the faithful, who were abandoned when young and then taken in by Christian families as a charitable gesture. This is the case of *Proiectus* and *Proiecticus*, which meant "exposed" and the unpleasant *Stercorius*[67], with the Greek parallel *Coprion*[68] that can be understood as "abandoned in the garbage". Further proof of the phenomenon of the abandonment of minors comes from the large number of *alumni* or "adoptive children" recorded in the Christian epigraphy of Rome. At the Catacomb of Pretestato, one of them was in fact named *Stercorius*[69]. Among the many famous examples, one might note the example from the Catacomb of Domitilla of *Dativus*, the adoptive parent, who dedicated a gravestone to *Vitalia* "very sweet adoptive daughter"[70].

Nevertheless, "humiliating" names, if they were all really such, in the end lost their original meaning and ended up as a fashionable phenomenon. This shift is demonstrated by the fact that pagans, who certainly did not have any intention of this sort behind their use[71], also used several of them.

Another characteristic of Christian nomenclature, but whose use was not unknown to pagans, consists in the spread of nicknames or *signa*. These were short names added to the personal ones, that could be de-

163 Catacomb of
Priscilla: *monograms of*
Rusticus *and* Rufilla *on
the front panel of a frag-
mentary sarcophagus
(ICUR IX, 25791)*

rived from specific physical characteristics, or pet names given at an early age that later remained attached to the people, or simply diverse names chosen for unknown reasons[72].

It was once thought that at times these names were connected with a new name that could have been given at the time of Baptism, particularly if the believer was already an adult. But, if this had been a standard practice, surviving examples are in fact too infrequent. Therefore, it seems more logical to think of it simply as a practice followed by only a small percentage of the Christian community.

These nicknames normally came immediately after the true personal *cognomen*, to which were added expressions such as "also called" (*qui et vocatur*), "by name of" (*nomine*), "by the nickname of" (*signo*), "that is" (*id est, sive*). For example, in the Catacomb of Priscilla, a boy, who died at a little more than 5 years old, was called Marcellus, but was nicknamed *Exsuperius*[73]. In the Catacomb of Pretestato, Valeria Calliope was known as *Anucella*[74], that is, "old lady", probably due to her facial features, which resembled an old woman. A believer, who exceptionally already had three names, *Marcia Augurina Maria*, also had the final nickname, *Carite*[75]; *Iulius [Sab]inus* was also known by the unique name of *Abenna*[76].

159

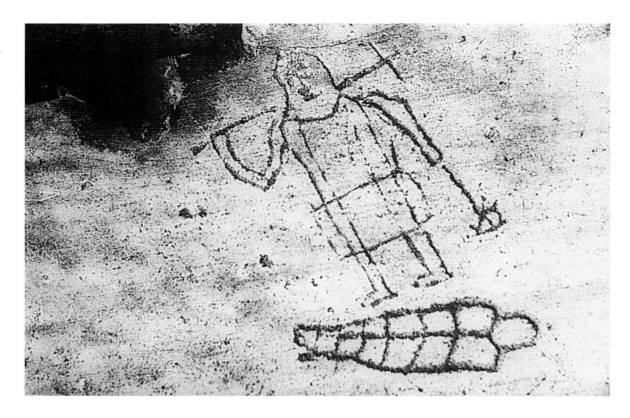

164 Catacomb of Commodilla: incised slab with a representation of a fossor and a body ready for burial (ICUR II, 6446)

Monograms

Monograms were found not only in cult buildings, where they normally recorded prosperous donors or popes or bishops who were very generous builders (or else rebuilders), but also sometimes in catacomb inscriptions. The most famous of these interwoven letters, within which a name was generally hidden, is the Christological one in its two most popular forms, the Cross with a looped rho, and that with a chi-rho[77]. But some faithful also indicated in this way their own identity as a result of personal habit. Unfortunately, in many cases, the decipherment of these initials remains problematic or at least open to different interpretations. In fact, one can never be certain of which was the initial letter or how many times single letters were repeated within the word. In addition, different names contained the same letters; therefore the possible solutions can be multiple.

For example, in the mausoleum annexed to the Basilica of S. Silvestro above the cemetery of Priscilla, a fragmentary sarcophagus lid displays only two monograms within the *tabula* for the inscription. Fortunately, they can be resolved with ease: on the left *Rusticus* and on the right *Rufilla* (fig. 163)[78]. On another mutilated gravestone from the same funerary area, in contrast, a symbol appears in which the letters E, S and perhaps L can be recognised, but in this case it has not yet been possible to propose a likely reading[79].

4. CHRISTIAN SOCIETY AND FUNERARY INSCRIPTIONS

A particularly precious element for the reconstruction of the composition of Early Christian communities consists of the daily activity carried out by the deceased during their lifetimes, since work was considered an essential component of the life of the faithful, a true social obligation. If, on the one hand, it was considered proper to help those who had insufficient means for survival, on the other, those who sank into idleness out of laziness or who idly awaited the charity of others were condemned[80].

Accordingly, it is not strange that references to occupations were inserted into funerary inscriptions, even though, compared to the high number of Roman epigraphs, these specifications occur in only a minimal percentage of the texts[81]. Nevertheless, when they do appear, they allow us to understand better the diverse components of ancient Christian society, where members of the most elevated as well as the most humble classes merged. They found rest, one beside the other, in the catacombs. In general, there were no clear hierarchical distinctions based on wealth, rather, they were united by one faith. Sometimes, however, the use of rather generic terms leaves doubts as to the exact roles that they fulfilled[82].

165 Catacomb of Priscilla: inscription of the milkman Pomponius Felix, *who bought the tomb for himself and his wife* Marcia *while he was still alive (ICUR IX, 25435)*

Incised representations

These representations are found particularly from the mid-fourth century onwards; they occur rather rarely in earlier periods. In addition to explicit references in the formulae, in several examples, knowledge of the activities carried out by Christians can also be discerned from the images incised on the gravestones, which represent the faithful busy at work or the tools of their trade. Thus, dozens of wine barrels[83], balances[84], chisels[85], axes, spindles[86], compasses, modii (unit of measurement for grain)[87], hammers[88], scissors and musical instruments[89] appear on Roman funerary slabs.

In an example from the Catacomb of Pretestato on Via Appia, a gravestone without a written inscription is incised with an orderly representation of surgical instruments, including scalpels, pliers or forceps (to extract teeth), spoons, a cupping glass (for blood-letting) and probes[90]. Next to a fragmentary Greek inscription, most probably belonging to a doctor/dentist, now in the cloister of the Basilica of S. Lorenzo fuori le mura, a pair of pliers holding an extracted molar is represented[91].

Vivacious and immediate, even though of rather shoddy quality, is the slab in the Catacomb of Domitilla on which *Constantius* is represented with his two pack horses, Barbarus and Germanus (to whom he must have been particularly attached)[92]. In the Catacomb of Commodilla, a roughly incised image depicts a *fossor* with a lamp in his hand and the *dolabra* (a sort of pick) on his shoulders, next to a dead body tightly wrapped in bandages and already prepared for burial (fig. 164)[93]. A gravestone in the Museo Pio Cristiano depicts a blacksmith forging a metal object on the anvil while stirring up the fire with bellows[94]. Less well known is an incised slab from the cemetery of Aproniano[95], on which a lumberjack seems to be identifiable. He is carrying a small bundle of cut wood, probably in the act of delivering them to a client; on the left appears a tree with large leaves.

Occupations and professions in the texts

The heterogeneity of the categories of occupations attested in the written texts has already been stressed. Amongst these, it is worth mentioning just a few examples included within the diverse sectors of human activity performed by the faithful in Rome. A

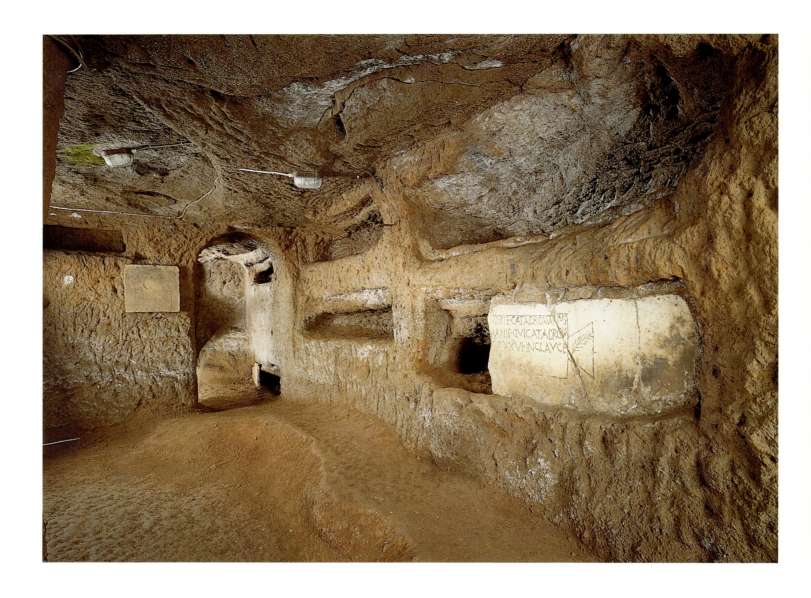

substantial group dedicated themselves to commerce or to small handicrafts. The sale of food products is amply documented by bakers[96] and pastry makers[97], butchers[98], salami vendors[99], fruit and vegetable grocers. The names of two milkmen can also be cited: one, *Pomponius Felix*, from the Catacomb of Priscilla[100] (fig. 165), and the other, *Quintus*, who was resident in the area of the Lateran and buried in the Catacomb of Pretestato[101].

Craftsmen are abundantly represented; examples include makers of nails[102], marble workers[103], engravers of gems and hard stones, glassmakers[104] and barbers[105]. At Commodilla, the inscription of *Olimpius*, an *elefantarius*, who probably worked and sold ivory objects, has been found[106]. Specialised craftsmen who were assigned a variety of tasks, from the sculpting of sarcophagi and decorative elements in cult buildings, to the incision of inscriptions, merit a separate discussion. An interesting example connected to the latter is depicted on a gravestone, now in the Museo Archeologico in Urbino, but originally from the Catacomb of SS. Marcellino e Pietro in Rome. Beneath the text, it contains the representation, so far unique, of a craftsman (Εὔτροπος) in his workshop, intent on sculpting a sarcophagus, probably helped by his son[107].

In the vast epigraphic repertoire of inscriptions, bricklayers, cleaners, dyers, seamstresses, shoemakers and cobblers are also present. Among the professionals and public officials are found many doctors and veterinarians[108], lawyers, notaries[109], stenographers[110], couriers[111], teachers[112] and clerks of grain administration[113]. As proof of the heterogeneity of Christian society, attestations also occur of famous individuals who held important roles in public administration or were of aristocratic families[114]. These included imperial clerks, senators, consuls, municipal judges and provincial officials. Among the most famous can be enumerated the senator *Iunius*, buried in 494[115] and the urban prefect, *Iunius Bassus*. The latter died in 359 and as a neophyte was buried in the magnificent sarcophagus decorated with biblical scenes (now in the Vatican Grottoes), that is the best-known example of Early Christian sculpture[116].

In the epigraphic documentation, not even the military are lacking; they belong to diverse specialities and every rank, including praetorians (the corps was disbanded by Constantine)[117], cavalry and *equites singulares*[118]. Thus, a rather widespread belief is discredited, that military service was prohibited to the faithful in the pre-Constantinian period[119].

Christians and the world of performance

Among the occupations explicitly recorded in written texts, jobs connected with the world of performance are sometimes also found. This might arouse surprise, since the rigorous position expressed by some Church Fathers in this regard is well known. In particular, Tertullian, in his work, *De spectaculis,* condemned not only those faithful who directly participated in the circus or theatre displays, but also all those present[120]. It was necessary to stay far away from these environments in which perversions and idolatric superstitions reigned and within which even Christians could not have preserved their pureness of spirit and body. All forms of spectacle, therefore, had to be forbidden to the faithful.

Attitudes similar to those of Tertullian were also expressed by other Church Fathers such as Origen, S. John Chrysostom and S. Augustine. Indeed, Augustine stressed the immorality and turmoil that a circus or theatre spectacle could exert on the conscience[121].

In contrast with this resolute position of the Church Fathers, it is known, however, that circus spectacles had a long life; even in the sixth century they were held regularly. Thus, a papyrus from Oxyrhynchus describes a programme of games, with chariot races, parades, singers, dancers, a gazelle chased by dogs, mimes and a group of athletes[122].

Roman epigraphic evidence provides further proof in this regard, attesting that some faithful calmly carried out activity connected with the world of performance. Therefore, one must conclude that in reality these jobs were not always prohibited to Christians, or at least not everywhere, or at least those that were not contrary to moral values or that did not involve violence.

Thus, a pantomime is represented on a mutilated gravestone at S. Paolo[123]; *Felix*, buried at Cyriaca, was probably an instructor of gladiators (*doctor*)[124]; *Eros* was a *pammusus gymnicus*, namely, an expert gymnast[125]. In addition, a now lost gravestone from S. Paolo fuori le mura referred to the charioteer *Eutumius*[126], and an acrobat (*catadromarius*) is recorded in a dedication (whose nature, nevertheless, has been questioned) at S. Sebastiano[127] (fig. 166).

Perhaps the best-known and most interesting example of a Christian involved in the world of performance is, however, that of *Vitalis*, a mime and impersonator who achieved great fame in the fifth century[128]. Only thirteen fragments have survived of his grandiose funerary verse stele, originally placed to cover a tomb in the floor of the Basilica of S. Sebastiano, but it can be completely reconstructed, since it was transmitted by Medieval syllogisms[129].

The very lively text reveals the great talent of this unique and extremely versatile individual[130]. Always happy, his presence alone was sufficient to chase away sadness or anger, making those present laugh. An excellent imitator, *Vitalis* changed voices and attitudes, "in such a way that you would have believed that from one single mouth many spoke"[131]. He was so good, in fact, as to be more credible and faithful to the originals than the individuals that he imitated. His speciality was female figures, who blushed when they saw how he imitated them. *Vitalis'* only regret was that most of those whom he had personified had suddenly vanished with his death and he ends by saying, "I beg you to read this (inscription) on my tomb mercifully! Say, mourning: how happy you were, Vitalis! May there be happy days for you now too!"[132].

It has been observed that the dedication, in itself, has a practically neutral formula, except for the final reference, which can be interpreted in the Christian sense. Yet, it must not be forgotten that in this late period such characteristics were rather common.

Women and work

Roman inscriptions also serve to confirm another interesting fact, namely, the presence in various communities of women engaged in diverse productive activities. Even though not extremely numerous, nevertheless, these examples refer to a rather extended range of occupations and professions, sometimes also of importance. One can note several saleswomen, such as the merchant of oil (*oliaria*), *Felicissima*[133] or *Pollecla – quae ordeu(m) bendet de bia Nova –* of wheat, both from the Catacomb of Domitilla[134]. *Ursa*, who was buried in the Catacomb of Commodilla, sold fruit[135]; *Leontia* was a *lagunara*, that is, she sold bottles (or fritters, according to another in-

terpretation)[136] at the Porta Trigemina of the Republican walls. One can also mention a "seller of food of long conservation" named *Aul(ia) Hilaritas*, whose memorial is attached to that of her husband, who carried out the same activity at the praetorian camp[137]; *Vincentia*, a goldsmith (*aurinetrix*) or more precisely "responsible for the manufacture of gold thread"[138], was buried at S. Callisto[139]; a worker *Bictora*, who loved the poor, died in 341[140].

From a comprehensive analysis of Christian epigraphy in Rome with allusions to occupations and professions, specific formulae connected to a type of occupation that was strictly Christian or at least new compared to the pagan world, have not normally emerged. The allusions are usually limited to a mere reference, or else to the representation of either the deceased at work or only the tools he commonly used when alive. No mention is made to exalt the dignity of work, intended as participation in the divine creative activity. Rather, work appears only as a necessity of life, as opposed to idleness, which the faithful should avoid. On the other hand, even the literary sources do not offer much information in this regard[141].

Only infrequently does one encounter noteworthy expressions that could, however, apply to a pagan text as well. For example, it is said of a doctor at S. Sebastiano that he was always a friend and dear to everyone, ingenious, prudent, not selfish towards the poor, and esteemed for his merit by all[142].

5. THE CLERGY

The oldest securely datable inscription that refers to a member of the Roman clergy is that of Pope Anterus, who died in 236 and was buried in the Crypt of the Popes in the Catacomb of S. Callisto[143].

As with other elements that only appear gradually, at first sporadically and then with greater frequency, in formulae, references to

ecclesiastical ranks spread from the fourth century onwards, not only in epitaphs but also in votive and dedicatory texts[144]. These inscriptions provide a rather broad range documentation for all the diverse functions of the clergy. Both bishops, priests, deacons, who constituted the so-called "major orders" as well as sub-deacons, lectors, exorcists, acolytes, cantors, ostiaries, who constituted the so-called "minor orders" are included.

According to a generally accepted theory, until the fifth century, the *fossores* also belonged to the clergy. It was they, who, in addition to actually digging the galleries of the catacombs, sometimes decorated the interiors, incised the gravestones and managed the sales of the tombs[145].

While in the early centuries, monks were commonly assimilated with lay people, later a certain number of them were included within the Church hierarchy. From the third century onwards, such a vocation was precluded to those exercising activities considered little suitable to the ministry. Up until the fourth century, a precise norm regarding the celibacy of clergy members must not have existed, since in several inscriptions they were recorded as married. These documents are not surprising since it is known that orig-

167 Catacomb of S. Callisto: inscription of the deacon Severus, *incised on a transenna, in which the term p(a)p(a) appears for the first time, here applied to Marcellinus (296–204) (ICUR IV, 10183)*

165

inally even the highest ranks of the clergy could be chosen from among lay people, and therefore those already married. This usage was later modified and more definite and regular requisites were progressively instituted[146].

Popes and bishops

Turning to ancient inscriptions of the popes, these were designated as "bishops", although the person who held the Roman post was considered the bishop "par excellence" of the Primate Roman See. This designation persisted for a long time, until around 304 when the first known example of the use of the term of Egyptian origin, "Papa" (father), occurs (fig. 167)[147]. In fact, it appears in an abbreviated form with a double P in a long inscription, also important from the dogmatic point of view. It was incised on a marble *transenna* reused by the deacon Severus, "through the inspiration of his Pope Marcellinus"[148]. Nevertheless, popes were sometimes also designated with the term *antistes*, literally, "high priest"[149].

At Rome, bishops from other dioceses are also attested, who died by chance during their stay or exile in the city, as in the case of Bishop Urbanus at S. Callisto[150]. Cemeteries under the authority of the suburban dioceses are different matters. The Catacomb of S. Alessandro on Via Nomentana in which the Bishop Adeodatus is remembered is one example[151].

An analysis of the epigraphic material reveals that some clergy members also carried out other activities in addition to their ministry. One need only recall the inscription at S. Callisto, still *in situ*, concerning "Dionysios, doctor and priest"[152]. This aspect has been considered only marginally until now[153], but it deserves to be re-examined, also in light of the concept of work in Early Christian society and the function of the clergy.

Sometimes a precious element was added to the qualifications of the numerous priests documented in Roman inscriptions, namely, the *titulus* to which these priests belonged[154]. Such is the case of *Basilius*, who carried out his ministry at S. Sabina[155], or his colleague of the "titulus" of Lucina whose name has been lost[156].

It is known that there was a college of seven deacons, the coadjutors of the pope, which was active at Rome for a long time. The first of these was designated in an inscription as "the first in the order of the Levites"[157]. Concerning the minor ranks, several inscriptions connected to exorcists can be pointed out, such as the two from the Catacomb *ad Decimum* near Grottaferrata. The first is of Faustus[158]; the second of *Proficius*, a lector and an exorcist[159], who dedicated the epitaph to his dead wife.

Widows and Consecrated Virgins

Inscriptions also transmit a record of other functions, not strictly pertinent to the ecclesiastical hierarchy but carried out within the organisation of the individual communities. For example, a rather ample documentation exists for widows. Within the Church, these women constituted a category with well-defined duties of a charitable nature. Widows could live within a community, under the direction of one of them, in a sort of monastic regime[160].

From the epigraphic evidence, no certain proof has emerged that they were consecrated persons, since they are only designated by the term "widow"[161]. Nevertheless, precisely the obviousness with which this epithet was indicated, even in very concise texts, may suggest that these faithful somehow lent their services to the community. Alternatively, the term may have been intended to emphasise their choice to remain widows, as a sign of their absolute fidelity to a single husband[162].

Among the Roman examples, one can cite that of *Prima*, a widow who died when she was over 100 years old and was buried at S. Ermete[163], and that of *Germana* at Panfilo[164]. The epitaphs of two other faithful that stress their widowhood, all datable to

the third century, also belong to this catacomb[165].

Regarding female monasticism, on the other hand, the term "virgin" (*virgo*, παρθένος) frequently occurs in inscriptions. With reasonable probability, it refers to consecrated people only, since it speaks explicitly of *virgines sacrae* or *virgines Dei*[166]. It is necessary, however, to wait until the fifth to sixth centuries to find explicit allusions to monasteries, the first of which probably appeared in Rome towards the end of the fourth century[167].

Among the occupations carried out within the Christian communities, one can mention again the *cubicularii*, instituted in Rome by S. Leo the Great for the care of the sacred relics of the Basilicas of SS. Pietro e Paolo[168]. Some believe that such a qualification could have been extended to other martyrs' sanctuaries[169], but this remains controversial[170].

6. The Transformation of Language

As had already been anticipated, Early Christian funerary texts display significant signs of the evolution of Latin and Greek from the third to the fourth centuries, as well as errors due to the distraction or ignorance of the stone carver responsible for transcription of the funerary dedication. Accordingly, it has recently been argued that Christian epigraphy is "a source of absolute importance" for the study of linguistic issues[171]. Sometimes the errors were somehow corrected, by inserting a forgotten letter between those already incised or by trying to erase that which was erroneously incised. Many other times, however, this did not happen, suggesting that not even the commissioners were educated enough to point out imperfections or solecisms to the craftsmen who had made the mistakes.

168 Catacomb of S. Sebastiano: transliterated inscription, written in Latin with Greek letters, of Siricus with a wish for peace. The incised representation shows the dead youth already as an orant figure in eternal beatitude (ICUR V, 13214)

169 Catacomb of S. Sebastiano: inscription of Bincentia, *a late form of Vincentia, flanked by an incised Christogram, a basket (probably filled with bread) and a dove holding an olive branch in his beak*

venemerenti) (fig. 169), the dropping of the nasals *m-n* at the end of the word *(annu, mecu, nove...)* and the metathesis between the dark vowels *o-u (cumpari, filiu...)*, or between *i-e (diposita, fecet, dilictae...)*. The same is true for Greek regarding the abridgement of diphthongs ει and αι to ι (κῖτε) or for the substitution of η for ι (θικι). At other times, some verbal forms were so distorted by the spoken language that they became almost unrecognisable. For example, this is the case of *quiescit*, "rest", which could be altered to *quesquest, cesquit*[174] or *cesquet*.

The presence of some forms which reflect pronunciation already similar to vulgate Italian is also documented. For example, the epitaph of *Apricla*, who *vissit annos deceotto in decenobem* (instead of *vixit annos duodeviginti in undeviginti*), that is, "lived 18 years (adding almost) to 19"[175]. Alternatively, in the gravestone of *Donmnula (!)*, who lived perhaps 5 years and *meses otto* (for *menses octo*), the numeral is already the Italian "otto"[176].

Finally, the contribution of Christian inscriptions to neologisms is also noteworthy, as proven by the publication a few years ago of a volume that contains hundreds of additions to the first four letters of the alphabet of the *Thesaurus Linguae Latinae*, derived from epigraphic texts[177]. Only among the names (family and cognomens), more than three hundred unedited names were added and many others were already included in the prestigious lexicon. This provides further proof of the great value of these inscriptions for a better understanding of the slow transformation of Classical languages in the late Antique period. Thus far, however, this aspect has been treated only marginally or in rather limited samples[178].

The forthcoming final publication of the edition of *the Inscriptiones Christianae Urbis Romae* and the preparation of complete indices of the series[179] will allow scholars to have at their disposition extremely useful material for this type of research.

It must be remembered that, until the period of Pope Damasus, Greek was the official language of the Roman liturgy and was the second language spoken in Rome, especially by foreigners and immigrants from the East. It is not surprising therefore to find thousands of catacomb inscriptions written in this language. The curious phenomenon of transliterated texts, that is, texts written in Latin with the Greek alphabet, is also tied to the widespread diffusion of Greek and bilingualism[172]. This was obviously due to commissioners (and to craftsmen) who knew only Greek and who tried to adopt the sounds to the Latin they had learned in Rome[173] (fig. 168).

An analysis of the inscriptions, nevertheless, does not always allow us to determine whether these phenomena were the result of the distraction or limited level of literacy of the craftsmen, or whether they were a reflection of the spoken language. Doubts do not exist for other well-documented examples, such as, the monophthong in place of the diphthong *ae* in Latin (*caste femine, Donate, pientissime...*), the interchange of the labials *b-v (bixit, bibas,*

7. Affection and Sentiments

Through funerary inscriptions, one can ideally penetrate into the Christian communities and gather some fresh details that reveal sentiments and aspects of the family life of couples, children, parents and friends. In contrast, the literary sources cannot do more than provide very scanty evidence concerning these elements, and that, only indirectly, since the documentation is mediated through the interpretations of their authors. These represent details of apparently little significance. Yet, they demonstrate the intensity of affection, human pain and grief for the loss of dear ones, even though tempered by the comfort of faith, and the values of certain virtues exercised by the deceased during their lifetimes. In other words, they reveal some aspects of Christian ideals, experienced daily by the faithful and expressed through concise and incisive formulae.

Relationships between spouses

Some general observations can also be deduced from the diversity of expressions used to describe matrimony. In the inscriptions, spouses emphasised their harmonious relationships, experienced serenely without squabbles or any conflicts. These concepts recurred with a certain frequency in formulae, expressed in various ways: "without any discord"[180], "without blame and with every tenderness"[181], "without rage"[182], "without bitterness"[183], "without any complaints" ...[184]. These are some of the more popular ways to exalt the perfect success of marriage[185].

Spouses, then, praised their mutual positive qualities with gratitude. The eulogies of husbands most often praise wives for their sanctity[186], the simplicity of their habits[187], prudence[188] and diligence[189]. Wives praise their deceased husbands for their meek-

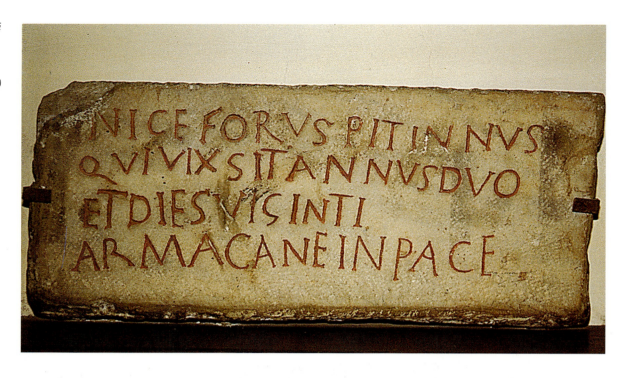

ness[190], affability[191], sweetness towards everyone[192], moral integrity[193], goodness, innocence[194] and integrity from every vice[195].

However, in these inscriptions relative to spouses, most often the formulae appear somewhat stereotyped or summary. In addition to the age of the deceased spouse, often scrupulously annotated down to the day and sometimes the hours lived, only generic attributes such as "worthy" or "remembered well" or wishes such as "rest in peace" can be added.

Moreover, not infrequently, the duration of the marriage is mentioned, an element that, combined with indications of the length of the life of the deceased, makes it possible to date the age at which the marriage was celebrated, sometimes with great precision[196]. In the presence of a homogeneous group of these facts, it has also been possible to perform statistical analyses that reveal that women married quite early (14–20 years of age), while men were distributed in a broader range, between the age of 20 and 30[197].

Parents and children

Probably however, this dearth of fantasy or inventiveness is due to the existence in the stone-cutters' workshops of manuals for the use of clients, who were often satisfied with the formulae of the repertoire that could express nothing more than a simple lament. Many references to family life are nevertheless expressed between the lines of diverse epitaphs. These reveal that affection, virtue, orderliness and morality were seen as important values in these early communities. The sense of friendship and fraternity appear almost as distinctive traits of inscriptions dedicated to men. To be amiable meant to be serene, of loyal character and helpful towards one's neighbour, all virtues that corresponded fully to Christian ideals[198].

In contrast, inscriptions dedicated to mothers expressed their love, chastity, industriousness, tenderness, and goodness as well as the gratitude of their children towards them in particular. Echoes of profound grief are found in texts dedicated by the parents of deceased children who often died at an early age, thus confirming the high incidence of infant mortality in the late Antique period (fig. 170). The affection and grief of these parents also led them to record exactly the duration of the brief lives of their dear ones. Thus, an inscription from S. Sebastiano speaks of *Libera* "who lived three years and two days, having been born on Thursday, 17 April, the twelfth day of the lunar cycle, and who died on Wednesday, 18 April, in the sixth hour of the night"[199].

Another piece of information that occurs relatively frequently is reference to the virtues of children, both young and old. For example, one inscription reads: "To *Dalmatius*, a very sweet son, full of genius and common sense, whom his unfortunate father could not enjoy for 7 whole years; a boy who studying Greek as well as Latin learned it quickly and in three days was snatched from life"[200].

Candour, goodness and intelligence were other virtues celebrated by parents (fig. 171). In every case, one notes that the attitude of the epitaphs was generally serene and indicated family relations based on widespread harmony. In addition to parents, children and spouses who dedicated epitaphs to each another, other relatives are also found, especially brothers and sisters, who demonstrated close affection for each other even in moments of grief.

In other cases, the dedicators were the grandparents. Often, married children went to live with their parents or in-laws, who behaved generously towards their grandchildren. Stepfathers, stepsons and stepdaughters, sisters-in-law, uncles and aunts as well as cousins are mentioned more rarely. For example, an inscription painted in red in the *Cappella Graeca* of Priscilla records *Palladius*, cousin and companion of *Obrimus*[201]; a stepfather, *Vitalis*, dedicated an epitaph to his stepdaughter *Victoria* in the Catacomb of Cyriaca[202].

In many Christian epitaphs mention is made of *alumni* and *alumnae*[203], but for the most part the term is not used in the sense of "scholar" but rather "adoptive child"[204]. It referred to abandoned children who were taken in by Christian families and brought up at home. Many of them must have died at

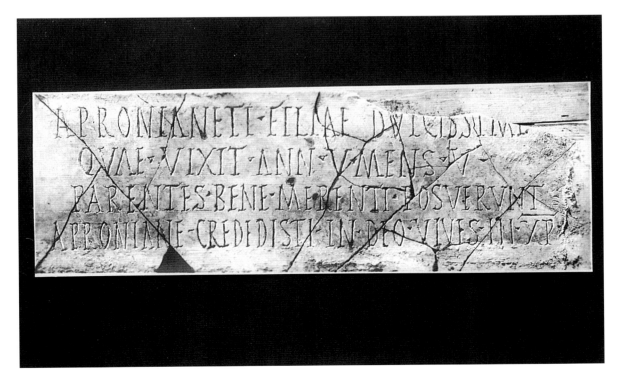

172 Catacomb of Panfilo: *inscription of Aproniane, who died when she was 5 years and five months old, with the closing formula "you believed in God, you will live in Christ!" (ICUR X, 26329)*

a tender age as a result of their precarious health or the difficulties they had undergone. The numerous tombs of small dimensions found in Roman cemeteries that lack inscriptions probably are to be connected with the charity of the faithful, who provided burial for those small children who had not survived. In a single gallery of the Catacomb of Panfilo, out of a total of 111 burials, 83 were of children and only 5 of these had epitaphs[205].

8. Faith and Religious Piety

"Here lies Quintilian, a man of God, a firm believer in the Trinity, who loved chastity and rejected the allurements of the world..." Thus reads a Roman inscription, unfortunately now lost, that is dated to 403[206]. An echo of this epitaph is found in the similar funerary dedication from the Catacomb of S. Sebastiano[207] of an Imperial Armenian official, *Edesius* "who believed in the Father, Son and Holy Spirit; he lived 25 years and rested in peace, 30 September". In the cemetery of Domitilla[208], one again finds reference to a believer "who believed in Jesus Christ, together with the Father, Son and Holy Spirit".

Those just mentioned are only a few of the numerous and heterogeneous examples of expressions, recurrent in funerary formulae, which reveal the sentiments of profound religious piety that the faithful experienced during these early centuries of Christianity and of which Roman epigraphy offers precious documentation. Brief but efficient phrases, as only the lapidary style could create, often reveal original and genuine sentiments. These certainly do not derive from the stereotypic models already available in the stone carvers' workshops. Nor should they be attributed to the clergy, who certainly had a greater theological background.

Rather, in the majority of cases, it was the simple faithful, even if of limited culture, who commissioned often mediocre craftsmen to incise these texts with a profound intrinsic content. They wished to proclaim some fundamental principles of their doctrine, especially those relative to the dogmas and spiritual values of the sacraments, and Baptism in particular.

Dogmas and sacraments

The concepts that occur with the greatest frequency refer to the Resurrection of the flesh, the coming of the celestial reign, the affirmation of the Oneness and the Trinity of God, and faith in Christ, whose divinity and salvation of mankind are proclaimed. It should suffice to think of the famous acrostic, $IX\Theta Y\Sigma$, that appeared extremely early in Christian inscriptions. The latter, in addition to the literal sense of the Greek word (fish), also represented for the faithful the confirmation that Jesus Christ was truly the Son of God and Saviour of mankind.

Undoubtedly, scanning the many thousands of funerary inscriptions found in Rome, one encounters numerous expressions that can be defined as "dogmatic", or that can be traced back in some way to the spirituality of the faithful of the first centuries. However, it should also be remembered that, in relation to the enormous quantity of epitaphs known, the inscriptions of religious character represent only a minority[209]. It is also relevant that they are largely datable to the Constantinian and later periods, when the formulae display a greater complexity and richness of content.

Sometimes, it was preferred to have recourse to the Bible to remind the faithful of fundamental concepts. Strangely, these citations are very rare in Rome; in contrast, they were rather widespread in many regions of the ancient Christian world, and especially in the East[210].

On numerous other occasions, however, it was the faithful themselves who drafted phrases that still impress the reader with their profoundness and simplicity of expression. Thus, a crystalline faith emerges from an epitaph that closed a grave on the pavement of a gallery on the first floor of the Catacomb of Priscilla[211]. It reads: "Here I rest, free from all anxiety. What I awaited has happened: when the coming of Christ occurs, I shall rise in peace". This believer expresses belief in the Resurrection and the anticipation of death as a moment of passage to a new life in a truly persuasive manner. His name was *Discolius*, a boy (*puer*), who was evidently ill for some time.

Aside from any other considerations, it also represents a typical case in which the poor quality of the writing contrasts with the richness of the content. Another beautiful expression comes to mind, that appeared on a gravestone, now lost, from Via Latina[212], of a priest named *Tigrinus*. He proclaims "I was kidnapped by the sweetness of the celestial kingdom".

The faith of the deceased is naturally matched by that of the surviving relatives, although they were afflicted by the loss of their loved ones. For example, in one funerary text, a father affirms that his child was "called by the angels"[213]; another addressed to the child *Magus* says "How happily the Mother Church will welcome you upon your return from this world!"[214]. Again, of the baby *Apronianus*, who died at the age of one year, nine months and five days[215], it is recorded that "much loved by his grandmother, when she saw that he was destined to die, she prayed to the Church that he might leave life on earth as a believer (baptised)".

In other cases, Christian acceptance of divine will emerges most clearly. For example, on a fragmentary gravestone from the Roman cemetery of S. Pancrazio[216], dated to 402, the text reads: "The Lord has given, the Lord has taken away". These words are quoted from the Book of Job (1,21), that suited these tragic circumstances extremely well.

It was a source of comfort for those remaining behind to entrust their loved ones to divine mercy, as can be seen in an inscription from a tomb in the Catacomb of Priscilla[217]. "Father of all, You had created them and (now) You welcome Irene, Zoe, and Marcellus. Glory to You in Christ!". Those who believed would certainly obtain salvation, as

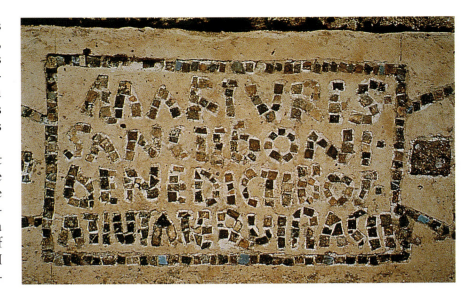

recall the parents of little *Aproniane*, who died at five years and five months old and was buried in the cemetery of Panfilo[218]. "*Aproniane*, you believed in God, you will live in Christ!" (fig. 172).

Wishes and prayers

A substantial number of epitaphs contain wishes and prayers. These document the close connection between the deceased and surviving relatives as well as profound faith in the communion of the saints, the value of prayers of the living for the deceased and vice versa.

The most common wish is certainly that of peace, that is, of life with the Lord in paradise, of participating in the heavenly banquet, the *refrigerium* of the chosen souls. Thus, in the catacombs, one often reads: "May the Lord grant the *refrigerium* to your soul" or "for his *refrigerium*". Thus, a graffito on a *loculus* in the cemetery of S. Croce prays: "Narcissus, may God grant you the *refrigerium*"[219].

As shall be seen, the martyrs could also intercede for the deceased devoted to them. For example, a believer buried in the cemetery of Panfilo addresses an invocation to them in rather late and corrupt Latin: "Martyrs, saintly, good and blessed, help Cyriacus!"[220] (fig. 173).

173 Catacomb of Panfilo: mosaic inscription of Cyriacus that invokes the help of the "saintly, good, and blessed martyrs" (ICUR X, 26350)

Prayer and remembrance

In various examples, the living ask their deceased loved ones to intervene in their favour: "pray for your parents"[221]; "Dear, remember me"[222]; "Marina, remember us both"[223]. At other times, the deceased addresses those who read the inscription, imploring them to remember him. Thus, the second part of the famous *carmen* of *Agape* in the Catacomb of Priscilla says: "I implore you, brothers, to pray whenever you come here and to invoke the Father and Son in all your prayers so that they might save *Agape* forever"[224]. In the same cemetery, another believer swears: "In the name of eternal hope (that is, of eternal life) you who read this, remember Epithetus!"[225].

Undoubtedly, the examples just cited differ considerably from the requests sometimes inserted in pagan inscriptions, in which only a greeting was addressed to the passer-by (*ave, salve*). In these pagan inscriptions, the deceased sometimes asked to be remembered, but naturally without spiritual implications, other than the concept expressed by Horace, according to whom the aspiration was "not to die completely", but to live at least in the memory of others.

The grace of Baptism

The great strength of the faithful rested in Baptism, in which the old man died and was reborn as a new man. Allusions to this sacrament, the source of new light and the moment of rebirth to spiritual life, could not fail to appear in funerary inscriptions. Thus, in the Catacomb of Marco e Marcelliano, the gravestone of *Julia*, born in Rome, addressed its reader in a very original and vivid manner: "now that I have received divine Grace (Baptism), I shall be welcomed in peace as a neophyte"[226]. Similarly, a beautiful expression is found in the inscription of the neophyte *Marcianus*, who was buried in the Roman cemetery of Ponziano: "The skies open for you. May you live in peace." The text is eloquently preceded by the Christological symbol of the fish[227].

Very important in this respect is another funerary inscription of less certain origin: "Here lies *Herculia*, purified by the holy waters, who recently was reborn in God and lives forever in eternity. This is due to her faith, her merits, her very pure life; walking on the saintly path, she has reached the kingdom of heaven"[228]. In the Catacomb of Priscilla, the inscription of little *Tyche*, who lived one year, 10 months and 15 days, records that she died on the very day on which she received Baptism[229].

Therefore, an analysis of funerary formulae clearly reveals a strict relationship between Baptism (sometimes received just before death) and entrance into paradise, as correctly stressed by Father Janssens[230]. Baptism not only allowed a man to be reborn in God, but also purified him from every guilt or sin. This rapid survey can be concluded with mention of the funerary dedication of *Restutus* in the Catacomb of Priscilla[231]. "I have become faithful in worldly death, in fact I am left with life in heaven... Here rests my body, but I live in the celestial ether, at the feet of the Lord, distinguished by the gift of Christ". One might add to this the verse inscription of the high-level Imperial official *Probus*[232]. "He lives beatified in the eternal dwelling place of paradise, who dying has put on the beautiful clothes of the celestial gift".

Finally, some significant information on catechumens can also be obtained from Roman funerary inscriptions. These, although they had not received the sacrament of Baptism before their death, were evidently considered members of the community of faithful among whom they were buried. All the inscriptions that refer to them date to the fourth century, a period in which the structures of the catechumenate had already been defined[233]. For example, *Viktor*, buried as a catechumen in the Catacomb of S. Ippolito, proclaims himself "servant of the Lord Jesus Christ"[234].

9. THE CULT OF THE MARTYRS IN FUNERARY INSCRIPTIONS

Multiple relationships between Christian inscriptions and the cult of the martyrs are to be expected given the devotion of the

HICCONGESTAIACE... ...VAE... ISSITVRBAPIORVM
CORPORASANCTOR... R... TIN... NVENERANDASEPVLC...
SVB... TMESANIMASRAPVITSIBIREGIACAELI
HICCOM... ESXYSTIPORTANTQVIEXHOSTE... OPAEA
HICNVMER... SPROCERV... SERVATQVIALTARI... XTI
HICPOSITVSLONGAVIXITQVIINPACESACERDOS
HICCONFESSORESSANCTIQVOSGRAECIA... ISIT
HIC... VENESPVERIQ SENE... ...SIQVENT... TES...
QVISMAGVIR... NE... MPTAC... ...T... V... REM
HICFATEORDAMASVS... OLVI... ...NE... EMBRA
...D... ...N... ...NE... ANCTOS... ...IORVM

174 Catacomb of S. Callisto: Crypt of the Popes, poem composed by Pope Damasus in honour of the martyrs of the complex of S. Callisto

faithful. Their strength of their devotion was such that it made them desire to rest in peace as close as possible to venerated tombs or led them to make long and difficult journeys to see the tombs of these witnesses to the faith.

An analysis of Roman dedications offers various insights on this subject, beginning with the poor pre-Constantinian epitaphs, followed by the famous epigrams of Pope Damasus and finally ending with humble graffiti. It was Pope Damascus who first worked to foster and expand the cult of the martyrs, commissioning the incision of what are still considered to be the most beautiful Christian inscriptions. Although their meaning was often complex, these inscriptions are extremely valuable for their references and allusions to the actual people buried in a specific catacomb. Undoubtedly, the documentation is heterogeneous, but precious in many ways, not infrequently also from the hagiographic point of view.

Epitaphs of martyrs

Occasionally, one has the good fortune of finding the original inscriptions that closed the tombs of martyrs. In underground Rome, in only one case was the tomb still completely preserved. On 21 March 1845, Father Giuseppe Marchi discovered the intact *loculus* of S. Hyacinth in the cemetery of S. Ermete; the tomb still contained his remains, which were later transferred to the church of the Collegio Urbaniano. What is surprising is the extreme simplicity of this gravestone, even though he was a witness to the faith and a victim of the persecution of 258. Only the date of burial (11 September), his name and the qualification of *martyr* are inscribed, without any other Christian symbols or laudatory expressions[235].

A similar conciseness with the absence of figurative elements of any sort, however, also

175

characterises the ancient gravestones of the martyred popes in the Crypt of the Popes at S. Callisto. Here, even the *dies natalis* is missing and the title of martyr is indicated only by a symbol joining several Greek letters (in some cases added later). Thus, one reads: "Fabian, pope, martyr"[236], or "Pontian, pope, martyr"[237]. In the Crypt of S. Cornelius, the famous inscription found by de Rossi reads: "Cornelius, martyr, pope"[238].

In slightly later inscriptions, however, the day of burial appears once again. For example, in the fragmentary dedication of Pope Gaius, who died in 296 and was buried in the cemetery of S. Callisto, one reads: "Deposition of Bishop Gaius on 22 April"[239].

Only during the period of Pope Damasus does one find true eulogies of martyrs, within the context of the work carried out by the pope to re-establish and spread the cult. But these were all commemorative epigrams that, although certainly important, were composed at least 60 years after the end of the last great persecutions and thus do not represent contemporary works.

The most beautiful Christian inscriptions

Speaking of the cult of the martyrs as reflected in epigraphy requires reference first of all to Pope Damasus (366–384), who composed circa 80 songs for saints and martyrs buried in the catacombs, as well as for his mother Laurentia and his sister Irene. He was proclaimed the patron of Christian archaeology by Pius XI in 1926 for his poetic activity, accompanied by an intensive exploration and study of venerated tombs, and for the monumental systematisation that he gave to many of these.

During his pontificate, in fact, Damasus commissioned the restoration and execution of diverse building projects in the cemeteries. New staircases were constructed, galleries widened, skylights opened, spaces created for the liturgy. In other words, he organised true centres for the cults of martyrs that, from then onwards for many centuries, were the destination of uninterrupted pilgrimages from every part of the ancient Christian world[240].

Following the tragic events that befell Rome, especially during the Graeco-Gothic wars in the course of the fourth century, many venerated places were devastated and damaged. Inscriptions often suffered the same fate; in several instances, they have survived thanks to the copies made in the Medieval period that were collected in epigraphic collections.

The value of the Damasan inscriptions from an historical, archaeological, as well as hagiographic point of view is undeniable, especially when they are the only source (or the most reliable one) for the reconstruction of events tied to specific individuals, such as Eutychian at S. Sebastiano[241]. This "witness to the faith" had to undergo atrocious torments in prison, from fasting to suffering from a lack a sleep, until when he was thrown off a cliff. In his poem, Damasus narrates that he was able to find the tomb of the martyr following a revelatory dream. He provided a dignified systematisation of it, inviting the faithful to venerate the memory of Eutychian.

The sources used by Damasus to document the different saints were often specified. For SS. Marcellinus and Peter, he claims to have gathered direct information about them when he was a boy, from the mouth of their executioner[242]. Other times, he guarantees the veracity of his statements with his own spiritual and moral authority[243]. For the martyr Agnes, however, he claims to have gathered information from the parents of the saint[244].

Perhaps the most famous epigram composed by Damasus is the one located in the Crypt of the Popes in the Catacomb of S. Callisto, where 9 popes and 3 bishops were buried in the third century. The poem ends with the phrase: "Here I confess, I, Damasus, would have wanted to repose my corpse but I was afraid to be a nuisance to the saintly ashes of the just" (fig. 174)[245].

The *carmen* in honour of Pope Sixtus II (257–258) was also composed for the same cemetery. Along with his four deacons, Sixtus was a victim of the persecution of Valerian, since he defied the edict that prohibited celebrations in the catacombs. Only two fragments of the song survive, but the text can be reconstructed with the help of Medieval transcriptions.

Much of the success of the Damasan epigrams is due to the beauty of the lettering, conceived by Furius Dionysius Philocalus, the calligrapher of the poet pope. He created a specific type of script for these large slabs, derived from the Classical square capital. This script is distinct from all other writings adopted by the Christians for its high quality and the careful preparation that preceded the incision of the texts, which were arranged

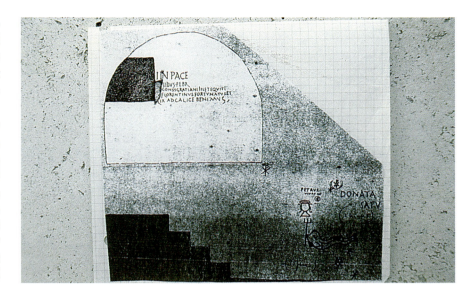

175 Catacomb of Priscilla: drawing of the lunette of an arcosolium with graffiti left by the faithful, that record a refrigerium in the catacomb, which took place in the month of March of 374 (or 375); Florentinus, Fortunatus, and Felix participated (ICUR IX, 24867)

176 Catacomb of S. Sebastiano: fragments of wall plaster from the so-called triclia (a covered pergola) with numerous graffiti that invoke the Apostles Peter and Paul

177 Catacomb of Pan-filo: cubiculum of the martyr with the altar that probably contained his relics

with great regularity and symmetry. Philo-calus adopted various solutions so that each line ended at the same point, like links. Thus, he inserted smaller letters within or beside others, or raised the T to save space.

The majority of these large gravestones were in verse, but prose inscriptions also oc-curred, such as the one in honour of S. Janu-arius in the Catacomb of Pretestato[246]. The slabs were placed so that they would be clearly visible within the crypt, the small basilicas in the cemeteries, or the liturgical spaces created along the galleries, which cor-responded to the venerated tombs. A clever play of *chiaroscuro* effect, obtained by lines incised in a more or less prominent fashion, and the regular use of decorative curly apices are two other characteristics of this script. Others attempted to imitate the script after the calligrapher's death but they lacked the

technical ability; thus, it is relatively easy to distinguish these less elegant replicas from the original gravestones.

Philocalus himself signed some inscrip-tions, such as the one dedicated to Eusebius "pope and martyr"[247] in which on the left and right in a vertical fashion, one can read "Furius Dionysius Philocalus, devoted friend of Pope Damasus, wrote (this gravestone)"[248]. About 20 inscriptions, datable to the decade between 370 and 380, are generally attributed to him. In addition, fragments of inscriptions signed by Philocalus, but not connected with the Damasan gravestones have been found; this is the case of a mutilated epitaph of unknown provenance now at the Musei Vaticani[249].

Expressed judgements on the poetic abil-ity of Damasus are conflicting. Although his style is, generally speaking, neither original nor of high quality in that he not infre-

178 Catacomb of Panfilo: drawing of the graffiti inscribed to the left of the altar in the cubiculum of the martyr, with the invocation s(a)c(tu)s Panfilu(s)

quently reflects and draws on Classical authors, undoubtedly he also displays sincerity of sentiments and intentions, often adopting images efficient in their conciseness. At any rate, Damasus and Philocalus represent two fundamental figures of importance for the rebirth of official monumental epigraphy, as compared to the common production of the Christian workshops.

Devotion of the faithful towards the martyrs

Inscriptions in the Roman catacombs can contain references of various kinds to the venerated martyrs, depending on whether they are votive or funerary. In the former case, the record of the work carried out in the historical crypts can be tied to important clergy members or to simple lay people, driven by carrying out a promise made or by other motives not specified. In the latter case, an allusion to the tomb of the martyr can be included to stress the proximity of the tomb of the faithful with the venerated site.

To provide an example of these inscriptions, it is sufficient to cite the dedication incised on the *transenna* of an altar in the cemetery of S. Alessandro on Via Nomentana. The inscription records that *Delicatus* donated that marble furnishing, dedicated to Bishop *Ursus*, to fulfil a promise made in honour of the local martyrs Eventius and Alexander[250].

Sometimes, commemorative gravestones have been preserved that include precise indications of the feasts of specific martyrs. Thus, in the *Coemeterium Maius* on Via Nomentana, one reads that "here on 16 September (the commemoration is celebrated) of the martyrs Viktor, Felix, Papias, Emerentiana and Alexander"[251]. The date specified corresponds to that recorded in the *Martyrologium Hieronymianum*. A believer, *Patricia*, dedicated a marble railing to these same individuals[252].

Among the numerous votive texts, one can cite also that of the deacon Gaudentius who carried out work in a catacomb on Via Tiburtina. This work, neglected by the sources, was in honour of the controversial martyr Novatian, identified by some as an anti-pope and promoter of a schism, martyred during the persecution of Valerian in 258[253].

In other cases, the faithful specify almost proudly on their gravestones that they were able to buy a burial place near a venerated tomb. Thus, *Felicissimus* and *Leoparda* in the Catacomb of Priscilla had a *bisomus*, that is, a *loculus* with two places, next to the entrance of the *cubiculum* of S. Crescentius[254]. At S. Callisto, *Serpentius* declares that he bought a tomb from the *fossor* Quintus near the Crypt of S. Cornelius[255], and *Iovina* bought herself an *arcosolium* near the tomb of S. Gaius[256] in the same catacomb. Apart from all other considerations, these explicit epigraphic references provide precious clues for the identification (or confirmation) of the presence of venerated tombs in a catacomb.

Sometimes allusions to martyrs were inserted instead in the invocations contained in the epitaphs. They entrusted their deceased loved ones to these martyrs, as in two inscriptions from the cemetery of S. Ermete[257]: "I recommend the innocence of Gemellus to Bassilla!"; "Lady Bassilla, we, Crescentinus and Micina, entrust to you our daughter Crescentia, who lived 10 months and a few days!"[258].

Finally, mention of martyrs can occur in relation to their feast day, if this happened to coincide with the death of a believer. In this case, this indication was not necessarily connected with the catacomb in which the martyr was buried. Thus, at Commodilla, *Pascasus* ended his life on earth on 12 October, "on the eighth day before the feast day of S. Asterius", that fell on 19 October 19[259].

Graffiti

Directly connected to the cult of the martyrs and the phenomenon of pilgrimages are numerous graffiti by Church members and the faithful. These graffiti are found in many catacombs, in particular, close to a venerated place (fig. 175). These humble inscriptions, incised with a hard point in the plaster or virgin tufa of the galleries, *arcosolia* or *cubicula*, often constitute proof of the existence (or the proximity) of a martyr's tomb. Unfortunately, some of these are either entirely or partially indecipherable, since the letters often appear deformed or almost unrecognisable, given as well the mixture of different types of scripts. In addition, it is not rare that these graffiti are intertwined and superimposed, so as to render their interpretation not infrequently complex (if not impossible).

The content of these graffiti is as variable as its chronology. The earliest (in the *triclia* of the Memoria Apostolorum on Via Appia)[260] (fig. 176) date to the second half of the third century. The latest ones immediately precede the phenomenon of the transfer of the remains of the martyrs, between the end of the eighth and the beginning of the ninth centuries.

In the majority of cases, only a name is incised by the faithful who desired to leave a sign of their presence in these holy places. Sometimes the graffiti reveal a possible "barbarian" origin of those who incised them. For example, the name of the Longobard *Liutprand* is incised in the Catacomb of SS. Marcellino e Pietro[261], and the name *Gaido* appears in the small niche with the destroyed votive painting of the Madonna and Child in the cemetery of Panfilo[262]. This same name occurs as well on the fresco depicting S. Luke at Commodilla[263], proof of the fact that pilgrims used to visit more than one sanctuary of the martyrs.

The only written evidence known in Rome until now in the runic alphabet has just recently been identified in the same catacomb. With all probability, a believer who arrived in Rome from central Europe to visit the tombs of the martyrs incised it[264]. Still in the small Basilica of Commodilla, above the magnificent votive painting of the widow *Turtura,* an anonymous believer incised a unique text. He wished to express his indignation, since, while attending the sacred rites in this place he had noted with surprise that the celebrant did not recite the prayers preceding the preface quietly as was prescribed, but so that everyone could hear. Having been scandalised by the event, he wrote on the fresco: "That man does not recite the *secreta* quietly!"[265].

The foreign origin of the faithful, and often of the clergy members who celebrated the rites *ad corpus*, was only explicitly mentioned in a few cases, such as by the Neapolitan *Pascalis* at the Catacomb of Panfilo[266] or *Iohan[nes]* from Rieti at SS. Marcellino e Pietro[267]. At other times, acclamations for the living and for their dead were incised, of the type, "Leontius, may you live in Christ!" that can be read in the Crypt of the Popes at S. Callisto[268].

The graffiti, therefore, turn out to be particularly valuable when they mention or invoke a martyr buried in a specific cemetery. The discovery of the name of Pamphilus, incised by an anonymous believer in the vener-

ated *cubiculum* of the catacomb of the same name (fig. 177), has provided a fundamental element for the reconstruction of the identity of an individual, who before was only conjectured hypothetically[269] (fig. 178). Thus, in a gallery near the Crypt of the Popes at S. Callisto, one reads among other things, "Saint Sixtus, remember Aurelius Repentinus in your prayers..."[270], in the cemetery of SS. Marcellino e Pietro, "Marcellinus (and) Peter, intercede for the Christian Gallicanus!"[271] and at Priscilla, "Save me, Saint Crescentius, my light"[272].

In addition to numerous clergy members, graffiti provide evidence for many monks, such as the "*Maiulus*, sinful monk" in the Catacomb of Panfilo[273] or "*Rapulus*, humble and unworthy monk" at SS. Marcellino e Pietro[274]. Unfortunately, in the majority of cases, it is not specified to which cloisters they belonged.

NOTES

1 Di Stefano Manzella 1997, p. 307.
2 Carletti 1997, p. 161.
3 Carletti 1988, pp. 119–128.
4 For a series of studies on Father Ferrua and his research, see *L'Accademia Selinuntina di Scienze Lettere Arti di Mazara del Vallo ed il Premio Sélinon 1987* (Trapani 1987).
5 Nuzzo 1997.
6 De Santis 1994, pp. 23–51; Felle-Del Moro-Nuzzo 1994, pp. 88–158.
7 On the symbols and biblical scenes incised on the slabs, see the contribution of F. Bisconti in this volume.
8 ICUR I, 1753: *Serbulus emit bisomu (!) / a Leontio fossore.*
9 Conde Guerri 1979.
10 Sanders 1991.
11 See most recently, Di Stefano Manzella 1997, pp. 99–101.
12 Nordberg 1963, pp. 211–222; Caldelli 1997. See, for example, an inscription from the Catacomb of S. Croce (ICUR V, 15330), preceded by the dedication D(is) M(anibus) (s(acrum)), "sacred to the Gods of the Underworld", to *Mavortius* who

lived 18 years, 1 month and 9 days; he was buried on the ides of October, three days after his death. There is a considerable difference, explicitly recorded, between the day that he died and that on which he was buried.
13 Nordberg 1963, pp. 223–229.
14 Raoss 1967.
15 Similar names occur also in the Jewish funerary inscriptions of Rome (Frey 1975²).
16 Colafranesco 1997, pp. 116–117.
17 Mazzoleni 1996; Carletti 1997, pp. 145–148.
18 The bibliography is extremely vast. See, amongst others, Ferrua 1943, pp. 279–305; Guarducci 1978, pp. 378–386 (with earlier biblio.); Wischmeyer 1980, pp. 22–47; Filippi 1996, pp. 182–184, nn. 24–25; Di Stefano Manzella 1997, pp. 220–222 (entry by G. Filippi).
19 Guarducci 1978, pp. 487–494.
20 Carletti 1988, pp. 128–131.
21 Carletti 1988, pp. 115–135.
22 Carletti 1997, p. 145. On the origins of the cemetery, see also Février 1959, p. 1–26.
23 Carletti 1988, pp. 119–120; Carletti 1997, pp. 145–146.
24 ICUR IX, 25046.

25 ICUR IX, 25166 and 25434.
26 ICUR IX, 25581.
27 Marucchi 1910, pl. LXI, wall XVIII.
28 On the origins of Christian figurative language, see Bisconti 1996.
29 ICUR VIII, 23243.
30 Ferrua 1978, pp. 583–616.
31 ICUR IV, 9516.
32 Pergola 1983, pp. 183–248; Carletti 1997, p. 146.
33 Nestori 1971, pp. 169–278; Carletti 1988, pp. 126–127.
34 Carletti 1997, p. 146.
35 Carletti 1997, pp. 146–147.
36 Carletti 1997, p. 146.
37 ICUR X, 26620: Κάρικος ὦ κῖτε | μνησθῆ ἡ ψυχὴ | αὐτοῦ ("Here lies Karikos; may his soul be remembered").
38 ICUR VI, 17246; R, 929, 1: *M(arco) Aurelio Augg(ustorum duorum) lib(erto) Proseneti / a cubiculo Aug(usti) / proc(uratori) thesaurorum / proc(uratori) patrimoni proc(uratori) / munerum proc(uratori) vinorum / ordinato a divo Commodo / in kastrense patrono piissimo / liberti bene merenti / sarcophagum de suo / adornaverunt.*
39 ICUR VI, 17246: *Prosenes receptus ad deum V non(is)*

181

[[Ma]]rtiis [- - -]nia Praesente et Extricato... scripsit Ampelius lib(ertus).

40 ICUR X, 27057: *Ti. Cl(audius) Marcianus et / Cornelia Hilaritas / Corneliae Paulae par(entes) fec(e)r(unt) quae vix(it) ann(is) X dieb(us) / VIII dec(essit) X kal(endas) Aug(ustas) Max(imo) et / Urb(ano) co(n)s(ulibus).*

41 ICUR II, 6021: *Aurelia dulcissima filia quae / de saeculo recessit / vixit ann(os) XV m(enses) IIII / Severo et Quinti(a)n(o) co(n)ss(ulibus).*

42 ICUR I, 1415: Ἡράκλιτος ὁ θεοφιλ|έστατος ἔζησεν ἔτ(η) η'| παρὰ ἡ(μέρας) ιγ' ἐνόσησεν ἡμ[έ]ρας ιβ' τελευτᾷ πρὸ ια' κ(αλανδῶν) μαί(ων)| Πίῳ καὶ Ποντιανῷ ὑπ(άτοις)... .

43 ICUR X, 27126: *Alexander / Augg(ustorum duorum) ser(vus) fecit /se bivo (!) Marcus filio / dulcisimo (!) caputa/fricesi qui deputa/batur inter bestito/res (!) qui vixit anni / XVIII mensibu(s) VIIII / diebu(s) V. peto a bobis (!) / fratres boni per / unum deum ne quis / (h)ui[[c]] titelo moles[tet] / pos(t) mor[tem meam].*

44 Perraymond 1980–1981, pp. 115–152.

45 ICUR II, 4246: *D(is) M(anibus)* Ἰχθὺς ζώντων / *Liciniae Amiati be/nemerenti vixit.* Now see, Di Stefano Manzella 1997, pp. 218–220 (entry by G. Filippi).

46 Biamonte 1992, pp. 95–123.

47 ICUR X, 27233: Πρῶτος ἐν ἁγίῳ | πνεύμα|τι θεοῦ | ἐνθάδε | κεῖται. | Φιρμίλλα | ἀδελφὴ | μνήμη|ς χάριν.

48 Zilliacus 1963, n. 156; Filippi 1996, n. 169; p. 276; Di Stefano Manzella 1997, pp. 216–218 (entry by G. Filippi): *D(is) M(anibus) / Iuliae / Calliste / Iulius Narcissus / coniunx et / Iulius Philadelphus / et Iulia Onesime / et Iulia Felicissima / matri b(ene) m(erenti) fecerunt / P IH XP.*

49 Ramsey 1975, pp. 526–528, n. 371.

50 Kajanto 1997, pp. 103–111.

51 ICUR VI, 16291.

52 *Hermes, Hercules, Afrodites, Apollo, Eros, Saturninus, Martialis, Asclepiodotus, Athenodorus, Achilles, Pentesilea, Posidonius, Isidorus, Aelius.*

53 Solin 1982.

54 At S. Ippolito, an *Ant(onius) Iudas*, perhaps an ostiary, is found (ICUR VII, 20012).

55 ICUR VII, *Indices. II. Nomina et cognomina*, p. 550.

56 See, for example, *Sufsuate* (ICUR, VII, 19386) or *Baguas* (ICUR VII, 20380).

57 *Ursus, Leo , Fomicula, Mus, Leopardus, Capreolus, Chelidonia, Palumba, Tinca.* See Kajanto 1965, pp. 325–334.

58 *Cara* (ICUR IX, 24662 and 26075 in Greek), *Pisinna* (ICUR, VIII, 21238), *Micina* (ICUR X, 27060).

59 ICUR X, 27357 a; Ferrua 1991a, p. 121–122, n. 98: *depositus Herila comes in pace fidei catholice.* The inscription, now lost, is dated to 462.

60 ICUR VIII, 23627; Ferrua 1991a, p. 123, n. 102.

61 Kajanto 1962 pp. 49–50, Kajanto 1965, pp. 55–56, Sgarlata 1991, pp. 134–137.

62 ICUR VI, 16077, *Asella coiu[gi].*

63 ICUR VI, 17285: *Licinius Gaudentius et Flavia Asellica...*

64 ICUR VI, 16433: *Sissinus et Onager iun(ior)....*

65 ICUR IV, 12303: *Locus Importuni acol(u)t(hi) s(an)c(ta)e / eccl(esiae) Rom(anae) t(i)t(uli) s(an)c(ta)e Anastasiae.*

66 ICUR V, 13594: *Hic requiescit Superbus / tantum in nomine dictus / quem innocentem mitemq(ue) sa(n)cti no/vere beati, in quo miserabilis pa/ter optaverat ante iacere....*

67 See, for example, ICUR VI, 16505: *Stercorio.*

68 For example, ICUR VI, 15704: *Coprion coiugi Florentine...*

69 ICUR V, 15307: *Sterco[riu]s qui vi[xit] / bene[me]renti / alumn[o su] o Nice.* On *alumni*, see Janssens 1981, pp. 181–190.

70 ICUR III, 9246: *Vitaliae, alumnae karissimae Dativus nutritor.*

71 Kajanto 1965, pp. 286–287.

72 Kajanto 1966.

73 ICUR IX, 25347: *Marcellus, qui et Exsuperius.*

74 ICUR X, 14067: *Valeria Calliope qui (!) et Anucella.* The correct form would be *anicula.*

75 ICUR V, 13975: *Marcia Augurina Maria que (e)t Carite.*

76 *Iulius [Sab?]inus qui et Abenna* (ICUR VI, 15528).

77 Mazzoleni 1997.

78 ICUR IX, 25791.

79 ICUR IX, 25794.

80 On the subject and its iconographical parallels, see, for example, Bisconti 1989, pp. 393–397.

81 Mazzoleni 1986. A statistical analysis with similar results was carried out in the cemetery of SS. Marco e Marcelliano (Saint-Roch 1983).

82 Di Stefano Manzella 1997, p. 316.

83 See, for example, a gravestone from the Catacomb of Panfilo (ICUR X, 26547).

84 A balance appears on the gravestone of the banker and money changer (*numul(arius)*) *Aurelius Venerandus* (ICUR VIII, 23104; Di Stefano Manzella 1997, pp. 320–321 (entry by C. Lega).

85 ICUR V, 13870 c.

86 ICUR V, 15253 b.

87 ICUR I, 327.

88 A hammer (and originally also a chisel) was incised on the gravestone of the sculptor (*artifici signario*) *Maecius Aprilis* (ICUR VII, 19054; Di Stefano Manzella 1997, p. 333 (entry by C. Lega)).

89 For example, the epitaph of *Gentilla* at the Catacomb of Commodilla includes a harp (ICUR II, 6204).

90 ICUR V, 15255.

91 ICUR VII, 19846; Mazzoleni, *et al* 1983, pp. 155–162.

92 ICUR III, 8474.

93 ICUR II, 6446.

94 ICUR III, 7372.

95 ICUR VI, 15584. According to Ferrua, the scene would best be interpreted as an anomalous representation of the sacrifice of Abraham (with the presumed Isaac unusually mature and bearded).

96 The tomb of Mercurius, a *pisturis*, that is, a baker, was probably located in the Vatican cemetery area (ICUR II, 4247: Di Stefano Manzella 1997, pp. 327–330 (entry by C. Lega)).

97 ICUR VII, 19027: *Locus Leopardi / dulciari et Fili/cissimes.*

98 *Primitivo ... lanius (!)* appears in the Catacomb of Domitilla (ICUR III, 9093; Di Stefano Manzella 1997, pp. 324–325 (entry by L. Chioffi)).

99 ICUR III, 6524 (*locus Adeodati porcinari*); ICUR V, 14193 (*Domitius Taurus pernarus de platia macelli*).

100 ICUR IX, 25435: *[[l]]ac[[t]]earius.*

101 ICUR V, 14583: *Quintus lactearius...qui fuit de domum (!) Laterani.*

102 ICUR IV, 12476; Di Stefano Manzella 1997, pp. 231–232 (entry by C. Lega and P. Liverani): *Leopardus de Belabru ... clabarus* (!).

103 See, for example, *Silbanus marmorarius* in the Musei Vaticani (ICUR I, 1761; Di Stefano Manzella 1997, pp. 331–332 (entry by C. Lega)).

104 ICUR II, 4675 (*Artis ispeclararie Sabinius Santias anima dulcis...*).

105 Such as *Octavianus tusor* (!) in the Musei Vaticani (ICUR I, 1706; Di Stefano Manzella 1997, pp. 335–336 (entry by C. Lega)).

106 ICUR II, 6111: *Locus Olympi elefantari* (!). The term *elephantarius*, unique up till now in Latin, is understood by some as the "elephant tamer in the circus games".

107 ICUR VI, 17225.

108 ICUR V, 15403 (*Secundinus mulomedicus*)

109 ICUR IX, 25812 (notario)

110 ICUR IX, 26113 (᾽Ολυμπίῳ σημιογράφῳ)

111 Such as *Rufus tabellarius* (ICUR VIII, 22635; Di Stefano Manzella 1997, pp. 322–323 (entry by C. Lega)).

112 See, for example, *Coritus magiter* (!) in ICUR IX, 23947; Di Stefano Manzella 1997, pp. 316–318 (entry by C. Lega).

113 ICUR III, 8669: *Leo officialis ann(onae)*.

114 Di Stefano Manzella 1997, pp. 266–267.

115 ICUR I, 1473; Di Stefano Manzella 1997, p. 275 (entry by C. Lega and S. Orlandi): *Hic quiescet* (!) *Iohannis v(ir) s(pectabilis)*....

116 ICUR II, 4164; R, n. 680: *Iun(ius) Bassus v(ir) c(larissimus) qui vixit ann(os) XLII men(ses) II, in ipsa praefectura urbi neofitus iit ad Deum*....

117 ICUR VIII, 21683.

118 ICUR IX, 25033: *Blossio Urbano eq(uiti) R(omano)*. The *equites singulares* also had the same fate as the praetorians. See, for example, ICUR VIII, 21973: *eq(ues) singularis Quartinus*.

119 Ferrua 1970, p. 209; Hornus 1973–1974, pp. 223–228.

120 Jurgens 1972; Pasquato 1984, cols. 3281–3284.

121 Pincherle 1984, p. 31. See, for example, August., *De fide et op.*

18.33: PL 40, 220; *De cat. rud.* 25.48; CCL 46, 172; *Conf.* VI.7.11: NBA I, 158.

122 Cornell-Matthews 1984, p. 187.

123 ICUR II, 5130: *hic requii[scit (!) - - -] / pantom[imus]*....

124 ICUR VII, 18774: *Felix doctor in p(ace)*.

125 ICUR I, 1983: *...Erotis a[[l]]umno / dulcisimo (!) et pammuso / gymnico*....

126 ICUR II, 4905: *Eutymius auriga...* The inscription dates to 439.

127 ICUR V, 13698: *m]emorie catadromarius [ludis ?- - -]*...

128 ICUR V, 13655.

129 De Rossi 1888, p. 94 n. 67.

130 An Italian translation is found in Janssens 1981, pp. 41–42.

131 *...Fingebam vultus habitus ac verba loquentur / ut plures uno crederis ore loqui...*"

132 *...vos ...deprecor.. / qui tumulum legitis cum pietate meum / o quam laetus eras Vitalis dicite maesti / sint tibi Vitalis sin (!) tibi laeta modo.*

133 ICUR III, 6699: *Felicissima oliaria.*

134 ICUR III, 7751.

135 *Ursa pomararia* (ICUR II, 6114).

136 ICUR V. 15389; Di Stefano Manzella 1997, pp. 233–234 (entry by C. Lega and P. Liverani): *Leontia ...ad porta Trigemina lagunara* (!).

137 ICUR I, 1519; Di Stefano Manzella 1997, pp. 235–236 (entry by C. Lega and P. Liverani): *...Aul(ius) Maximus / [con]-ditarius de castris pra/[etor]ibus Aul(ia) Hilaritas condita/riae eos in pace.*

138 Di Stefano Manzella 1997, pp. 323–324 (entry by C. Lega).

139 ICUR IV, 12503.

140 ICUR I, 1420: *...Bictora...amatrix pauperotum et operaria.*

141 Grossi-Di Berardino 1984, p. 212.

142 ICUR V, 13800: *hic iacet amicus et caru[s omnibus - - -] /medecus (!) ingeniosus pru[dens - - - in suis o]/peribus non cupidus ne[mini]/cuius beneficia omnibus cop[iosa fuerunt - - -]*...

143 ICUR IV 10558: ᾽Αντέρως ἐπί(σκοπος). His predecessor, Pontian (230–235) was transferred to Rome by Pope Fabian, from his burial place in Sardinia (ICUR IV, 10670; Baruffa 1992, pp. 55–56).

144 Carletti 1997, pp. 155–156.

145 Guyon 1974; Conde Guerri 1979.

146 Di Berardino 1983, col.719.

147 The term, however, began to be used during the fourth century; Damasus himself normally still uses the term *episcopus*.

148 ICUR IV, 10183: *Cubiculum duplex cum arcisoliis et lu[[m]]inare / iussu p(a)p(ae) sui Marcellini diaconus iste / Severus fecit...*

149 ICUR IV, 11751: *[sub Iulio a]ntistite).*

150 ICUR IV, 10664: Οὐρβάνος ἐ[πί(σκ(οπος)].

151 ICUR VIII, 22985: + *Hic requiescit in pace Adeodatus episc(opus), qui vixit ann(os) / pl(us) m(inus) LXVII et sed(it) ann(os) II et m(enses) VIIII. Dep(ositus) su[[b]] d(ie) prid(ie) kal(endas) Decemb(res).* It is specified that his episcopate lasted two years and nine months.

152 ICUR IV, 9483:

153 Wipzycka 1972, pp. 154–173.

154 On this subject, see most recently Fiocchi Nicolai 1997, pp. 134–136.

155 ICUR II, 5154: *[pres]byteri Basili tituli Sabine.*

156 ICUR X, 27537: *[- - - pre]sb(ytero) tituli Lucin[ae]*...

157 ICUR V, 12601: *levitarum primus in ordine.*

158 ICUR VI, 15700: *Faustus exorc(ista).*

159 ICUR VI, 15721: *Proficius lect(or) et exorcista.*

160 Stahlin 1974; Janssens 1981, pp. 210–214.

161 *Vidua*, χῆρα.

162 Mazzoleni 1989, p. 341.

163 ICUR X, 27148: *Primae biduae (!) deces/sit ann(is) centu(m)*...

164 ICUR X, 26377: *Bidua* (!) *Germana*

165 Mazzoleni 1989a, pp. 465–482.

166 Janssens 1981, pp. 207–208.

167 Janssens 1981, ibid.; Colombás 1974–5.

168 Fiocchi Nicolai 1983, cols. 872–873.

169 See, for example, ICUR VII, 17759 and 17865, both from the Catacomb of Cyriaca: *[- - -]us cubicula/[rius - - -] e locus Ioh[annis] / cub(icularii) t(i)t(uli).*

170 Cavallaro 1972, pp. 158–175.

171 Colafrancesco 1997, p. 113.

172 See, for example, ICUR X, 27226: Κυριακο φιλιω | Κουιν–

τιανους | πατερ φηκιτ, that is, *Quiriaco filio/ Quintianus / pater fecit.*

173 Felle 1997, pp. 669–676.

174 Zilliacus 1963, n. 262, p. 216.

175 ICUR VII, 18436; Di Stefano Manzella 1997, p. 354 (entry by A.E. Felle).

176 ICUR X, 26566.

177 Ferrua 1985.

178 Zilliacus 1963.

179 Mazzoleni 1994.

180 ICUR VI, 15625: *sine ulla discordia*

181 ICUR VII, 17765: *inculpabiliter et cum omni suavitate*

182 ICUR III, 7497; V, 13338, 14245: *sine bile.*

183 ICUR III, 8175: *[sine a]maritudine.*

184 ICUR III, 9170; V, 13130, 15273; VIII, 23101: *sine ulla querela.*

185 Testini 1976, pp. 150–164.

186 ICUR VII, 18892: *sancta ac venerabilis.*

187 ICUR II, 4928 a: *simplex.*

188 ICUR V, 13196: *prudens.*

189 ICUR II, 5333: *sollers.*

190 ICUR VII, 18170: *mitissimo.*

191 ICUR VII, 17549: *adfabilis.*

192 ICUR I, 1770: *dulcis omnibus suis et amicis acceptus.*

193 ICUR II, 4895: *moribus probus.*

194 ICUR IV, 11904: *mirae bonitatis et innocentiae.*

195 ICUR II, 4219 b: *cunctis integer a vitiis.*

196 ICUR X, 27168: *Silvana Niciati mari/to benemerenti cum quo / vixit annis tribus mesibus (!) / duobus oris (!) undecim.* "Silvana (dedicated this) for her husband *Nicias*, with whom she lived three years, two months, and 11 hours".

197 Carletti 1977, pp. 39–51.

198 See esp. Janssens 1981, pp. 163–165.

199 ICUR V, 13104: *Libera que vixit annos tres et dies duos / nata est XV kal(endas) Maias dies Jovis et mortua / est XIIII kal(endas) Maias dies Mercuri ora noctis sexta...*

200 ICUR I, 1978: *Dalmatio filio dulcissimo, toti/us ingeniositatis ac sapienti/ae puero, quem plenis septem an/nis perfui patri infelici non licu/it; qui studens litteras graecas, non /monstratas sibi latinas adripuit et in / triduo ereptus est rebus humanis...*

201 ICUR IX, 26122: Ὄβριμος Παλλαδίῳ | γλυκυτάτῳ ἀνεψίῳ | συνσχολάστῃ μνήμης | χάριν.

202 ICUR VII, 19501: *Vitali patra/ter filiatrae / suae Victo/riae meren/ti iscrisi (!) / in paece (!).*

203 ICUR III, 9246: *Vitaliae alumnae karissimae / Dativus nutritor* ("to his dearest adopted daughter *Vitalia*, her adoptive father *Dativus*").

204 Janssens 1981, pp. 181–190.

205 Josi 1926, p. 134.

206 ICUR I, 3221: *Quintilianus homo Dei [- - -] / confirmans tri nitatem [- - -] / amans castitatem [- - -] / respuens mundum [- - -] / requiescet (!)...*

207 ICUR V, 13443: *Aedesius neo/fitus qui credi/dit in Patre et Fi/lio et Spiritu Sa/ncto...*

208 ICUR III, 7666: *[Se]/cundianu[s credidit] / Cristum Iesu[m cum Patr]/e et filio e Isp[iritu Sancto].*

209 Carletti 1997, pp. 145–146.

210 Felle 1994. ICUR IX, 25962 a, with the citation from *Gen.* 3, 19, is not included in the examples collected.

211 ICUR IX, 25102; Mazzoleni 1985, pp. 269–271.

212 ICUR VI, 15842: *...ego caelestis captus dulcedine regni...*

213 ICUR III, 9155: *...accersitus ab angelis...*

214 ICUR I, 1678: *quam te letum (!) excipet mater ecclesia de oc (!) / mundo revertentem...*

215 ICUR VIII, 23087:*...cum soldu (!) amatus fuisset a maiore sua et vidit / hunc morti constitu[tu]m esse [[p]]etivit de aeclesia (!) ut fidelis / de seculo (!) recessisset.*

216 ICUR II, 4272: *[- - - de]dit deus deus tulit...*

217 ICUR IX, 26027: Ὁ πατὴρ τῶν πάντων οὕς ἐποίησες κ(αὶ) | παρελάβης Εἰρήνην Ζόην κ(αὶ) Μάρκελλον. | σοὶ δόξα ἐν Χρ(ιστῷ).

218 ICUR X, 26329: *Aproniane, crededisti in deo vives in XP (= Christo).*

219 ICUR V, 15331: *Nar{e}cissus, deus tibi refrigeret.*

220 ICUR X, 26350: *Martures / sancti boni / benedicti, bos(!) / atiutate Quiracu (!).*

221 ICUR III, 8452: *.Attice...ora pro paren/tibus tuis*

222 ICUR IX, 26075: Κάρα μνημονεύε μου.

223 ICUR IX, 25356: *Marine in mente{m} nos habeto...duobus.*

224 ICUR IX, 25962 b: *Vos precor, o fratres, orare huc quando veni[tis] / et precibus totis patrem natumque rogatis / ut deus omnipotens Agapen (!) in saecula servet.*

225 ICUR IX, 26034: Τὴν αἰώνι|όν σοι ἐλπί|δα ἀναγεινώ|σκων, μνήσθη|τι 'Επικ|τήτου.

226 ICUR IX, 11927: *...mox gratia dei percepi suscepta in pace neofyta.*

227 ICUR II, 4640: *Marcia/nus enon/fitus (!) / recesi (!) / celi (!) tibi pa/ten(t) bisbes (!) / in pace.*

228 ICUR I, 396: *Herculia hic sita est sacratis abluta lymbis / quae nuper [r]ena[ta] deo vivit per saecula semper...*

229 ICUR IX, 25562: *Tyche dulcis / vixit anno uno / mensibus X dieb(us) XV / accepit VIII ka[l](endas) - - -] / reddidit die s(upra) s(cripta)*

230 Janssens 1981, p. 33.

231 ICUR IX, 25966: *Restutus nomen factus in morte fidelis / terrena nam vita manet caeli mihi iugis.../ Hic corpus iaceo caeli sed in aethere vivo / ante pedes domini praecellens munere Christi...*

232 ICUR II, 4219 b: *...vivit in aeterna paradisi sede beatus / qui nova decedens muneris aetherii / vestimenta tulit...*

233 Mazzoleni 1993a, pp. 168–170.

234 ICUR VII, 20300: Κῖτε Βίκτορ κατηχούμενος | αἰτῶν εἴκοσι παρθένος | δοῦλος τοῦ κυρίου Εἰησοῦ Χρ(ιστοῦ).

235 ICUR X, 26672: *d(e)p(ositus) III idus septe(m)br(es) / Yacinthus / martyr.*

236 ICUR IV, 10694: Φαβιανὸς ἐπί(σκοπος) μ(ά)ρτ(υς).

237 ICUR IV, 10670: Ποντιανὸς ἐπί(σκοπος) μ(ά)ρτ(υς).

238 ICUR IV, 9367: *Cornelius martyr ep(iscopus).*

239 ICUR IV, 10584: Γ[α΄ίο]υ ἐπι[σκ(όπου)] | κατ(άθησις) | πρ[ὸ ι΄] καλ(ανδῶν) μαΐω[ν].

240 On the various aspects of the personality of Damasus, see, for example, the articles published in the Proceedings of the International Congress for the 1600 Anniversary of the Death of Pope Damasus, held in Rome, 10–12 December 1984 (Città del Vaticano 1986).

241 Ferrua 1942, n. 21; ICUR V, 13274; Ferrua-Carletti 1985, pp. 32–34.

242 Ferrua 1942, n. 28; ICUR, VI, 16961: *percussor rettulit mihi, cum puer essem...*

243 Ferrua 1942, n. 8; ICUR III, 8132; Ferrua-Carletti 1985, pp. 13–16:..*credite per Damasum...*

244 Ferrua 1942, n. 37; ICUR VIII, 20753; Ferrua-Carletti 1985, pp. 39–42: *fama refert sanctos dudum retulisse parentes....*

245 Ferrua 1942, n. 16; ICUR IV, 9513; Ferrua-Carletti 1985, pp. 19–23: ... *hic fateor Damasus volui mea condere membra / sed cineres timui sanctos vexare piorum.*

246 ICUR V, 13871: *Beatiss[i]mo martyri / Ianuario / Damasus epis[c]op(us) / fecit.*

247 Ferrua 1942, n. 18; ICUR IV, 9514; Ferrua-Carletti 1985, pp. 26–28: ... *Eusebio episcopo et martyri.*

248 *Damasi papae cultor adque (!) amator / Furius Dionysius Filocalus scribsit (!).*

249 Di Stefano Manzella 1997, pp. 260–261 (entry by C. Lega and G. De Felix)

250 ICUR VIII, 22958: *[s(an)c(t)is martyrib(us) Eventio] et Alexandro Delicatus voto posuit / dedi/can/te ae/pis/cop(o) / Urs[o]..*

251 ICUR VIII, 21590: XVI *kal(endas) octob(res) marturotu(m) h[i]c in cimi/teru maiore Victor[[i]]s Felicis Papiantis / Emerentianetis et Alexandri*

252 ICUR VIII, 21592: *[Alexa]ndro Victo[ri Mau]ro Papie et Felici Patricia [- - - vot]un solvit.*

253 ICUR VII, 20334: *Novatiano beatissimo / marturi Gaudentius diac(onus) f[ecit].*

254 ICUR IX, 25165: *Filicissimus (!) et Leopar[da] / bisomum at Criscent[ionem] / introitu.*

255 ICUR IV, 9441: ...*Ser[[pe]]ntiu/s emit loc(u)/m a Quinto / fossore ad / santum (!) Co/rnelium*

256 ICUR IV, 9924: ...*Iovine...conpa[ra]bit sibi arco[so]lium in Callisti at domn[um] Gaium...*

257 ICUR X, 27034: ...*conmando Bassila (!) innocentia Gemelli*

258 ICUR X, 27060: *domina Bassilla com/mandamus tibi Cres/centinus et Micina / filia nostra Crescen(tiam?) /que vixit men(ses) X et d(i)es.*

259 ICUR II, 6094: *fecit fatu IIII idus / Octtrobis (!) GII ante / natale domni As/teri depositus in / pace.*

260 The numerous invocations to Peter and Paul represent, for some scholars, valid evidence to support the presence of Apostolic relics in that place from the second half of the third to the first decades of the fourth centuries. On this controversial subject, see, for example, Ferrua

1991a, pp. 297–314 and Carletti 1997, pp. 148–149.

261 ICUR VI, 15979: *[L]uitprandiu* (!)

262 ICUR X, 26320.

263 ICUR II, 6449, 7 and 19; Carletti 1984–5, p. 132.

264 Carletti 1984–5, p. 132 and 141–142: *Eadbald.*

265 ICUR II, 6449,39: *non dice/re il/le se/crita / abboce (!). See also* Bagatti 1936, p. 113.

266 ICUR X, 26316: *Pascal(is a) Neapoli.*

267 ICUR VI, 15984 b: *Iohan[nes] / Reat[inus].*

268 ICUR IV, 9524, 20: *Leonti vib[as] in Chr(isto).*

269 ICUR X, 26317; Mazzoleni 1993, pp. 108–113.

270 ICUR IV, 9521: *Sante Suste in mente / habeas in horationes (!) / Aureliu Repentinu (!). See also* Baruffa 1992, p. 51.

271 ICUR VI, 15963: *Marcelline / Petre petite / [p]ro Gallicanu (!) [c]hristiano.*

272 ICUR IX, 24853: *salba me / domne Crescnetionem / meam luce (!).*

273 ICUR X, 26315: *Maiulus mon(achus) peccator.*

274 ICUR VI, 15969: *eg(o) Rapulus humilis et indignus monachus.*

BIBLIOGRAPHY

AHLQUIST 1995 — A. Ahlquist, *Pitture e mosaici nei cimiteri paleocristiani di Siracusa. Corpus iconographicum*, Venezia 1995.

ALLODI-LEVI 1885 — L. Allodi - G. Levi, *Il Regesto Sublacense del secolo XI*, Roma 1885.

ALPIGIANO 1988 — Aristide di Atene, *Apologia*, ed. C. Alpigiano, Firenze 1988.

AMANTE SIMONI 1990 — C. Amante Simoni, 'Sepoltura e moneta: obolo, viatico, obolo-offerta', *Le sepolture in Sardegna dal IV al VII secolo, IV Convegno sull'Archeologia Tardoromana e Altomedievale. Cuglieri 27-28 giugno 1987*, Oristano 1988, pp. 231-244.

ANDREAE 1980 — B. Andreae, *Die Sarkophage mit Darstellungen aus dem Menschenleben. Die römischen Jagdsarkophage*, Berlin 1980.

APOLLONJ GHETTI-FERRUA-JOSI-KIRSCHBAUM 1951 — B. M. Apollonj Ghetti - A. Ferrua - E. Josi - E. Kirschbaum, *Esplorazioni sotto la Confessione di San Pietro in Vaticano eseguite negli anni 1940-1949*, I-II, Città del Vaticano 1951.

ARMELLINI 1880 — M. Armellini, *Il cimitero di S. Agnese sulla via Nomentana*, Roma 1880.

ARMELLINI 1893 — M. Armellini, *Gli antichi cimiteri cristiani di Roma e d'Italia*, Roma 1893.

ATLANTE FORME CERAMICHE 1981 — 'Atlante delle forme ceramiche I, Ceramica fine romana nel bacino mediterraneo (medio e tardo impero)', *Enciclopedia dell'Arte Antica Classica e Orientale*, Roma 1981.

AUGENTI 1991 — A. Augenti, «Ipsi lapides ululant nobiscum». Il suburbio sudorientale di Roma tra la tarda antichità e l'alto medioevo, *Mélanges de l'École Française de Rome, Moyen Âge 103*, 1991, pp. 41-82.

BAGATTI 1936 — B. Bagatti, *Il cimitero di Commodilla o dei martiri Felice ed Adautto presso la via Ostiense*, Città del Vaticano 1936.

BARGEBUHR 1991 — F. P. Bargebuhr, *The Paintings of the New Catacomb of the via Latina and the Struggle of Christianity against Paganism*, Heidelberg 1991.

BARUFFA 1992 — A. Baruffa, *Le catacombe di S. Callisto. Storia, archeologia, fede*, Città del Vaticano 1992.

BARUFFA 1994 — A. Baruffa, *Giovanni Battista de Rossi. L'archeologo esploratore delle catacombe*, Città del Vaticano 1994.

BENDINELLI 1922 — G. Bendinelli, *Il monumento sepolcrale degli Aureli al Viale Manzoni in Roma (Monumenti Antichi dei Lincei, XXVIII)*, Roma 1922.

BERTONIÈRE 1985 — G. Bertonière, *The Cult Center of the Martyr Hippolytus on the via Tiburtina*, Oxford 1985.

BIAMONTE 1992 — G. Biamonte, 'Dal segno pagano al simbolo cristiano', *Studi e Materiali di Storia delle Religioni 58*, 1992, 1, pp. 98-123.

BIANCHI BANDINELLI 1976 — R. Bianchi Bandinelli, *Roma. L'arte romana al centro del potere*, Milano 1976.

BIANCHI BANDINELLI 1978 — R. Bianchi Bandinelli, *Dall'Ellenismo al Medioevo*, Roma 1978.

BIANCHI BANDINELLI 1984 — R. Bianchi Bandinelli, 'I problemi dell'arte romana. La sua importanza', *L'arte romana*, ed. L. Franchi dell'Orto, Roma 1984, pp. 87-95.

BIDEZ 1924 — J. Bidez (ed.), *L'Empéreur Julien. Oeuvres complètes, I, 2, Lettres et fragments*, Paris 1924.

BISCONTI 1979 — F. Bisconti, 'Aspetti e significati del simbolo della fenice nella letteratura e nell'arte del Cristianesimo primitivo', *Vetera Christianorum 16*, 1979, pp. 21-40.

BISCONTI 1980 — F. Bisconti, 'Contributo all'interpretazione dell'atteggiamento di orante', *Vetera Christianorum 17*, 1980, pp. 17-27.

BISCONTI 1981 — F. Bisconti, 'Lastra inedita del cimitero di Priscilla', *Rivista di Archeologia Cristiana 57*, 1981, pp. 43-67.

BISCONTI 1981a — F. Bisconti, 'Sull'unità del linguaggio biblico nella pittura cimiteriale romana', *Miscellanea S. Cipriani*, Brescia 1981, pp. 731-740.

BISCONTI 1983-1984 — F. Bisconti, headword *fossore*, DPAC, I, cols. 1389-1391.

BISCONTI 1985   F. Bisconti, 'L'ipogeo degli Aureli in viale Manzoni: Un esempio di sincresi privata', *Augustinianum* 25, 1985, pp. 889-903.

BISCONTI 1987   F. Bisconti, 'La rappresentazione dei defunti nelle incisioni sulle lastre funerarie paleocristiane aquileiesi e romane', *Antichità Altoadriatiche* 30, 1987, pp. 289-308.

BISCONTI 1988   F. Bisconti, 'Un fenomeno di continuità iconografica: Orfeo citaredo, Davide salmista, Cristo pastore, Adamo e gli animali', *Augustinianum* 28, 1988, pp. 429-436.

BISCONTI 1989   F. Bisconti, 'Letteratura patristica e iconografia paleocristiana', *Complementi interdisciplinari di Patrologia*, Roma 1989, pp. 367-412.

BISCONTI 1989a   F. Bisconti, 'Un piccolo museo al Casale di S. Tarcisio nel comprensorio di S. Callisto', *Rivista di Archeologia Cristiana* 65, 1989, pp. 21-47.

BISCONTI 1990   F. Bisconti, 'Sulla concezione figurativa dell'«habitat» paradisiaco: a proposito di un affresco romano poco noto', *Rivista di Archeologia Cristiana* 66, 1990, pp. 25-80.

BISCONTI 1992   F. Bisconti, 'Altre note di iconografia paradisiaca', *Bessarione* 9, 1992, pp. 89-117.

BISCONTI 1992a   F. Bisconti, 'Un singolare esempio di iconografia «attitudinale»: Note su una pittura del cimitero «ad duas lauros»', *Memoriam Sanctorum Venerantes. Miscellanea in onore di V. Saxer*, Città del Vaticano 1992, pp. 21-48.

BISCONTI 1993   F. Bisconti, 'La catechesi di Pietro. Una scena controversa', *Esegesi e catechesi nei padri (secc. II-IV)*, Roma 1993, pp. 171-179.

BISCONTI 1993a   F. Bisconti, 'Cristo e S. Paolo in un frammento di sarcofago della tricora orientale di S. Callisto', *Rivista di Archeologia Cristiana* 69, 1993, pp. 7-24.

BISCONTI 1994   F. Bisconti, 'Memorie classiche nelle decorazioni pittoriche delle catacombe romane. Continuità grafiche e variazioni semantiche', *Historiam Pictura Refert. Miscellanea in onore di p. Alejandro Recio Veganzones*, Città del Vaticano 1994, pp. 28-66.

BISCONTI 1994a   F. Bisconti, 'Materiali epigrafici dal cimitero dei Ss. Pietro e Marcellino. Spunti e conferme per la cronologia della regione I', *Rivista di Archeologia Cristiana* 70, 1994, pp. 7-42.

BISCONTI 1995   F. Bisconti, 'Dentro e intorno all'iconografia martiriale romana: dal «vuoto figurativo» all'«immaginario devozionale»', *Martyrium* 1995, pp. 247-292.

BISCONTI 1995a   F. Bisconti, 'Riflessi iconografici del pellegrinaggio nelle catacombe romane. Genesi e primi sviluppi dell'iconografia martiriale a Roma', *Akten des XII Internationalen Kongresses für Christliche Archäologie, Bonn 22-28 september 1991*, 2, Città del Vaticano 1995, pp. 552-558.

BISCONTI 1995b   F. Bisconti, 'Il restauro della cripta dei vescovi nelle catacombe napoletane di S. Gennaro', *Associazione Italiana per lo Studio e la Conservazione del Mosaico, Atti del II Colloquio, Roma 5-7 dicembre 1994*, Bordighera 1995, pp. 311-320.

BISCONTI 1995c   F. Bisconti, 'L'abbraccio tra Pietro e Paolo ed un affresco inedito del cimitero romano dell'ex Vigna Chiaraviglio', *XLII Corso di Cultura sull'Arte Ravennate e Bizantina, Ravenna, 14-19 maggio 1995*, Ravenna 1995, pp. 71-93.

BISCONTI 1996   F. Bisconti, 'L'arte delle catacombe', AA.VV., *Dalla terra alle genti. La diffusione del Cristianesimo nei primi secoli*, Milano 1996, pp. 94-106.

BISCONTI 1996a   F. Bisconti, 'Genesi e primi sviluppi dell'arte cristiana: i luoghi, i modi, i temi', AA.VV., *Dalla terra alle genti. La diffusione del Cristianesimo nei primi secoli*, Milano 1996, pp. 71-93.

BISCONTI 1996b   F. Bisconti, 'La Madonna di Priscilla: interventi di restauro ed ipotesi sulla dinamica decorativa', *Rivista di Archeologia Cristiana* 72, 1996, pp. 7-34.

BISCONTI 1997   F. Bisconti, 'L'apparato figurativo delle iscrizioni cristiane di Roma', Di Stefano Manzella, 1997, pp. 173-179.

BISCONTI 1997a   F. Bisconti, 'La «coronatio» di Pretestato. Storia delle manomissioni del passato e riflessioni sui recenti restauri', *Rivista di Archeologia Cristiana* 73, 1997, pp. 7-49.

BISCONTI 1997b   F. Bisconti, 'Il lucernario di S. Cecilia. Recenti restauri e nuove acquisizioni nella cripta callistiana di S. Cecilia', *Rivista di Archeologia Cristiana* 73, 1997, pp. 307-339.

BISCONTI 1998   F. Bisconti, 'La pittura paleocristiana',

BISCONTI 1998a

F. Bisconti, 'Il cubicolo dell'Esodo nel cimitero dei Giordani. Ultime manifestazioni pittoriche nelle catacombe romane', *Domum Tuam Dilexi. Miscellanea in onore di Aldo Nestori*, Città del Vaticano 1998, pp. 81-108.

BISCONTI
in press

F. Bisconti, *Pastori eccezionali: a proposito di due affreschi romani appena restaurati*, in press.

BISCONTI-GIULIANI-TOMMASI 1995

F. Bisconti - R. Giuliani - F. Tommasi, 'Nuove indagini nella catacomba dei Ss. Pietro e Marcellino sulla via Labicana', *Atti del XII Incontro di Studio organizzato dal Comitato per l'Archeologia Laziale (CNR)*, Roma 1995, pp. 293-302.

BISCONTI-MAZZOLENI 1996

F. Bisconti - D. Mazzoleni, headword *mosaico*, Enciclopedia dell'Arte Antica Classica e Orientale, II supplemento, Roma 1996, pp. 821-827.

BOLDETTI 1720

M. A. Boldetti, *Osservazioni sopra i cimiteri de' Santi Martiri ed antichi cristiani di Roma*, Roma 1720.

BORDIGNON
1991-1992

C. Bordignon, *La tecnica pittorica negli affreschi delle catacombe romane*, unprinted treatise at Pontificio Istituto di Archeologia Cristiana, 1991-1992.

BOSIO 1632

A. Bosio, *Roma Sotterranea*, Roma 1632.

BOSIO 1993

P. Bosio, 'Frammenti di rilievo con scene agropastorali del comprensorio callistiano', *Rivista di Archeologia Cristiana* 69, 1993, pp. 25-30.

BOZZINI 1975-1976

P. Bozzini, 'Coperchi di sarcofago di Pretestato e di S. Callisto', *Rendiconti della Pontificia Accademia Romana di Archeologia* 48, 1975-1976, pp. 325-365.

BRANDENBURG 1978

H. Brandenburg, 'Überlegungen zum Ursprung der frühchristlichen Bildkunst', *Atti del IX Congresso Internazionale di Archeologia Cristiana, Roma 21-27 settembre 1975*, Città del Vaticano 1978, pp. 3-28.

BRANDENBURG 1979

H. Brandenburg, *Roms frühchristliche Basiliken des 4. Jahrhunderts*, München 1979.

BRANDENBURG
1983

H. Brandenburg, headword *Archeologia Cristiana*, DPAC, I, cols. 317-330.

BRANDENBURG
1984

H. Brandenburg, 'Überlegungen zu Ursprung und Entstehung der Katakomben Roms', *Vivarium. Festschrift Theodor Klauser zum 90. Geburtstag*, Münster i. Westfalen 1984, pp. 11-49.

BRANDENBURG
1994

H. Brandenburg, 'Coemeterium. Der Wandel des Bestattungswesens als Zeichen des Kulturumbruchs der Spätantike', *Laverna* 5, 1994, pp. 206-232.

BROCCOLI 1981

U. Broccoli, *Corpus della scultura altomedievale*, VII, *La diocesi di Roma*, V, *Il suburbio*, 1, Spoleto 1981.

BROWN 1974

P. Brown, *Il mondo tardo antico. Da Marco Aurelio a Maometto*, Torino 1974.

BROWN 1983

P. Brown, *Il culto dei santi. L'origine e la diffusione di una nuova religiosità*, Torino 1983.

BUONARROTI 1716

F. Buonarroti, *Osservazioni sopra alcuni frammenti di vasi antichi di vetro ornati di figure trovati nei cimiteri di Roma*, Firenze 1716.

CALDELLI 1997

M. L. Caldelli, 'Nota su «D(is) M(anibus)» e «D(is) M(anibus) s(acrum)» nelle iscrizioni cristiane di Roma', Di Stefano Manzella 1997, pp. 185-187.

CAMIRUAGA et Alii
1994

I. Camiruaga et Alii, *La arquitectura del hipogeo de la via Latina en Roma*, Città del Vaticano 1994.

CAPRINO 1974

C. Caprino, 'Un nuovo contributo alla conoscenza dello Hermes che si allaccia il sandalo', *Bollettino d'Arte* 59, 1974, pp. 106-112.

CARLETTI 1977

C. Carletti, 'Aspetti biometrici del matrimonio nelle iscrizioni cristiane di Roma', *Augustinianum* 17, 1977, pp. 39-51.

CARLETTI 1981

C. Carletti, 'Pagani e cristiani nel sepolcreto della «piazzola» sotto la Basilica Apostolorum a Roma', *Vetera Christianorum* 18, 1981, pp. 287-307.

CARLETTI 1984-85

C. Carletti, 'I graffiti sull'affresco di S. Luca nel cimitero di Commodilla', *Rendiconti della Pontificia Accademia Romana di Archeologia* 57, 1984-85, pp. 129-143.

CARLETTI 1985   C. Carletti, 'Linguaggio biblico e comunità a Roma nel III secolo: il contributo delle iscrizioni dell'«arenario» di Priscilla', *Annali di Storia dell'Esegesi* 2, 1985, pp. 201-207.

CARLETTI 1988   C. Carletti, «Epigrafia cristiana» - «epigrafia dei cristiani»: alle origini della terza età dell'epigrafia, AA.VV., *La terza età dell'epigrafia. Colloquio AIEGL-Borghesi 86*, Faenza 1988, pp. 115-135.

CARLETTI 1989   C. Carletti, 'Origine, committenza e fruizione delle scene bibliche nella produzione figurativa romana del III secolo', *Vetera Christianorum* 26, 1989, pp. 207-219.

CARLETTI 1992   C. Carletti, 'Gli affreschi della cripta di Milziade nel cimitero di S. Callisto. Interventi di restauro', *Rivista di Archeologia Cristiana* 68, 1992, pp. 141-168.

CARLETTI 1994   C. Carletti, 'Quod multi cupiunt et rari accipiunt. A proposito di una nuova iscrizione della catacomba dell'ex Vigna Chiaraviglio', *Historiam Pictura Refert. Miscellanea in onore di p. Alejandro Recio Veganzones*, Città del Vaticano 1994, pp. 111-126.

CARLETTI 1994a   C. Carletti, 'Nuove iscrizioni dalla catacomba della ex Vigna Chiaraviglio sulla via Appia', *Mélanges de l'École Française de Rome, Antiquité*, 106, 1994, pp. 29-41.

CARLETTI 1994b   C. Carletti, 'Storia e topografia della catacomba di Commodilla', J. G. Deckers - G. Mietke - A. Weiland, *Die Katakombe «Commodilla». Repertorium der Malereien*, Città del Vaticano 1994, pp. 3-27.

CARLETTI 1995   C. Carletti, 'Viatores ad martyres. Testimonianze scritte altomedievali nelle catacombe romane', *Epigrafia medievale greca e latina. Ideologia e funzione. Atti del Seminario di Erice (12-18 settembre 1991)*, Spoleto 1995, pp. 197-225.

CARLETTI 1997   C. Carletti, 'Nascita e sviluppo del formulario epigrafico cristiano: prassi e ideologia', Di Stefano Manzella 1997, pp. 143-164

CARLETTI 1998   C. Carletti, 'Un monogramma tardoantico nell'epigrafia funeraria dei cristiani', *Domum Tuam Dilexi. Miscellanea in onore di Aldo Nestori*, Città del Vaticano 1998, pp. 127-142.

CASALONE 1962   C. Casalone, 'Note sulle pitture dell'ipogeo di Trebio Giusto a Roma', *Cahiers Archéologiques* 11, 1962, pp. 53-64.

CASEL 1932   O. Casel, 'Älteste christliche Kunst und Christusmysterium', *Jahrbuch für Liturgiewissenschaften* 1932, pp. 1-36.

CAVALLARO 1972   M. A. Cavallaro, 'Intorno ai rapporti tra cariche statali e cariche ecclesiastiche nel basso impero. Note storico-epigrafiche sul cubiculariato', *Athenaeum* 50, 1972, pp. 158-175.

CAVAZZINI 1994-1995   S. Cavazzini, *La componente cosmica nelle volte dei cubicoli delle catacombe romane. L'esempio del cimitero dei Ss. Pietro e Marcellino*, Tesi di licenza presso il Pontificio Istituto di Archeologia Cristiana, AA. 1994-1995.

CCL   *Corpus Christianorum, Series Latina*, Turnhout 1953 ff.

CECCHELLI 1929   C. Cecchelli, 'Origini romane dell'archeologia cristiana', *Roma. Rivista di studi e di vita romana* 7, 1929, pp. 105-112.

CECCHELLI 1938   C. Cecchelli, *Il Cenacolo Filippino e l'archeologia cristiana*, Roma 1938.

CECCHELLI 1944   C. Cecchelli, *Monumenti cristiano-eretici di Roma*, Roma 1944.

CHALKIA 1991   E. Chalkia, *Le mense paleocristiane. Tipologia e funzioni delle mense secondarie nel culto paleocristiano*, Città del Vaticano 1991.

CHICOTEAU 1976   M. Chicoteau, *Glanures au viale Manzoni*, Brisbane 1976.

CIANFRIGLIA-FILIPPINI 1985   L. Cianfriglia - P. Filippini, 'Via G. Ravizza: tomba ipogea', *Bullettino della Commissione Archeologica Comunale* 90, 1985, pp. 217-234.

COLAFRANESCO 1997   P. Colafranesco, 'La lingua latina nelle iscrizioni del tardo-impero', Di Stefano Manzella 1997, pp. 113-120.

COLOMBÁS 1974-75   G. M. Colombás, *El monacato primitivo*, 2 vols, Madrid 1974-75.

CONDE GUERRI 1979   E. Conde Guerri, *Los «fossores» de Roma paleocristiana (Estudio iconográfico, epigráfico y social)*, Città del Vaticano 1979.

CORNELL-MATTHEWS
1984
T. Cornell - G. Matthews, *Atlante del mondo romano*, Novara 1984.

CSEL
Corpus Scriptorum Ecclesiasticorum Latinorum, Wien 1865 ff.

D'ANGELA 1985
C. D'Angela, 'L'obolo a Caronte. Usi funerari medievali tra paganesimo e cristianesimo', *Quaderni Medievali* 15, 1985, pp. 82-91.

DAGENS 1971
C. Dagens, 'A propos du cubiculum de la «velatio»', *Rivista di Archeologia Cristiana* 47, 1971, pp. 119-129.

DAL COVOLO 1989
E. Dal Covolo, *I Severi e il cristianesimo. Ricerche sull'ambiente storico-istituzionale delle origini cristiane tra il secondo e il terzo secolo*, Roma 1989.

DANIÉLOU-MARROU
1970
J. Daniélou - H. I. Marrou, *Nuova storia della Chiesa*, I, *Dalle origini a S. Gregorio Magno*, Torino 1970.

DASSMANN 1973
E. Dassmann, *Sündenvergebung durch Taufe, Buße und Martyrerfürbitte in den Zeugnissen frühchristlicher Frömmigkeit und Kunst*, Münster 1973.

DE BRUYNE 1959
L. De Bruyne, 'Les lois de l'art paléochrétien comme instrument herméneutique', *Rivista di Archeologia Cristiana* 35, 1959, pp. 183-211.

DE BRUYNE 1968
L. De Bruyne, 'L'importanza degli scavi lateranensi per la cronologia delle prime pitture catacombali', *Rivista di Archeologia Cristiana* 44, 1968, pp. 81-116.

DE BRUYNE 1969
L. De Bruyne, 'La peinture cémeteriale constantinienne', *Akten des VII Internationalen Kongresses für Christliche Archäologie, Trier 5-11 Sept. 1965*, Berlin-Città del Vaticano 1969, pp. 29-159.

DE BRUYNE
1969-1970
L. De Bruyne, 'Aristote ou Socrate? A propos d'une peinture de la via Latina', *Rendiconti della Pontificia Accademia Romana di Archeologia* 42, 1969-1970, pp. 173-183.

DE BRUYNE 1970
L. De Bruyne, 'La cappella greca di Priscilla', *Rivista di Archeologia Cristiana* 46, 1970, pp. 291-330.

DE FRANCESCO
1998
D. De Francesco, 'Proprietà fondiaria ed evergetismo privato: considerazioni e problemi a proposito della donazione di Gallicanus nella «Vita Silvestri»', *Il Lazio tra antichità e medioevo. Studi in memoria di Jean Coste*, Roma 1998.

DE MARIA
1991-1992
L. De Maria, *Contributo alla conoscenza del fenomeno del «trasporto dei corpi santi» nella Roma del Seicento: La collezione epigrafica del portico di Santa Maria in Trastevere*, Unprinted thesis, Scuola Nazionale di Archeologia. Università degli Studi di Roma «La Sapienza», Roma 1991-1992.

DE ROSSI 1864
G. B. de Rossi, 'Patena vitrea adorna di immagini bibliche scoperta in Colonia', *Bullettino di Archeologia Cristiana* 2, 1864, pp. 89-91.

DE ROSSI
1864-1877
G. B. de Rossi, *La Roma sotterranea cristiana*, I-III, Roma 1864-1877.

DE ROSSI 1874
G. B. de Rossi, 'Scoperta della basilica di S. Petronilla col sepolcro dei martiri Nereo ed Achilleo nel cimitero di Domitilla', *Bullettino di Archeologia Cristiana*, ser. II, 5, 1874, pp. 5-35; 68-74.

DE ROSSI
1884-1885
G. B. de Rossi, 'Scoperta d'una cripta storica nel cimitero di Massimo ad sanctam Felicitatem sulla via Salaria Nuova', *Bullettino di Archeologia Cristiana*, ser. IV, 3, 1884-1885, pp. 149-184.

DE ROSSI 1888
G. B. de Rossi, *Inscriptiones Christianae Urbis Romae septimo saeculo antiquiores*, II vol., Roma 1888.

DE ROSSI
1888-1889
G. B. de Rossi, 'L'ipogeo degli Acilii Glabrioni nel cimitero di Priscilla', *Bullettino di Archeologia Cristiana*, ser. IV, 6, 1888-1889, pp. 15-66; 103-133.

DE ROSSI 1891
G. B. de Rossi, 'L'Accademia di Pomponio Leto e le sue memorie scritte sulle pareti delle catacombe romane', *Bullettino di Archeologia Cristiana*, ser. V, 1, 1891, pp. 81-94.

DE ROSSI 1994
Giovanni Battista de Rossi e le catacombe romane. Mostra fotografica e documentaria in occasione del I Centenario della morte di Giovanni Battista de Rossi (1894-1994), Città del Vaticano 1994.

DE ROSSI-FERRUA
1944   G. B. de Rossi, *Sulla questione del vaso di sangue. Memoria inedita con introduzione storica e appendici di documenti inediti per cura del P. Antonio Ferrua S. I.*, Città del Vaticano 1944.

DE SANTIS 1994   P. De Santis, 'Elementi di corredo nei sepolcri delle catacombe romane: l'esempio della regione di Leone e della galleria Bb nella catacomba di Commodilla', *Vetera Christianorum*, 31, 1994, pp. 23-51.

DE VISSCHER 1951   F. De Visscher, 'Le régime juridique des plus anciens cimetières chrétiens à Rome', *Art Bulletin* 69, 1951, pp. 39-54.

DECKERS 1992   J. G. Deckers, 'Wie genau ist eine Katakombe zu datieren?', *Memoriam Sanctorum Venerantes. Miscellanea in onore di V. Saxer*, Città del Vaticano 1992, pp. 217-238.

DECKERS-MIETKE-
WEILAND 1991   J. G. Deckers - G. Mietke - A. Weiland, *Die Katakombe «Anonima di via Anapo». Repertorium der Malereien*, Città del Vaticano 1991.

DECKERS-MIETKE-
WEILAND 1994   J. G. Deckers - G. Mietke - A. Weiland, *Die Katakombe «Commodilla». Repertorium der Malereien*, Città del Vaticano 1994.

DECKERS-SEELIGER-
MIETKE 1987   J.G. Deckers - H.R. Seeliger - G. Mietke, *Die Katakombe «Santi Marcellino e Pietro». Repertorium der Malereien*, Città del Vaticano-Münster 1987.

DEICHMANN 1970   F. W. Deichmann, 'Märtyrerbasilika, Martyrion, Memoria und Altargrab', *Mitteilungen des Deutschen Archäologischen Instituts (Rom)* 77, 1970, pp. 144-169.

DEICHMANN 1993   F. W. Deichmann, *Archeologia Cristiana*, Roma 1993.

DEICHMANN-TSCHIRA
1957   F. W. Deichmann - A. Tschira, 'Das Mausoleum der Kaiserin Helena und die Basilika der Heiligen Marcellinus und Petrus an der Via Labicana vor Rom', *Jahrbuch des Deutschen Archäologischen Instituts* 72, 1957, pp. 44-110.

DI BERARDINO 1983 A. Di Berardino, headword *Clero*, DPAC, I, cols. 716-721.

DI STEFANO
MANZELLA 1997   I. Di Stefano Manzella (ed.), *Le iscrizioni dei cristiani in Vaticano*, (Inscriptiones Sanctae Sedis, 2), Città del Vaticano 1997.

DORIGO 1966   W. Dorigo, *Pittura tardoromana*, Milano 1966.

DPAC   *Dizionario Patristico e di Antichità Cristiane*, 3 vols., Casale Monferrato 1983-1988

DUCHESNE 1907   L. Duchesne, *Histoire ancienne de l'Église*, II, Paris 1907.

DULAEY 1977   M. Dulaey, 'L'entretien des cimetières romains du 5e au 7e siècle', *Cahiers Archéologiques* 26, 1977, pp. 7-18.

DUVAL 1988   Y. Duval, *Auprès des saints, corps et âme. L'inhumation «ad sanctos» dans la chrétienté d'Orient et d'Occident du IIIe au VIIe siècle*, Paris 1988.

DUVAL 1991   Y. Duval, «Sanctorum sepulcris sociari», *Les fonctions des saints dans le monde occidental (IIIe-XIIIe siècle). Actes du colloque organisé par l'École Française de Rome avec le concours de l'Université de Rome «La Sapienza», Rome, 27-29 octobre 1988*, Rome 1991, pp. 333-351.

ECK 1996   W. Eck, *Tra epigrafia, prosopografia e archeologia. Scritti scelti, rielaborati ed aggiornati*, Roma 1996.

ENGEMANN
1968-1969   J. Engemann, 'Bemerkungen zu spätrömischen Gläsern mit Goldfolien-Dekor', *Jahrbuch für Antike und Christentum* 11-12, 1968-1969, pp. 7-25.

ENGEMANN 1973   J. Engemann, *Untersuchugen zur Sepulkralsymbolik der späteren römischen Kaiserzeit*, Münster 1973.

ENGEMANN 1983   J. Engemann, 'Altes und neues zu Beispielen heidnischer und christlicher Katakombenbilder im spätantiken Rom', *Jahrbuch für Antike und Christentum* 26, 1983, pp. 128-151.

ENGEMANN 1990   J. Engemann, headword *Hirt*, Reallexikon für Antike und Christentum 116, 1990, cols. 577-607.

ENNABLI 1976   A. Ennabli, *Lampes chrétiennes de Tunisie (Musées du Bardo et de Carthage)*, Paris 1976

FAEDO 1978   L. Faedo, 'Per una classificazione preliminare dei vetri dorati tardoromani', *Annali della Scuola Normale Superiore di Pisa, Classe di Lettere e Filosofia* III, 8, 3, 1978, pp. 1025-1070.

FAEDO 1985   L. Faedo, 'Su alcuni vetri dorati della raccolta oliveriana di Pesaro. Contributi per l'esegesi iconografica e la cronologia', *Atti del VI Congresso Nazionale di Archeologia Cristiana, Pesaro-Ancona 19-23 settembre 1983*, II, Ancona 1985, pp. 473-487.

FAEDO 1995   L. Faedo, 'Nuovi contributi sui vetri dorati tardoromani', *XLII Corso di Cultura sull'Arte Ravennate e Bizantina, Ravenna 14-19 maggio 1995*, Ravenna 1995, pp. 311-336.

FARIOLI 1963   R. Farioli, *Pitture di epoca tarda nelle catacombe romane*, Ravenna 1963.

FASOLA 1954-1955   U. M. Fasola, 'Le recenti scoperte agiografiche nel Coemeterium Majus', *Rendiconti della Pontificia Accademia Romana di Archeologia* 28, 1954-1955, pp. 75-89.

FASOLA 1956   U. M. Fasola, 'Topographische Argumente zur Datierung der «Madonna orans» im Coemeterium Majus', *Römische Quartalschrift für christliche Altertumskunde und für Kirchengeschichte* 51, 1956, pp. 137-147.

FASOLA 1961   U. M. Fasola, 'La regione delle cattedre nel Cimitero Maggiore', *Rivista di Archeologia Cristiana* 37, 1961, pp. 237-267.

FASOLA 1965   U. M. Fasola, *La basilica dei SS. Nereo ed Achilleo e la catacomba di Domitilla* (*Le chiese di Roma illustrate*, 44), Roma 1965.

FASOLA 1970   U. M. Fasola, 'La basilica sotterranea di S. Tecla e le regioni cimiteriali vicine', *Rivista di Archeologia Cristiana* 46, 1970, pp. 193-288.

FASOLA 1972   U. M. Fasola, 'Le recenti scoperte nelle catacombe sotto Villa Savoia. Il «Coemeterium Iordanorum ad S. Alexandrum»', *Actas del VIII Congreso Internacional de Arqueologia Cristiana, Barcelona, 5-11 octubre 1969*, Città del Vaticano 1972, pp. 273-297.

FASOLA 1974   U. M. Fasola, 'La «Regio IV» nel cimitero di S. Agnese', *Rivista di Archeologia Cristiana* 50, 1974, pp. 175-205.

FASOLA 1975-1976   U. M. Fasola, *Enrico Josi*, in *Rendiconti della Pontificia Accademia Romana di Archeologia* 48, 1975-1976, pp. 3-9.

FASOLA 1976   U. M. Fasola, 'Les catacombes entre la légende et l'histoire', *Dossiers de l'Archéologie* 18, 1976, pp. 54-62.

FASOLA 1980   U. M. Fasola, 'Indagini nel sopratterra della catacomba di S. Callisto', *Rivista di Archeologia Cristiana* 56, 1980, pp. 221-278.

FASOLA 1982-1984   U. M. Fasola, 'Scoperta di un probabile santuario di martiri in una regione post-costantiniana della catacomba «ad duas lauros»', *Rendiconti della Pontificia Accademia Romana di Archeologia* 55-56, 1982-1984, pp. 341-359.

FASOLA 1983   U. M. Fasola, headword *cimitero*, DPAC, I, cols. 666-677.

FASOLA 1985   U. M. Fasola, 'Un tardo cimitero cristiano inserito in una necropoli pagana della via Appia', *Rivista di Archeologia Cristiana* 61, 1985, pp. 13-57.

FASOLA 1987   U. M. Fasola, 'Scoperte recenti nell'ultima catacomba visitata da Padre Bruzza. La sua attività in favore delle catacombe romane', *Atti del convegno di studi nel centenario della morte di Luigi Bruzza, 1883-1983, Vercelli, 6-7 ottobre 1984*, Vercelli 1987, pp. 209-230.

FASOLA 1994   U. M. Fasola, headword *catacombe*, Enciclopedia dell'Arte Antica Classica e Orientale, II, *supplemento* 2, 1994, cols. 49-57.

FASOLA-FIOCCHI NICOLAI 1989   U. M. Fasola - V. Fiocchi Nicolai, 'Le necropoli durante la formazione della città cristiana', *Actes du XIe Congrès International d'Archéologie Chrétienne, Lyon, Vienne, Grenoble, Genève et Aoste, 21-28 september 1986*, II, Città del Vaticano 1989, pp. 1153-1205.

FASOLA-TESTINI 1978   U. M. Fasola - P. Testini, 'I cimiteri cristiani', *Atti del IX Congresso Internazionale di Archeologia Cristiana, Roma 21-27 settembre 1975*, Città del Vaticano 1978, pp. 103-139; pp. 191-198.

FELLE 1995   A. E. Felle, 'Loci scritturistici nella produzione epigrafica romana', *Vetera Christianorum* 32, 1995, pp. 61-89.

FELLE 1997   A. E. Felle, 'Manifestazioni di bilinguismo nelle iscrizioni cristiane di Roma', *Preatti dell'XI Congresso Internazionale di Epigrafia Greca e Latina, Roma 18-24 settembre 1997*, Roma 1997, pp. 669-676.

193

FELLE-DEL MORO-
NUZZO 1994   A. E. Felle - M.P. Del Moro - D. Nuzzo, 'Elementi di «corredo-arredo» delle tombe del cimitero di S. Ippolito sulla via Tiburtina', *Rivista di Archeologia Cristiana* 70, 1994, pp. 89-158.

FELLE-GIULIANI
in press   A. E. Felle - R. Giuliani, 'Nuove indagini sulla catacomba dell'ex Vigna Chiaraviglio nel comprensorio callistiano dell'Appia antica a Roma (1990-91)', *Atti del VII Congresso Nazionale di Archeologia Cristiana*, Cassino 20-24 settembre 1993, in press.

FERRARY 1996   J.-L. Ferrary, *Onofrio Panvinio et les antiquités romaines*, Rome 1996.

FERRETTO 1942   G. Ferretto, *Note storico-bibliografiche di archeologia cristiana*, Città del Vaticano 1942.

FERRUA 1938   A. Ferrua, 'Le tre Rome Sotterranee', *La Civiltà Cattolica* 89, III, 1938, pp. 399-412.

FERRUA 1942   A. Ferrua, *Epigrammata Damasiana*, Città del Vaticano 1942.

FERRUA 1943   A. Ferrua, 'Nuove osservazioni sull'epitaffio di Abercio', *Rivista di Archeologia Cristiana* 20, 1943, pp. 279-305.

FERRUA 1944   A. Ferrua, «Novatiano beatissimo martyri», *La Civiltà Cattolica* 95, IV, 1944, pp. 232-239.

FERRUA 1949   A. Ferrua, headword *Bosio Antonio*, Enciclopedia Cattolica, II, Città del Vaticano 1949, cols. 1943-1944.

FERRUA 1957   A. Ferrua, 'Scoperta di una nuova regione nella catacomba di Commodilla', *Rivista di rcheologia Cristiana* 33, 1957, pp. 7-43.

FERRUA 1958   A. Ferrua, 'Scoperta di una nuova regione della catacomba di Commodilla (II parte)', *Rivista di Archeologia Cristiana* 34, 1958, pp. 5-56.

FERRUA 1960   A. Ferrua, 'Una catacomba di diritto privato', *La Civiltà Cattolica* 111, III, 1960, pp. 473-480.

FERRUA 1960a   A. Ferrua, *Le pitture della nuova catacomba di via Latina*, Città del Vaticano 1960.

FERRUA 1961   A. Ferrua, «Qui filius diceris et pater inveniris». Mosaico novellamente scoperto nella catacomba di S. Domitilla, *Rendiconti della Pontificia Accademia Romana di Archeologia* 33, 1961, pp. 209-224.

FERRUA 1968   A. Ferrua, 'I primordi della Commissione di Archeologia Sacra 1851-1852', *Archivio della Società Romana di Storia Patria* 91, 1968, pp. 251-278.

FERRUA 1970   A. Ferrua, 'Problemi archeologici per l'insegnamento della Storia Ecclesiastica', *La Chiesa antica nei secoli II-V*, Milano 1970, pp. 207-221.

FERRUA 1971   A. Ferrua, 'La catacomba di Vibia', *Rivista di Archeologia Cristiana* 47, 1971, pp. 7-62.

FERRUA 1978   A. Ferrua, 'L'epigrafia cristiana prima di Costantino', *Atti del IX Congresso Internazionale di Archeologia Cristiana*, Roma 21-27 settembre 1975, Città del Vaticano 1978, pp. 583-613.

FERRUA 1985   A. Ferrua, *Note al Thesaurus Linguae Latinae. Addenda et corrigenda (A-D)*, Bari 1985.

FERRUA 1986   A. Ferrua, *Sigilli su calce nelle catacombe*, Città del Vaticano 1986.

FERRUA 1990   A. Ferrua, *San Sebastiano*, Bari 1990.

FERRUA 1991   A. Ferrua, *La polemica antiariana nei monumenti paleocristiani*, Città del Vaticano 1991.

FERRUA 1991a   A. Ferrua, *Scritti vari di antichità cristiane*, Bari 1991.

FERRUA-CARLETTI
1985   A. Ferrua - C. Carletti, *Damaso e i martiri di Roma*, Città del Vaticano 1985.

FÉVRIER 1959   P.-A. Février, 'Étude sur les catacombes romaines', *Cahiers Archéologiques* 10, 1959, pp. 1-26.

FÉVRIER 1977   P.-A. Février, 'A propos du repas funéraire. Culte et sociabilité. «In Christo Deo pax et concordia sit convivio nostro»', *Cahiers Archéologiques* 26, 1977, pp. 29-45.

FÉVRIER 1978   P.-A. Février, 'Le culte des morts dans les communautés chrétiennes durant le IIIe siècle', *Atti del IX Congresso Internazionale di Archeologia Cristiana*, Roma, 21-27 settembre 1975, I, Città del Vaticano 1978, pp. 11-274.

FÉVRIER 1983 · P.-A. Février, 'Une approche de la conversion des élites au IVᵉ siècle: le décor de la mort', *Miscellanea Historiae Ecclesiasticae*, VI, *Congrès de Varsovie 1978*, Bruxelles 1983, pp. 22-45.

FÉVRIER 1983a · P.-A. Février, 'Images et société' (IIIᵉ-IVᵉ siècles), *Crise et redressement dans les provinces européennes de l'Empire (milieu du IIIᵉ - milieu du IVᵉ siècle ap. J.-C.). Actes du colloque de Strasbourg (décembre 1981)*, Strasbourg 1983, pp. 27-48.

FÉVRIER 1985 · P.-A. Février, 'La morte cristiana: immagini e vissuto quotidiano', *Storia vissuta del popolo cristiano*, Torino 1985.

FÉVRIER 1989 · P.-A. Février, 'A propos de la date des peintures des catacombes romaines', *Rivista di Archeologia Cristiana* 65, 1989, pp. 105-133.

FÉVRIER 1992 · P.-A. Février, 'Un plaidoyer pour Damase. Les inscriptions des nécropoles romaines', *Institutions, société et vie politique dans l'Empire Romain au IVᵉ siècle ap. J. C. Actes de la table ronde autour de l'oeuvre d'André Chastagnol (Paris, 20-21 janvier 1989)*, Rome 1992, pp. 497-506.

FILIPPI 1996 · G. Filippi, AA.VV., *Dalla terra alle genti. La diffusione del Cristianesimo nei primi secoli*, Milano 1996, No. 24-25, pp. 182-184.

FINOCCHIARO 1995 · G. Finocchiaro, 'La «Roma sotterranea» e la Congregazione dell'Oratorio. Inediti e lacune del manoscritto vallicelliano G.31', *Messer Filippo Neri, santo: l'apostolo di Roma*, Roma 1995, pp. 189-193.

FIOCCHI NICOLAI 1982 · V. Fiocchi Nicolai, 'L'ipogeo detto di Scarpone presso Porta S. Pancrazio', *Rivista di Archeologia Cristiana* 58, 1982, pp. 7-28.

FIOCCHI NICOLAI 1983 · V. Fiocchi Nicolai, headword *Cubiculario*, DPAC, I, cols. 872-873.

FIOCCHI NICOLAI 1991 · V. Fiocchi Nicolai, 'Storia e topografia della catacomba anonima di via Anapo', Deckers-Mietke-Weiland 1991, pp. 3-23.

FIOCCHI NICOLAI 1994 · V. Fiocchi Nicolai, 'Evergetismo ecclesiastico e laico nelle iscrizioni paleocristiane del lazio', *Historiam Pictura Refert. Miscellanea in onore di Padre Alejandro Recio Veganzones*, Città del Vaticano 1994, pp. 237-252.

FIOCCHI NICOLAI 1995 · V. Fiocchi Nicolai, «Itinera ad sanctos». Testimonianze monumentali del passaggio dei pellegrini nei santuari del suburbio romano, *Akten des XII. Internationalen Kongresses für Christliche Archäologie, Bonn, 22.-28. September 1991*, II, Città del Vaticano 1995, pp. 763-775.

FIOCCHI NICOLAI 1995a · V. Fiocchi Nicolai, 'Una nuova basilica a deambulatorio nel comprensorio della catacomba di S. Callisto a Roma', *Akten des XII. Internationalen Kongresses für Christliche Archäologie, Bonn, 22.-28. September 1991*, II, Città del Vaticano 1995, pp. 776-786.

FIOCCHI NICOLAI 1997 · V. Fiocchi Nicolai, 'Strutture funerarie ed edifici di culto paleocristiani di Roma dal III al VI secolo', Di Stefano Manzella 1997, pp. 121-141

FIOCCHI NICOLAI 1997a · V. Fiocchi Nicolai, 'La nuova basilica paleocristiana «circiforme» della via Ardeatina', *Via Appia. Sulle ruine della magnificenza antica*, Milano 1997, pp. 78-83.

FIOCCHI NICOLAI 1998 · V. Fiocchi Nicolai, 'Considerazioni sulla funzione del cosiddetto battistero di Ponziano sulla via Portuense', *Il Lazio tra antichità e medioevo. Studi in memoria di Jean Coste*, Roma 1998, pp. 307-316.

FIOCCHI NICOLAI in press · V. Fiocchi Nicolai, 'Giovanni Battista de Rossi e le catacombe romane (1894-1994)', *Atti del XIII Congressus Internationalis Archaeologiae Christianae, Split-Poreć, 25-9 / 1-10 1994*, in press.

FIOCCHI NICOLAI in press · Fiocchi Nicolai, 'S. Filippo Neri, le catacombe di S. Sebastiano e le origini dell'archeologia cristiana', *S. Filippo Neri nella realtà del XVI secolo, Roma, 11-13 maggio 1995*, in press.

FIOCCHI NICOLAI et Alii 1992 · V. Fiocchi Nicolai - R. Martorelli - G. Chiarucci - L. Spera - P. Di Marco - P. M. Barbini, 'Scavi nella catacomba di S. Senatore ad Albano Laziale', *Rivista di Archeologia Cristiana* 68, 1992, pp. 7-140.

FIOCCHI NICOLAI-
DEL MORO-NUZZO-
SPERA
in press · V. Fiocchi Nicolai - M. P. Del Moro - D. Nuzzo - L. Spera, 'La nuova basilica circiforme della via Ardeatina', *Rendiconti della Pontificia Accademia Romana di Archeologia*, in press.

FORNARI 1932 · F. Fornari, 'Il rilievo del complesso monumentale di San Sebastiano sulla via Appia', *Rivista di Archeologia Cristiana* 9, 1932, pp. 201-213.

FREMERSDORF 1962 · F. Fremersdorf, *Die römischen Gläser mit aufgelegten Nuppen in Köln*, Köln 1962.

FREMIOTTI 1926 · P. Fremiotti, *La Riforma Cattolica del secolo decimosesto e gli studi di Archeologia Cristiana*, Roma 1926.

FREND 1996 · W. H. C. Frend, *The Archaeology of Early Christianity: A History*, London 1996.

FREY 1975² · J. B. Frey, *Corpus Inscriptionum Iudaicarum*, vol. I, New York 1975².

FRUTAZ 1976 · A. P. Frutaz, *Il complesso monumentale di Sant'Agnese*, Città del Vaticano 1976.

GARRUCCI 1864 · R. Garrucci, *Vetri ornati di figure in oro trovati nei cimiteri cristiani di Roma*, Roma 1864.

GCS · *Die griechischen christlichen Schriftsteller*, Leipzig-Berlin 1897 ff.

GEERTMAN 1995 · H. Geertman, 'Cripta anulare 'ante litteram'. Forma, contesto e significato del monumento sepolcrale di San Lorenzo a Roma', *Martyrium* 1995, pp. 125-155.

GESTA EPISCOPORUM · *Gesta Episcoporum Neapolitanorum, Monumenta Germaniae Historica. Scriptores rerum Langobardicarum et Italicarum saec. VI-IX*, Hannoverae 1878.

GHEDINI 1990 · F. Ghedini, 'Raffigurazioni conviviali nei monumenti funerari romani', *Rivista di Archeologia* 14, 1990, pp. 35-62.

GIORDANI 1978 · R. Giordani, 'Probabili echi della crisi ariana in alcune figurazioni paleocristiane', *Rivista di Archeologia Cristiana* 54, 1978, pp. 229-263.

GIULIANI 1994 · R. Giuliani, 'Il restauro dell'arcosolio di Veneranda nelle catacombe di Domitilla sulla via Ardeatina', *Rivista di Archeologia Cristiana* 70, 1994, pp. 61-87.

GIULIANI 1996 · R. Giuliani, 'Il restauro del cubicolo detto «delle stagioni» nella catacomba dei Ss. Marcellino e Pietro sulla via Labicana', *Rivista di Archeologia Cristiana* 72, 1996, pp. 35-64.

GIULIANI 1997 · R. Giuliani, 'Il mosaico nelle catacombe romane', *Riscoperta del mosaico* 1, 2, 1997, pp. 4-9.

GIULIANI 1997a · R. Giuliani, 'Un arcosolio mosaicato nel secondo piano del cimitero di Priscilla. Il contributo delle analisi di fluorescenza da ultravioletti e da raggi x per la conoscenza di una decorazione musiva in avanzato stato di degrado', *Associazione Italiana per lo Studio e la Conservazione del Mosaico, Atti del IV Colloquio, Palermo 9-13 dicembre 1996*, Ravenna 1997, pp. 791-806.

GIULIANI 1997b · R. Giuliani, 'Gli affreschi salvati', *Archeo* 143, 1997, pp. 52-56.

GIULIANI 1998 · R. Giuliani, 'Un'interessante novità epigrafica dalla catacomba della ex Vigna Chiaraviglio sulla via Appia antica. Ancora sull'attività dei presbiteri Proclino e Urso a S. Sebastiano', *Domum Tuam Dilexi. Miscellanea in onore di Aldo Nestori*, Città del Vaticano 1998, pp. 375-397.

GIULIANI
in press · R. Giuliani, 'Il restauro del cubicolo detto «degli atleti» nella catacomba dei Ss. Marcellino e Pietro sulla via Labicana', *Atti del XIII Congressus Internationalis Archaeologiae Christianae, Split-Poreč, 25-9 / 1-10 1994*, in press.

GIUNTELLA 1985 · A. M. Giuntella, *Mense e riti funerari in Sardegna*, Taranto 1985.

GOFFREDO
in press · D. Goffredo, *Le cosiddette scene di ingresso nell'arte paleocristiana*, in press.

GRABAR 1966 · A. Grabar, *Le premier art chrétien*, Paris 1966.

GRABAR 1968 · A. Grabar, *Christian Iconography. A Study of its origins*, London 1968.

GRAZIANI ABBIANI
1969 · M. Graziani Abbiani, *Lucerne fittili paleocristiane nell'Italia Settentrionale*, Bologna 1969.

GROSSI-DI BERARDINO
1984   V. Grossi - A. Di Berardino, *La Chiesa antica: ecclesiologia e istituzioni,* Roma 1984.

GUARDUCCI 1966   M. Guarducci, 'La morte di Cleopatra nella catacomba della via Latina', *Rendiconti della Pontificia Accademia Romana di Archeologia* 38, 1966, pp. 259-281.

GUARDUCCI 1978   M. Guarducci, *Epigrafia greca,* IV, Roma 1978.

GUIDOBALDI-GUIGLIA
1983   F. Guidobaldi - A. Guiglia, *Pavimenti marmorei di Roma dal IV al IX secolo,* Città del Vaticano 1983.

GUYON 1974   J. Guyon, 'La vente des tombes à travers l'épigraphie de la Rome chrétienne (IIIe-VIIe siècles): le rôle des fossores, mansionarii, praepositi et prêtres', *Mélanges de l'École Française de Rome, Antiquité,* 86, 1974, pp. 549-596.

GUYON 1987   J. Guyon, *Le cimetière aux deux lauriers. Recherches sur les catacombes romaines,* Città del Vaticano 1987.

GUYON 1994   J. Guyon, 'Peut-on vraiment dater une catacombe? Retour sur le cimitière «aux deux lauriers» ou catacombe des saints Marcellin et Pierre, sur la via Labicana à Rome', *Boreas* 14, 1994, pp. 89-103.

GUYON 1995   J. Guyon, 'L'église de Rome du IVe siècle à Sixte III (312-432)', *Histoire du christianisme des origines à nos jours,* II, *Naissance d'une chrétienté (250-430),* Paris 1995, pp. 771-798.

HIMMELMANN 1973   N. Himmelmann, *Typologische Untersuchungen an römischen Sarkophagreliefs des 3. und 4. Jahrhunderts n. Chr.,* Mainz am Rhein 1973.

HIMMELMANN 1975   N. Himmelmann, 'Das Hypogäum der Aurelier am viale Manzoni', *Akademie der Wissenschaften und der Literatur,* Mainz am Rhein 1975, pp. 7-26.

HIMMELMANN 1980   N. Himmelmann, *Über Hirten-Genre in der antiken Kunst,* Opladen 1980.

HORNUS 1973-1974   H. M. Hornus, 'Les inscriptions funéraires militaires chrétiennes anciennes', *Archiv für Papyrusforschung* 22-23, 1973-1974, pp. 223-228.

ICUR   A. Silvagni - A. Ferrua - D. Mazzoleni - C. Carletti, *Inscriptiones Christianae Urbis Romae septimo saeculo antiquiores, nova series,* vols I-X, Roma-Città del Vaticano 1922-1992.

ILCV   E. Diehl, *Inscriptiones Latinae Christianae Veteres,* I-III, Berolini 1925-1931.

JANSSENS 1981   J. Janssens, *Vita e morte del cristiano negli epitaffi di Roma anteriori al sec. VII,* Roma 1981.

JASTRZEBOWSKA
1970   E. Jastrzebowska, 'Les scènes de banquet dans les peintures et sculptures des IIIe et IVe siècles', *Recherches Augustiniennes* 14, 1979, pp. 3-90.

JOSI 1924   E. Josi, 'Il cimitero di Panfilo', *Rivista di Archeologia Cristiana* 1, 1924, pp. 15-119.

JOSI 1926   E. Josi, 'Il cimitero di Panfilo, parte II', *Rivista di Archeologia Cristiana* 3, 1926, pp. 51-211.

JOSI 1954   E. Josi, headword *Ugonio Pompeo,* Enciclopedia Cattolica, XII, Città del Vaticano 1954, cols. 715-716.

JURGENS 1972   H. Jurgens, *Pompa diaboli. Die lateinischen Kirchenväter und das Theater,* Stuttgart 1972.

KAJANTO 1962   I. Kajanto, 'On the problem of names of humility', *Arctos* 3, 1962, pp. 45-53.

KAJANTO 1965   I. Kajanto, *The latin cognomina,* Helsinki 1965.

KAJANTO 1966   I. Kajanto, *Supernomina,* Helsinki 1966.

KAJANTO 1997   I. Kajanto, 'Roman Nomenclature during the Late Empire', Di Stefano Manzella 1997, pp. 103-111.

KIRSCHBAUM 1957   E. Kirschbaum, *Die Gräber der Apostelfürsten,* Frankfurt am Main 1957.

KITZINGER 1963   E. Kitzinger, 'The Hellenistic Heritage in Byzantine Art', *Dumbarton Oaks Papers* 17, 1963, pp. 63-79.

KITZINGER 1989   E. Kitzinger, *L'arte bizantina,* Milano 1989.

KLAUSER 1958   Th. Klauser, 'Studien zur Entstehungsgeschichte der christlichen Kunst', *Jahrbuch für Antike und Christentum* 1, 1958, pp. 20-51.

KOLLWITZ 1969   J. Kollwitz, 'Die Malerei der Konstantinischen Zeit', *Akten des VII Internationalen*

Kongresses für Christliche Archäologie, Trier 5-11 Sept. 1965, Berlin-Città del Vaticano 1969, pp. 29-158.

KÖTZSCHE
BREITENBRUCH 1976   L. Kötzsche Breitenbruch, *Die neue Katakombe an der via Latina in Rom. Untersuchungen zur Ikonographie der Alttestamentlichen Wandmalereien*, Münster i. Westfalen 1976.

KRAUTHEIMER
1937-1980   R. Krautheimer, *Corpus Basilicarum Christianarum Romae. Le basiliche paleocristiane di Roma (sec. IV-IX)*, I-V, Città del Vaticano 1937-1980.

KRAUTHEIMER
1980-1982   R. Krautheimer, 'Intorno alla fondazione di San Paolo fuori le mura', *Rendiconti della Pontificia Accademia Romana di Archeologia* 53-54, 1980-1981 / 1981-1982, pp. 207-220.

L'HEUREUX 1856   G. L'Heureux (Macario), *Hagioglypta sive picturae et sculpturae sacrae antiquiores, praesertim quae Romae reperiuntur*, ed. R. Garrucci, Lutetiae Parisiorum 1856.

LA ROCCA 1988   C. La Rocca, 'Morte e società. Studi recenti sulle necropoli altomedievali', *Quaderni Medievali* 26, 1988, pp. 236-245.

LECLERCQ 1950   H. Leclercq, headword *Rossi (J.-B. de)*, Dictionnaire d'Archéologie chrétienne et de Liturgie, XV, 1, Paris 1950, cols. 93-99.

LP   *Le Liber Pontificalis. Texte, introduction et commentaire*, ed. L. Duchesne, I-II, Paris 1886-1892; III, ed. C. Vogel, Paris 1957.

LUISELLI 1986   B. Luiselli, 'In margine al problema della traslazione delle ossa di Pietro e Paolo', *Mélanges de l'École Française de Rome, Antiquité* 98, 1986, pp. 843-854.

LUMBROSO 1889   G. Lumbroso, 'Gli Accademici nelle catacombe', *Archivio della R. Società Romana di Storia Patria* 12, 1889, pp. 215-239.

MAC MULLEN 1989   R. Mac Mullen, *La diffusione del cristianesimo nell'Impero Romano. 100-400*, Roma-Bari 1989.

MANSI 1766   J. D. Mansi, *Sacrorum Conciliorum Nova et Amplissima Collectio*, XII, Florentiae 1766.

MARANGONI 1744   G. Marangoni, *Delle cose gentilesche e profane trasportate ad uso e a adornamento delle chiese*, Roma 1744.

MARCHI 1844   G. Marchi, *Monumenti delle arti cristiane primitive nella metropoli del cristianesimo. Architettura*, Roma 1844.

MARCONI
COSENTINO-RICCIARDI
1993   R. Marconi Cosentino - L. Ricciardi, *Catacomba di Commodilla. Lucerne e altri materiali delle gallerie 1, 8, 13*, Roma 1993.

MARKTHALER 1927   P. Markthaler, 'Die dekorativen Konstruktionen der Katakombendecken', *Römische Quartalschrift für christliche Altertumskunde und für Kirchengeschichte* 35, 1927, pp. 53-112.

MARTINEZ FAZIO
1976   L. M. Martinez Fazio, 'La eucarestia, banquete y sacrificio en la iconografia paleocristiana', *Gregorianum* 57, 1976, pp. 459-521.

MARTYRIUM 1995   *Martyrium in Multidisciplinary Perspective. Memorial Louis Reekmans*, Leuven 1995.

MARUCCHI 1910   O. Marucchi, *I monumenti del Museo Cristiano Pio Lateranense*, Milano 1910.

MARUCCHI 1914   O. Marucchi, *Monumenti del cimitero di Domitilla sulla via Ardeatina (Roma Sotterranea Cristiana, Nuova Serie, I, 2)*, Roma 1914.

MARUCCHI 1921   O. Marucchi, 'Un singolare gruppo di antiche pitture dell'ipogeo del viale Manzoni', *Nuovo Bollettino di Archeologia Cristiana* 27, 1921, pp. 83-93.

MARUCCHI 1933   O. Marucchi, *Le catacombe romane. Opera postuma*, Roma 1933.

MAZZARINO 1973   S. Mazzarino, *L'Impero Romano*, I-III, Roma-Bari 1973.

MAZZARINO 1974   S. Mazzarino, *Antico, tardoantico ed era costantiniana*, I, Bari 1974.

MAZZOLENI 1985   D. Mazzoleni, 'Tre iscrizioni della catacomba di Priscilla', *Rivista di Archeologia Cristiana* 61, 1985, pp. 265-273.

MAZZOLENI 1986   D. Mazzoleni, 'Il lavoro nell'epigrafia cristiana', *Spiritualità del lavoro nella catechesi dei Padri del III-IV secolo. Convegno di studio e aggiornamento, Roma, 15-17 marzo 1985*, Roma 1986, pp. 263-271.

MAZZOLENI 1989   D. Mazzoleni, 'Patristica ed epigrafia', *Complementi interdisciplinari di Patrologia*, Roma 1989, pp. 319-365.

MAZZOLENI 1989a   D. Mazzoleni, 'Iscrizioni inedite dalla catacomba di Panfilo', *Quaeritur inventus colitur, Miscellanea in onore del P. U. M. Fasola*, Città del Vaticano 1989, pp. 465-482.

MAZZOLENI 1993   D. Mazzoleni, 'Novità epigrafiche dalla catacomba di Panfilo', *Rendiconti della Pontificia Accademia Romana di Archeologia* 63, 1990-91, [1993], pp. 95-113

MAZZOLENI 1993a   D. Mazzoleni, 'Riferimenti alla catechesi nelle iscrizioni cristiane del IV secolo', *Esegesi e Catechesi dei Padri (secc. II-IV), Atti del Convegno di Studio e aggiornamento, Roma 26-28 marzo 1992*, Roma 1993, pp. 163-170.

MAZZOLENI 1994   D. Mazzoleni, 'Le «Inscriptiones Christianae Urbis Romae septimo saeculo antiquiores» (ICUR): stato attuale e prospettive', *Rivista di Archeologia Cristiana* 70, 1994, pp. 313-320.

MAZZOLENI 1997   D. Mazzoleni, 'Origine e cronologia dei monogrammi riflessi nelle iscrizioni dei Musei Vaticani', Di Stefano Manzella 1997, pp. 173-179.

MAZZOLENI
in press   D. Mazzoleni, 'L'epigrafia cristiana al tempo dei Severi', *Atti del I Convegno Internazionale di Studi Severiani, Albano Laziale, 31 maggio-1 giugno 1996*, in press.

MAZZOLENI et Alii
1983   D. Mazzoleni *et Alii*, 'Dentisti nell'arte paleocristiana', *La Nuova Stampa Medica Italiana* 3, 1983, 5, pp. 155-162.

MAZZOLENI-BISCONTI
1992   D. Mazzoleni - F. Bisconti, 'I martiri cristiani', *Archeo-Dossier* 87, 1992, pp. 52-97.

MEEKS 1992   W. A. Meeks, 'Il cristianesimo', *Storia di Roma*, II, *L'impero mediterraneo*, 3, *La cultura e l'Impero*, Torino 1992, pp. 283-319.

MENEGHINI-
SANTANGELI
VALENZANI 1993   R. Meneghini - R. Santangeli Valenzani, 'Sepolture intramuranee e paesaggio urbano a Roma tra V e VII secolo', *La storia economica di Roma nell'alto medioevo alla luce dei recenti scavi archeologici, Atti del Seminario, Roma 2-3 aprile 1992*, Firenze 1993, pp. 89-111.

MENEGHINI-
SANTANGELI
VALENZANI 1995   R. Meneghini - R. Santangeli Valenzani, 'Sepolture intramuranee a Roma tra V e VII secolo d. C. Aggiornamenti e considerazioni', *Archeologia Medievale* 22, 1995, pp. 283-290.

MERCATI 1937   G. Mercati, *Opere minori*, II (1897-1906) (*Studi e Testi*, 77), Città del Vaticano 1937.

MIELSCH 1978   H. Mielsch, 'Zur Stadtrömischen Malerei des 4. Jahrhundert n. Chr.', *Mitteilungen des Deutschen Archäologischen Instituts, Röm. Abt.* 85, 1978, pp. 187-192.

MINASI 1997   M. Minasi, 'Le vicende conservative dell'affresco di Turtura nel cimitero di Commodilla', *Rivista di Archeologia Cristiana* 73, 1997, pp. 65-97.

MINASI 1998   M. Minasi, 'Madonna col Bambino tra i santi Felice ed Adautto e la donatrice Turtura', *Romana pictura. La pittura romana dalle origini all'età bizantina*, Milano 1998, pp. 296-298.

MOORMANN 1998   E. Moormann, 'La pittura romana fra costruzione architettonica e arte figurativa', *Romana pictura. La pittura romana dalle origini all'età bizantina*, Milano 1998, pp. 14-32.

MOREY 1959   Ch. R. Morey, *The gold-glass collection of the Vatican Library*, Città del Vaticano 1959.

MURRAY 1981   S. Ch. Murray, *Rebirth and Afterlife. A Study of the Trasmutation of some pagan Imagery in Early Christian funerary Art*, Oxford 1981, pp. 98-111.

NESTORI 1959   A. Nestori, 'Un cimitero cristiano anonimo nella villa Doria Pamphilj a Roma', *Rivista di Archeologia Cristiana* 35, 1959, pp. 5-47.

NESTORI 1969   A. Nestori, 'Un ipogeo pagano fatto cristiano', *Akten des VII Internationalen Kongresses für Christliche Archäologie, Trier 5-11 Sept. 1965*, Berlin-Città del Vaticano 1969, pp. 637-642.

NESTORI 1971   A. Nestori, 'La catacomba di Calepodio al III miglio dell'Aurelia Vetus e i sepolcri dei papi Callisto I e Giulio I'. I parte, *Rivista di Archeologia Cristiana* 47, 1971, pp. 169-278.

NESTORI 1990   A. Nestori, *La basilica anonima della via Ardeatina*, Città del Vaticano 1990.

NORDBERG 1963   H. Nordberg, 'Éléments païens dans les tituli chrétiens de Rome', *Zilliacus* 1963, pp. 211-229

NR
A. Nestori, *Repertorio topografico delle pitture delle catacombe romane. II edizione riveduta e aggiornata*, Città del Vaticano 1993.

NUZZO 1997
D. Nuzzo, 'Provinciali a Roma nelle testimonianze dell'epigrafia sepolcrale tardoantica', *Preatti dell'XI Congresso Internazionale di Epigrafia Greca e Latina Roma, 18-24 settembre 1997)*, Roma 1997, pp. 705-712.

OSBORNE 1985
J. Osborne, 'The Roman Catacombs in the Middle Ages', *Papers of the British School at Rome 53*, 1985, pp. 278-328.

PAINTER 1988
K. Painter, 'Frammenti di coppa', AA.VV. *Vetri dei Cesari*, Milano 1988, pp. 279-281.

PALEANI 1993
M. T. Paleani, *Le lucerne paleocristiane. Monumenti, Musei e Gallerie Pontificie. Antiquarium Romanum*, Roma 1993.

PALEANI-LIVERANI 1984
M. T. Paleani - A. R. Liverani, *Lucerne paleocristiane conservate nel Museo Oliveriano di Pesaro*, Roma 1984.

PANI ERMINI 1969
L. Pani Ermini, 'L'ipogeo detto dei Flavi in Domitilla', *Rivista di Archeologia Cristiana 45*, 1969, pp. 119-174.

PANVINIO 1568
O. Panvinio, *De Ritu sepeliendi mortuos apud veteres christianos, et eorundem coemeteriis liber*, Coloniae 1568.

PARISE 1969
N. Parise, headword *Boldetti Marcantonio*, Dizionario Biografico degli Italiani, 11, Roma 1971, pp. 247-249.

PARISE 1971
N. Parise, headword *Bosio Antonio*, Dizionario Biografico degli Italiani, 11, Roma 1971, pp. 257-259.

PASQUATO 1984
O. Pasquato, headword *Spettacoli*, DPAC, 2, cols. 3281-3284

PAVOLINI 1981
C. Pavolini, 'Le lucerne dell'Italia romana. Merci, mercati e scambi nel Mediterraneo', *Società romana e produzione schiavistica*, II, Bari 1981, pp. 139-184; 278-288.

PERGOLA 1975
Ph. Pergola, 'La région dite du Bon Pasteur dans le cimetière de Domitilla sur l'Ardeatina. Étude topographique de son origine', *Rivista di Archeologia Cristiana 51*, 1975, pp. 65-96.

Pergola 1978
Ph. Pergola, 'La condamnation des Flaviens «chrétiens» sous Domitien: persécution religieuse ou répression à caractèr politique?', *Mélanges de l'Ecole Française de Rome, Antiquité 90*, 1978, pp. 407-423.

PERGOLA 1979
Ph. Pergola, 'Il «praedium Domitillae» sulla via Ardeatina: analisi storico-topografica delle testimonianze pagane fino alla metà del III sec. d. C.', *Rivista di Archeologia Cristiana 55*, 1979, pp. 313-335.

PERGOLA 1983
Ph. Pergola, 'La région dite des Flavii Aurelii dans la catacombe de Domitille: contribution à l'analyse de l'origine des grandes nécropoles souterraines de l'antiquité tardives à Rome', *Mélanges de l'École Française de Rome, Antiquité 95*, 1983, pp. 183-248.

PERGOLA 1985-1986
Ph. Pergola, 'L'origine della regione detta dello «scalone del 1897» nella catacomba di Domitilla', *Rendiconti della Pontificia Accademia Romana di Archeologia 58*, 1985-1986, pp. 49-60.

PERGOLA 1986
Ph. Pergola, 'Le catacombe romane: miti e realtà (a proposito del cimitero di Domitilla)', *Società Romana e Impero Tardoantico*, II, *Roma: politica, economia, paesaggio urbano*, Roma-Bari 1986, pp. 333-348.

PERGOLA 1986a
Ph. Pergola, 'Nereus et Achilleus martyres: l'intervention de Damase à Domitille (avec un appendice sur les résultats des fouilles récentes de la Basilique de Damase à Generosa)', *Saecularia Damasiana. Atti del convegno internazionale per il XVI centenario della morte di papa Damaso I 11-12-384 - 10/12-12-1984*, Città del Vaticano 1986, pp. 203-224.

PERGOLA 1990
Ph. Pergola, 'Mensores frumentarii christiani et Annone à la fin de l'Antiquité. Relecture d'une cycle de peintures', *Rivista di Archeologia Cristiana 66*, 1990, pp. 167-184.

PERGOLA 1992
Ph. Pergola, «Petronella martyr»: une évergète de la fin du IVe siècle?, *Memoriam Sanctorum Venerantes. Miscellanea in onore di V. Saxer*, Città del Vaticano 1992, pp. 627-636.

PERGOLA-BARBINI 1997
Ph. Pergola - P. M. Barbini, *Le catacombe romane. Storia e topografia*, Roma 1997.

PERRAYMOND 1980-81
M. Perraymond, 'Formule imprecatorie ('APAI) nelle iscrizioni funerarie paleocristiane', *Quaderni dell'Istituto di Lingua e Letteratura Latina 1-2*, 1980-81, pp. 115-152.

PETRUCCI 1995	A. Petrucci, *Le scritture ultime*, Torino 1995.
PG	*Patrologiae cursus completus. Accurante J.-P. Migne, Series Graeca*, Parisiis 1857 ff.
PICARD 1992	J.-Ch. Picard, *Cristianizzazione e pratiche funerarie. Tarda antichità e alto medioevo (IV-VIII sec.)*, Torino 1992.
PIETRI (L.) 1995	L. Pietri, 'Les résistances: de la polémique païenne à la persécution de Dioclétien', *Histoire du Christianisme des origines à nos jours*, II, *Naissance d'une chrétienté (250-430)*, Paris 1995, pp. 155-185.
PIETRI 1976	Ch. Pietri, *Roma christiana. Recherches sur l'Église de Rome, son organisation, sa politique, son idéologie de Miltiade à Sixte III (311-440)*, I-II, Rome 1976.
PIETRI 1993	Ch. Pietri, 'La Roma cristiana', *Storia di Roma*, III, *L'età tardoantica, 1, Crisi e trasformazioni*, Torino 1993, pp. 697-721.
PIETRI 1995	Ch. Pietri, 'La conversion: propagande et réalités de la loi et de l'évergétisme', *Histoire du Christianisme des origines à nos jours*, II, *Naissance d'une chrétienté (250-430)*, Paris 1995, pp. 189-227.
PILLINGER 1984	R. Pillinger, *Studien zu römischen Zwischengoldgläsern*, Wien 1984.
PINCHERLE 1984	A. Pincherle, *Vita di S. Agostino*, Bari 1984.
PL	*Patrologiae cursus completus. Accurante J.-P. Migne, Series Latina*, Parisiis 1844 ff.
POHL 1962	G. Pohl, 'Die frühchristliche Lampe vom Lorenzberg bei Epfach, Landkreis Schongau. Versuch einer Gliederung der Lampen vom mediterranen Typus', *Schriftenreihe zur Bayerischen Landesgeschichte* 62, München 1962, pp. 219-228.
PRANDI 1949-1951	A. Prandi, 'La cripta di S. Sebastiano', *Rendiconti della Pontificia Accademia Romana di Archeologia* 25-26, 1949-1950 / 1950-1951, pp. 139-152.
PROVOOST 1970	A. Provoost, 'Les lampes à récipient allongé trouvées dans les catacombes romaines. Essai de classification typologique', *Bullettin de l'Institut Historique Belge de Rome* 41, 1970, pp. 17-55.
PURCELL 1987	N. Purcell, 'Tomb und Suburb', *Römische Gräberstraßen. Selbstdarstellung, Status, Standard. Kolloquium in München vom 28. bis 30. Oktober 1985*, München 1987, pp. 25-41.
R	F. W. Deichmann - G. Bovini - A. Brandenburg, *Repertorium der christlich-antiken Sarkophage. Rom und Ostia*, Wiesbaden 1967.
RAMIERI 1978	A. M. Ramieri, 'Gruppo di lucerne tardoantiche da S. Prisca', *Rivista di Archeologia Cristiana* 54, 1978, pp. 303-318.
RAMIERI 1993	A. M. Ramieri, 'Ritratti femminili nella catacomba di Priscilla', *Rivista di Archeologia Cristiana* 69, 1993, pp. 47-61.
RAMSAY 1975	W. Ramsay, *The cities and bishoprics of Phrygia*, Oxford 1975[2]
RAOSS 1967	M. Raoss, headword *Loculus*, E. De Ruggiero, *Dizionario Epigrafico di Antichità Romane*, IV, Roma 1964-67, pp. 1460-1829.
RECIO VEGANZONES 1968	A. Recio Veganzones, *La «Historica Descriptio Urbis Romae», obra manuscrita de Fr. Alfonso Chacon O.P. (1530-1599)*, Roma 1968.
RECIO VEGANZONES 1974	A. Recio Veganzones, 'Alfonso Chacon, primer estudioso del mosaico cristiano de Roma y algunos diseños chaconianos poco conocidos', *Rivista di Archeologia Cristiana* 50, 1974, pp. 295-329.
RECIO VEGANZONES 1978	A. Recio Veganzones, 'Iconografia en estuco del pastor en les catacumbas de Roma', *Atti del IX Congresso Internazionale di Archeologia Cristiana, Roma 21-27 settembre 1975*, Città del Vaticano 1978, pp. 425-440.
RECIO VEGANZONES 1980	A. Recio Veganzones, 'La cappella greca vista y diseñada entre los años 1783 y 1786 por Seroux D'Agincourt', *Rivista di Archeologia Cristiana* 56, 1980, pp. 49-84.
REEKMANS 1964	L. Reekmans, *La tombe du pape Corneille et sa région cémétériale*, Città del Vaticano 1964.
REEKMANS 1973	L. Reekmans, 'La chronologie de la peinture paléochrétienne. Notes et réflexions', *Rivista di Archeologia Cristiana* 49, 1973, pp. 273-291.

REEKMANS 1984   L. Reekmans, 'Zur Problematik der römischen Katakombenforschung', *Boreas 7*, 1984, pp. 242-260.

REEKMANS 1986   L. Reekmans, 'Spätrömische Hypogea', *Studien zur spätantiken und byzantinischen Kunst Friedrich Wilhelm Deichmann gewidmet*, Mainz 1986, pp. 11-37.

REEKMANS 1986a   L. Reekmans, 'Quelques observations sur la stratification sociale et la «tumulatio ad sanctos» dans les catacombes romaines', *L'inhumation privilégiée du IVe au VIIIe siècle en Occident. Actes du colloque tenu à Créteil le 16-18 mars 1984*, Paris 1986, pp. 245-249.

REEKMANS 1988   L. Reekmans, *Le complexe cémétérial du pape Gaius dans la catacombe de Callixte*, Città del Vaticano-Leuven 1988.

RUSSO 1979   E. Russo, 'L'affresco di Turtura nel cimitero di Commodilla, l'icona di S. Maria in Trastevere e le più antiche feste della Madonna a Roma', *Bullettino dell'Istituto Storico Italiano per il Medio Evo e Archivio Muratoriano*, 88, 1979, pp. 35-85.

SAINT-ROCH 1981   P. Saint-Roch, 'La région centrale du cimetière connu sous le nom de: «cimetière des Saints Marc et Marcellien et Damase»', *Rivista di Archeologia Cristiana 57*, 1981, pp. 209-251.

SAINT-ROCH 1983   P. Saint-Roch, 'Enquête «sociologique» sur le cimetière dit «coemeterium Sanctorum Marci et Marcelliani Damasique»', *Rivista di Archeologia Cristiana*, 59, 1983, pp. 411-423.

SAINT-ROCH 1986   P. Saint-Roch, 'Un cubicule important dans le cimetière de Damase et des Saints Marc et Marcellien', *L'inhumation privilégiée du IVe au VIIIe siècle en Occident. Actes du colloque tenu à Créteil les 16-18 mars 1984*, Paris 1986, pp. 189-190.

SALAMITO 1995   J.-M. Salamito, 'La christianisation et les nouvelles règles de la vie sociale', *Histoire du Christianisme des origines à nos jours, II, Naissance d'une chrétienté (250-430)*, Paris 1995, pp. 675-717.

SALVETTI 1978   C. Salvetti, 'Il catalogo degli oggetti minuti conservati presso la Pontificia Commissione di Archeologia Sacra', *Rivista di Archeologia Cristiana 54*, 1978, pp. 103-130.

SALVETTI 1993   C. Salvetti, 'Su alcuni frammenti di sarcofagi nella basilica di S. Silvestro a Priscilla', *Rivista di Archeologia Cristiana 69*, 1993, pp. 63-88.

SANDERS 1991   G. Sanders, *Lapides memores. Païens et chrétiens face à la mort: le témoignage de l'épigraphie funéraire latine*, Faenza 1991.

SANTAGATA 1980   G. Santagata, 'Su due discusse figurazioni conservate nel cimitero di S. Tecla', *Esercizi 3*, 1980, pp. 7-14.

SAUER 1926   J. Sauer, *Wesen und Wollen der christlichen Kunst*, Freiburg i. Br. 1926.

SAXER 1980   V. Saxer, *Morts, martyrs, reliques en Afrique chrétienne aux premiers siècles. Les témoignages de Tertullien, Cyprien et Augustin à la lumière de l'archéologie africaine*, Paris 1980.

SAXER 1984   V. Saxer, *Atti dei martiri dei primi tre secoli*, Padova 1984.

SAXER 1989   V. Saxer, 'L'utilisation par la liturgie de l'espace urbain et suburbain: l'exemple de Rome dans l'Antiquité et le Haut Moyen Âge', *Actes du XIe Congrès International d'Archéologie Chrétienne, Lyon, Vienne, Grenoble, Genève et Aoste 21-28 septembre 1986*, II, Città del Vaticano 1989, pp. 917-1033.

SCH   *Sources Chrétiennes*, Paris 1941 ff.

SCHUDDEBOOM 1996   C. Schuddeboom, *Philips van Winghe (1560-1592) en het ontstaan van de christelijke archeologie*, Groningen 1996.

SCHUMACHER 1977   W.N. Schumacher, *Hirt und Guter Hirt*, Rom-Freiburg-Wien 1977.

SGARLATA 1991   M. R. Sglarlata, *Ricerche di demografia storica. Le iscrizioni tardo-imperiali di Siracusa*, Città del Vaticano 1991.

SOLIN 1982   H. Solin, *Die griechische Personennamen in Rom. Ein Namenbuch*, Berlin-New York 1982.

SORDI 1965   M. Sordi, *Il cristianesimo e Roma*, Bologna 1965.

SORDI 1984   M. Sordi, *I cristiani e l'Impero Romano*, Milano 1984.

SPAGNOLI 1993   E. Spagnoli, 'Alcune riflessioni sulla circolazione monetaria in epoca tardoantica a Ostia (Pianabella) e a Porto', *La storia economica*

SPERA 1992   L. Spera, 'Un cubicolo monumentale nella catacomba di Pretestato', *Rivista di Archeologia Cristiana* 68, 1992, pp. 271-307.

di Roma nell'Altomedioevo alla luce dei recenti scavi archeologici, *Atti del Seminario, Roma 2-3 aprile 1992*, Firenze 1993, pp. 256-267.

SPERA 1992   L. Spera, 'Un cubicolo monumentale nella catacomba di Pretestato', *Rivista di Archeologia Cristiana* 68, 1992, pp. 271-307.

SPERA 1994   L. Spera, 'Interventi di papa Damaso nei santuari delle catacombe romane: il ruolo della committenza privata', *Bessarione* 11, 1994, pp. 111-127.

SPERA 1994a   L. Spera, 'Un'immagine di Cristo nel santuario di Ippolito sulla via Tiburtina: note su alcuni casi di frequentazione tarda dei complessi martiriali a Roma', *Bessarione* 11, 1994, pp. 39-51.

SPERA 1995   L. Spera, 'Decorazioni in marmo delle catacombe romane: Osservazioni preliminari', *Atti del II Colloquio dell'Associazione Italiana per lo Studio e la Conservazione del Mosaico, Roma 5-7 dicembre 1994*, Bordighera 1995, pp. 433-446.

SPERA 1997   L. Spera, 'Cantieri edilizi a Roma in età carolingia: gli interventi di papa Adriano I (772-795) nei santuari delle catacombe. Strategie e modalità di intervento', *Rivista di Archeologia Cristiana* 73, 1997, pp. 185-254.

SPERA in press   L. Spera, '«Sanctorum limina adornans»: note sull'intervento monumentale di papa Damaso nella Cripta dei Papi a S. Callisto', *Krater*, 1, in press.

SPERA in press   L. Spera, 'Scoperta di nuove testimonianze monumentali per lo studio dell'arenario centrale della catacomba di Priscilla a Roma', *Atti del VII Congresso Nazionale di Archeologia Cristiana, Cassino, 20-24 settembre 1993*, in press.

SPIGNO 1975   L. Spigno, 'Considerazioni sul manoscritto vallicelliano G.31 e la Roma Sotterranea di Antonio Bosio', *Rivista di Archeologia Cristiana* 51, 1975, pp. 281-311.

SPIGNO 1976   L. Spigno, 'Della Roma Sotterranea del Bosio e della sua biografia', *Rivista di Archeologia Cristiana* 52, 1976, pp. 277-301.

STEINGRÄBER 1981   S. Steingräber, *Etrurien. Städte, Heiligtümer, Nekropolen*, München 1981.

STOMMEL 1954   E. Stommel, *Beiträge zur Ikonographie der Konstantinischen Sarkophagplastik*, Bonn 1954.

STOMMEL 1958   E. Stommel, 'Zum Problem der frühchristlichen Jonasdarstellungen', *Jahrbuch für Antike und Christentum* 1, 1958, pp. 112-115.

STUIBER 1957   A. Stuiber, *Refrigerium interim*, Bonn 1957.

STUTZINGER 1982   D. Stutzinger, *Die frühchristlichen Sarkophagreliefs aus Rom. Untersuchungen zur Formveränderung im 4. Jahrhundert n. Chr.*, Bonn 1982.

STYGER 1925-1926   P. Styger, 'L'origine del cimitero di S. Callisto sull'Appia', *Rendiconti della Pontificia Accademia Romana di Archeologia* 4, 1925-1926, pp. 91-153.

STYGER 1933   P. Styger, *Die römischen Katakomben*, Berlin 1933.

STYGER 1935   P. Styger, *Römische Märtyrergrüfte*, Berlin 1935.

TESTINI 1963   P. Testini, 'Osservazioni sull'iconografia del Cristo in trono fra gli apostoli. A proposito dell'affresco di un distrutto oratorio cristiano presso l'aggere severiano a Roma', *Rivista dell'Istituto Nazionale di Archeologia e Storia dell'Arte* 11-12, 1963, pp. 230-300.

TESTINI 1966   P. Testini, *Le catacombe e gli antichi cimiteri cristiani in Roma*, Bologna 1966.

TESTINI 1968   P. Testini, 'Tardoantico e paleocristiano. Postilla per una positiva definizione della più antica iconografia cimiteriale cristiana', *Tardoantico e Altomedioevo*, Roma 1968, pp. 120-127.

TESTINI 1976   P. Testini, 'Aspetti di vita matrimoniale in antiche iscrizioni funerarie cristiane', *Lateranum* 42, 1976, pp. 150-164.

TESTINI 1978   P. Testini, 'Nuove osservazioni sul cubicolo di Ampliato a Domitilla', *Atti del IX Congresso Internazionale di Archeologia Cristiana, Roma 21-27 settembre 1975*, Città del Vaticano 1978, pp. 143-157.

TODISCO 1980   L. Todisco, 'Modelli classici per le prime espressioni figurative del peccato originale', *Annali della Facoltà di Lettere di Bari* 23, 1980, pp. 12-21.

TOLOTTI 1953   F. Tolotti, *Memorie degli Apostoli in Cata-cumbas*, Città del Vaticano 1953.

TOLOTTI 1970   F. Tolotti, *Il cimitero di Priscilla. Studio di topografia e architettura*, Città del Vaticano 1970.

TOLOTTI 1977   F. Tolotti, 'Ricerca dei luoghi venerati nella Spelunca Magna di Pretestato', *Rivista di Archeologia Cristiana* 53, 1977, pp. 7-102.

TOLOTTI 1978   F. Tolotti, 'Le cimetière de Priscille. Synthèse d'une recherches', *Revue d'Histoire Ecclesiastique* 73, 1978, pp. 306-307.

TOLOTTI 1978a   F. Tolotti, 'Origine e sviluppo delle escavazioni nel cimitero di Pretestato', *Atti del IX Congresso Internazionale di Archeologia Cristiana, Roma 21-27 settembre 1975*, Città del Vaticano 1978, pp. 159-187.

TOLOTTI 1980   F. Tolotti, 'Influenza delle opere idrauliche sull'origine delle catacombe', *Rivista di Archeologia Cristiana* 56, 1980, pp. 7-48.

TOLOTTI 1983   F. Tolotti, 'Le confessioni succedutesi sul sepolcro di S. Paolo', *Rivista di Archeologia Cristiana* 59, 1983, pp. 87-149.

TOLOTTI 1985   F. Tolotti, 'Contributo alla datazione della basilica dei SS. Nereo e Achilleo sulla via Ardeatina', *Rivista di Archeologia Cristiana* 61, 1985, pp. 374-378.

TOYNBEE 1993   J. M. C. Toynbee, *Morte e sepoltura nel mondo romano*, Roma 1993.

TRONZO 1986   W. Tronzo, *The Via Latina Catacomb. Imitation and Discontinuity in Fourth-Century Roman Painting*, London 1986.

UGONIO 1588   P. Ugonio, *Historia delle Stationi di Roma*, Roma 1588.

VALENTINI-ZUCCHETTI 1941-1942   R. Valentini - G. Zucchetti, *Codice topografico della città di Roma*, Roma 1940 (I), 1942 (II).

VALERI 1900   A. Valeri, *Cenni biografici di Antonio Bosio*, Roma 1900.

VAN DAEL 1978   P. S. G. Van Dael, *De Dode: Een Hoofolfiguur in de oudchristelijke Kunst*, Amsterdam 1978.

VAN ESSEN 1956-1958   C. C. Van Essen, 'Studio cronologico delle pitture parietali di Ostia', *Bollettino Comunale* 76, 1956-1958, pp. 115-181.

VISMARA 1986   C. Vismara, 'I cimiteri ebraici di Roma', *Società Romana e Impero Tardoantico*, II, Bari 1986, pp. 351-392.

VITALE 1995   M. Vitale, 'Mosaici pavimentali a Roma nel IV secolo: il caso dell'ipogeo di Villa Cellere', *Associazione Italiana per lo Studio e la Conservazione del Mosaico. Atti del II Colloquio, Roma 5-7 dicembre 1994*, Bordighera 1995, pp. 395-402.

VON HARNACK 1924   A. Von Harnack, *Die Mission und Ausbreitung des Christentums in den ersten drei Jahrhunderten*, I-II, Leipzig 1924.

VON HESBERG 1994   H. Von Hesberg, *Monumenta. I sepolcri romani e la loro architettura*, Milano 1994.

VOPEL 1899   H. Vopel, *Die altchristlichen Goldgläser*, Freiburg i. B. 1899.

WATAGHIN CANTINO 1980   G. Wataghin Cantino, 'Roma sotterranea. Appunti sulle origini dell'archeologia cristiana', *Ricerche di Storia dell'Arte* 10, 1980, pp. 5-14.

WEILAND 1994   A. Weiland, '«Conposuit tumulum sanctorum limina adornans». Die Ausgestaltung des Grabes der hl. Felix und Adauctus durch Papst Damasus in der Commodillakatakombe in Rom', *Historiam Pictura Refert. Miscellanea in onore di p. Alejandro Recio Veganzones O.F.M.*, Città del Vaticano 1994, pp. 625-645.

WILPERT 1891   J. Wilpert, *Fractio panis. Die älteste Darstellung des eucharistischen Opfers in der Cappella Greca*, Freiburg 1891.

WILPERT 1903   J. Wilpert, *Le pitture delle catacombe romane*, Roma 1903.

WILPERT 1910   G. Wilpert, *La cripta dei papi e la cappella di Santa Cecilia nel cimitero di Callisto*, Roma 1910.

WILPERT 1916   J. Wilpert, *Die römischen Mosaiken und Malereien der kirchlichen Bauten vom IV. bis XIII. Jahrhundert*, Freiburg im Breisgau 1916.

WILPERT 1924   G. Wilpert, 'Le pitture dell'ipogeo di Aurelio Felicissimo presso viale Manzoni in Roma', *Memorie dell'Accademia Romana di Archeologia* 1, 2, 1924, pp. 5-43.

WILPERT 1929-1936   G. Wilpert, *I sarcofagi cristiani antichi*, I-III, Roma 1929-1936.

WILPERT 1938   J. Wilpert, *La fede della Chiesa nascente secondo i monumenti dell'arte funeraria antica*, Città del Vaticano 1938.

WIPSZYCKA 1972   E. Wipszycka, *Les ressources et les activités économiques des églises en Égypte*, Paris 1972.

WIRTH 1934   F. Wirth, *Römische Wandmalerei vom Untergang Pompejis bis ans Ende des dritten Jahrhunderts*, Berlin 1934.

WISCHMEYER 1980   W. Wischmeyer, 'Die Aberkiosinschrift als Grabepigramm', *Jahrbuch für Antike und Christentum* 23, 1980, pp. 22-47.

WURMBRAND STUPPACH 1927   K. Wurmbrand Stuppach, 'Die Jägerkatakombe an der via Appia', *Belvedere* 3, 1927, pp. 289-294.

ZANCHI ROPPO 1969   F. Zanchi Roppo, *Vetri paleocristiani a figure d'oro conservati in Italia*, Bologna 1969.

ZILLIACUS 1963   H. Zilliacus, *Sylloge Inscriptionum Christianarum Veterum Musei Vaticani*, 2 vols, Helsinki 1963

ZIMMER 1982   G. Zimmer, *Römische Berufsdarstellungen*, Berlin 1982.

Sources of Illustrations

From Augenti 1991: 56
From Baruffa 1992: pl. III, p. 146
From Bendinelli 1922: 19
From Bertonière 1985: 66
From Stefano Bottai (ed.), *Tesori d'arte cristiana*,
    vol. I, Bologna, n. d.: 74
From Camiruaga, *et al* 1994: 51
From de Rossi 1864–1877, II: 37, 48
From de Rossi 1864–1877, III: 39
From Fasola 1987: 43
From Fasola-Testini 1978: 20
From Fiocchi Nicolai 1995: 58
From Guyon 1987: 27, 29, 38, 54, 69
From ICUR X: 25
From Krautheimer 1937-1980, III: 73
From Marchi 1844: 35
From Nestori 1959: 28
From Nestori 1971: 7
From Nestori 1990: 71
From Pergola 1975: 17
From Pergola 1983: 9
From Solin-Volpe 1983: 18
From Styger 1925–26: 6
From Testini 1966: 60
From Tolotti 1970: 8
From Tolotti 1977: 10, 57

Revision of Deckers-.Mietke-Weiland 1994 by B. Mazzei: 61
Revision of Fasola 1961 and Fasola-Fiocchi Nicolai 1989 by
    B. Mazzei: 36
Revision of Frutaz 1976 and Fasola 1974 by B. Mazzei: 23
Revision of Reekmans 1988 and Fasola 1980 by B. Mazzei: 30
Revision of Styger 1933 and Tolotti 1970 by B. Mazzei: 20

Biblioteca Vativana, Codice Vaticano-Latino 10545, fol. 183: 1
By kind permission of the Ordine dei Cavalieri di Malta: 12

Danilo Mazzoleni: 152, 171, 177, 178

All other illustrations: Pontificia Commissione di Archeologia
    Cristiana, Roma

We would like to that Dr. Barbara Mazzei for her help in the
revision of the text, bibliography and plans, and in the selection
of illustrations.

VINCENZO FIOCCHI NICOLAI teaches Christian Archaeology at the Università degli Studi di Roma Tor Vergata and the Scuola di Specializzazione del Pontificio Istituto di Archeologia Cristiana. He is also a member of the Pontificia Commissione di Archeologia Sacra.

FABRIZIO BISCONTI teaches at the Scuola di Specializzazione del Pontificio Istituto di Archeologia Cristiana. He is also a member and secretary of the Pontificia Commissione di Archeologia Sacra.

DANILO MAZZOLENI teaches Christian Archaeology at the Università degli Studi di Roma Tre and at the Scuola di Specializzazione del Pontificio Istituto di Archeologia Cristiana. He is also a member of the Pontificia Commissione di Archeologia Sacra.